Bella Merlin

Bella Merlin is an actor, writer and actor-trainer. Acting includes seasons at the Colorado Shakespeare Festival with Tina Packer, the National Theatre with Max Stafford-Clark's Out of Joint company, roles in theatre, film, television and radio throughout the UK, and the US premieres of her two fact-based dramas, *Tilly No-Body: Catastrophes of Love* and *Nell Gwynne: A Dramatick Essaye on Acting and Prostitution.* Writing includes *Acting: The Basics* and *Konstantin Stanislavsky* (Routledge), *With the Rogue's Company:* Henry IV *at the National Theatre* (Oberon), *Beyond Stanislavsky: The Psycho-Physical Approach to Actor Training* and *The Complete Stanislavsky Toolkit* (Nick Hern Books) and chapters and articles on subjects including Stanislavsky's Active Analysis, 'acting with facts', and Shakespeare and Stanislavsky. She is currently Professor of Acting and Directing at the University of California, Riverside, and Visiting Professor at Rose Bruford College of Theatre and Performance. She lives in Los Angeles with her husband, Miles Anderson.

www.bellamerlin.com

Also by Bella Merlin
and published by Nick Hern Books

Beyond Stanislavsky
The Psycho-Physical Approach to Actor Training

The Complete Stanislavsky Toolkit

FACING THE FEAR

An Actor's Guide to Overcoming Stage Fright

Bella Merlin

N H B

NICK HERN BOOKS
London
www.nickhernbooks.co.uk

A Nick Hern Book

Facing the Fear: An Actor's Guide to Overcoming Stage Fright
first published in Great Britain in 2016
by Nick Hern Books Limited,
The Glasshouse, 49a Goldhawk Road, London W12 8QP

Cover image: iStockPhoto.com/GeorgePeters
Author photo: The Riker Brothers

Designed and typeset by Nick Hern Books
Printed and bound in Great Britain by
Ashford Colour Press, Gosport, Hampshire

A CIP catalogue record for this book is available
from the British Library

ISBN 978 1 84842 313 8

FSC www.fsc.org
MIX
Paper from
responsible sources
FSC® C011748

'Stage fright is always waiting outside the door, waiting to get you. You either battle or walk away...'

Laurence Olivier

Let's not battle.

Let's not walk away.

Let's face the fear.

Contents

Acknowledgements

This book wouldn't exist without the stories and shared experiences of the actors and directors who have contributed to this journey, either in dialogue with me or through their published accounts. Personal thanks go to Mike Alfreds, Anthony Bianco, John Cariani, Donald Carrier, Winslow Corbett, Ben Diskant, Matthew Dunster, Giles Fagan, Amy Cole-Farrell, Sam Graham, David Hare, Georgia Hatzis, Jeff Horger, Caroline Hunt, Ron Hutchinson, Tanya Moodie, Rufus Norris, Maggie O'Brien, Tim Orr, Jonno Roberts, Richard Seer and Jay Whittaker. Their honesty and open-heartedness have been enormously generous. I am ever grateful to Max Stafford-Clark and Tina Packer, for giving me wonderful opportunities to play and teaching me so much. Thanks, too, to voice coach Margaret Jansen. To Adrian Noble, for letting me sit in on three seasons of rehearsals at the Old Globe San Diego and eavesdrop on his wisdom. To Anna Kritikos, for tirelessly transcribing hours of interviews while being an inspirational young actor in her own right. To my agents, Natasha, Jen, Lindsay and Perry, for being ever patient and loyal. To the terrific faculty, staff and students of the Theatre, Film and Digital Production Department at the University of California, Riverside. To Michael Nott, for his perspicacious comments, and to Margaret Nott, for her invaluable help with the biology. To Dr Dee Silver, for running through the neuroscience with a fine-tooth comb. To the brilliant team at Nick Hern Books (not least Matt Applewhite, Jon Barton and Jodi Gray). And finally to the two people without whom I simply couldn't have written this book. It's rare for any author to have the kind of personal mentorship that I have been privileged to receive from Nick Hern over the last fifteen years. I owe much to his absolute precision, impeccable vision, and wonderful sense of humour. And to Miles Anderson, a great actor, an inspirational director, a devoted reader of chapters (even when they weren't in a fit state to be read by anybody), and a patient and nurturing husband. Without him, I really wouldn't be able to face the fear.

Preface

It was the summer of 2011 when I started thinking seriously about writing a book on stage fright. I was with my husband, Miles Anderson, at the Old Globe Theatre in San Diego, California, where he was playing two vast roles in one Shakespeare festival under the direction of Adrian Noble. Knowing that he would only have a few weeks' rehearsals – for Prospero in *The Tempest* and Salieri in *Amadeus* – Miles started learning his lines months in advance. A strict schedule of so many lines every day for so many weeks dictated his life. And each day, for hours on end, he would labour over his scripts – sitting on the sofa, walking in the woods, staring at the stars – muttering and musing and magicking the roles. His hard work certainly paid off that summer to overwhelming critical acclaim, yet still the little demon of performance nerves would wink from the wings on the odd occasion and nibble away at his confidence.

The following year I found myself facing a similar challenge, when I was cast in the Colorado Shakespeare Festival under the direction of Shakespeare guru Tina Packer. Months in advance of the dauntingly short rehearsal period, I began the inevitable line-bashing. I knew that I had to be totally confident from the minute I entered the rehearsal room: there could be no room for self-doubt. And why? Because I was harbouring a 'dirty secret'.

Back in 2004, I'd suffered chronic stage fright. I wasn't very proud of it, so I didn't talk about it much. Nor did I seek help beyond just getting back on the 'horse' of acting and reading lots of books. Nonetheless, the experience had haunted me for years. Yet the desire to get to the bottom of it had haunted me in equal measure. So when Nick Hern agreed to the proposed book, I was extremely excited. My excitement was spurred during the writing process when serendipitously more and more prominent actors came out of the stage-fright closet. In the autumn of 2013, Derek Jacobi's autobiography, *As Luck Would Have It*, was published, and he appeared in a number of interviews talking frankly about his performance fears. Earlier that summer, Michael Gambon had admitted in the national press to the crippling stage fright that had hounded him for years, even leading to his hospitalisation twice.[1] Their brave and public admissions of stage fright galvanised my belief that this book – *Facing the Fear* – could perhaps be very useful to the acting community at large.

It's hard for anyone who hasn't suffered stage fright to know what it's actually like. It's hard for directors to truly understand what actors are going through in rehearsal or performance, unless they've been actors themselves. It's hard for audience members – however versed they might be in theatre – to comprehend the inner chaos. 'I'm alone – oh, God, how alone I am!' bewailed Laurence Olivier, as he waited in the wings to go on as Shylock. 'Nobody understands this... nobody.'[2] And that's part of the imperative of writing this book. To enable directors, writers, stage managers, critics, audiences – in fact, anyone engaged in making or watching performance – to have more understanding of what acting really entails. And stage fright clearly fascinates the public, as evidenced by the various books on public speaking as well as the wide-scale appeal of pianist Sara Solovitch's heartfelt account of *Playing Scared* (also published while I was writing this book, in summer 2015).[3]

This book is different, though. It's not about public speaking. Nor is it about performing music. It's about the specific challenges facing actors. The challenges of taking on another character. Of speaking somebody else's words. Of trying to synchronise our own feelings with those of the fictional character. And what do we do if our feelings are completely different from the character – such as when we're suffering stage fright? How on earth do we reconcile our own nerves with a cool, calm or confident character? That's an unnerving 'schizophrenia' that maybe only actors can understand.

It's common knowledge that many musicians use beta blockers to reduce the physiological effects of their performance anxiety (indeed, Solovitch talks about it openly) – though I've never heard an actor share this practice. Maybe that's because our art relies on us being absolutely present to our feelings, sensations, and emotions. Acting is all about opening our heart and being emotionally thin-skinned, whereas beta blockers are all about blocking our heart's adrenalin receptors. That said, maybe my actor-friends *are* taking beta blockers and it's just another 'dirty secret'. Who knows? I *do* know that what we do as actors is complex and subtle, as indeed is stage fright. So while this book offers insights for directors, stage managers, critics, audiences, et al., ultimately it's for all fellow actors and companions on the path. How much more could we help each other if we knew what we might be secretly going through?

Introduction

The actor's nightmare

You're standing on the stage in front of a packed auditorium. All eyes are on you. The lights. The darkness. The moment of glory. Then suddenly – out of nowhere – the dry mouth... the sweaty palms... the shaking knees... and the empty head. Lines well learnt – now lost in space. The feeling of falling... failing... freaking out... and fainting. And then you wake up!

Yet for many of us as actors, the nightmare becomes a reality. Stage fright – or 'The Fear', as Antony Sher famously calls it – has the power of a monster to drive seasoned professionals and acolyte beginners away from the stage for months, years, and even lifetimes. Laurence Olivier suffered stage fright from his teens to his sixties. Barbra Streisand avoided live performance for twenty-seven years. Marilyn Monroe, Ian Holm, Carly Simon, Kenneth Branagh – not to mention the great actor-trainers, Lee Strasberg and Konstantin Stanislavsky – the list of sufferers (in varying degrees) goes on and on...

There are lots of reasons why we suffer stage fright. It could be the way in which a play was rehearsed. It could be our relationship with the director. The fact that our agent is in the audience. The size of the part (and small roles can be more terrifying than leads). Added to which, the sensations of stage fright are mysterious. Sometimes the monster hunts us down ferociously; sometimes it's little more than a butterfly. Sometimes it's the press night that can be paralysing; sometimes it's the hundredth performance of a six-month run. Sometimes the monster has the girth of Godzilla. Sometimes it's a demon with the blackness of Beelzebub. Sometimes it's a pesky imp. Sometimes it's just an ugly worm. Yet, however it manifests itself (as I said in the Preface), we don't talk about our stage fright very often. After all, there's a certain shame attached to it. We feel our professionalism is at stake: we might be found wanting or unreliable – or, at worst, unemployable. So there are very few in-depth analyses of actors' anxieties, unlike the myriad studies in sport and stories in music, including that of Sara Solovitch.

Facing the Fear addresses the actor's silence. It provides – amongst other things – an outlet for actors to share their stage fright and to understand that it's not shameful. It's not unprofessional or amateur. It's normal. It's human. And it's part of the profession. We look the monster in the eye – often using first-person narratives to conjure up the immediacy. And my intention is to prove that, if the monster has to exist – as indeed it probably does – then we can live with it productively and maybe even pleasurably.

Facing the Fear is not a quick-fix manual. (Though, if that's what you're looking for, you could cut to Chapter 5. Alternatively, you could do what many musicians do and take a beta blocker; though I don't recommend it, as quick fixes rarely work.) Nor is it a book on how to act. If all is going well for you, you don't need to follow any of the tips. That said, there's something for most kinds of actors in most kinds of situations – whether or not there's an issue with performance anxiety. We focus mainly on theatre, as that's the environment in which the stakes are highest. By which I mean that there are people present who have paid to see our work, and it's hard to stop and start again if anything goes wrong. Live theatre is a tightrope in a way that television and film aren't. Though there's plenty in this book that applies to screen as well as stage.

Facing the Fear is ultimately a journey. A journey into the mysterious truths of stage fright. Truths such as the fact that we start to fear what we thought we loved. That we become our own enemy. That the human mind is complex, as indeed is the acting craft. This journey has many stories, along with some science, some history, some psychology, and some practical strategies. We'll do a little time-travelling, as well as voyaging into our own minds. And, like all journeys, it takes time. As I said, this book is not a quick fix (though it might save you a fortune in psychotherapist's fees!).

But why do I want to talk about stage fright in the first place?

Where this journey began

In 2004, I was smitten with an overwhelming bout of stage fright. It was very near the end of a five-month run of David Hare's powerful verbatim play *The Permanent Way*, directed by Max Stafford-Clark for his company Out of Joint in collaboration with the National Theatre. I'll let my production journal reveal the pride and fall:

> *May 1st 2004: Last night at the National Theatre*
>
> The last night at the National and the end of something very special. I've never before felt so strongly that performing a play could be so important. The audiences have been incredible, with all kinds of eulogies – from critics, public, theatre professionals, stage-door staff and ushers. It has been extraordinary.
>
> It'll be good to get out of London, though. Not that I've been nervous, not that it's ever worried me who's in and what they might think. But who knows? – There might be a sense of 'pressure off' among us all, so that we can finish this long run with some playful fun.

May 5th: First night at the West Yorkshire Playhouse, Courtyard Studio Theatre

What a nightmare!

Tonight I had every actor's worst possible scenario. I get mid-way through a sentence – and my brain shuts down. All those thoughts I'd had about being out of London – the pressure off and the fun on – couldn't have been further from the truth. Earlier in the day during the tech rehearsal, my fellow actor Matthew Dunster looked out into the auditorium of the intimate Courtyard Theatre, where the front row is barely a foot from the stage. 'God, they're close!' he said. 'This is scary!' I didn't think anything of it at the time, apart from being surprised that any of us should find anything scary so far into the run.

Then – during the show – I walk to the front of the stage in the role of the Investment Banker and, as always during this moment, I address a member of the audience. 'Well, I don't know about you, but I can only work when I feel the hot breath of a competitor down my neck.' Well, that's what I'm supposed to say...

Instead, I manage to say, 'Well, I don't know about you...' but then, as I look at this man on the fourth row, I can see the whites of his eyes. 'Wow!' I think. 'You really *are* close, aren't you?' And at that moment, any connection to the play is cut in my brain. I have no idea what I'm supposed to say next.

Strangely, I don't get the mad pumping of adrenalin that I've had in the past when I've momentarily tripped over a word. No heart pounding, no instant sense of fight or flight. Just a feeling of floating away... Into oblivion... As if I'm in a dream and nothing really matters... In this fleeting moment, it doesn't matter that I'm eyeballing a total stranger and saying whatever nonsensical words come out of my mouth. It doesn't matter that Max Stafford-Clark and Ian Brown (Artistic Director of the West Yorkshire Playhouse) are watching, *and* his casting director, *and* a full house of audience from Leeds. It's just me and this kind of floating-away feeling.

The moment maybe lasts a split second, yet it seems like a thousand years. Somehow I retrieve the next line and manage to get to the end of the scene seemingly in control. But all the time, I just want to slip into this strange kind of fainting place. I get off stage feeling totally, utterly spaced out.

And then it hits. The shakes and the palpitations kick in. It's as if my legs from pelvis to knee don't exist – it's just thin air. My peripheries have vanished. I can't feel my hands. Maybe I'd experienced some kind of 'connection overload' out there. What I mean is that in the National's Lyttelton Theatre, I hadn't really been able to see the eyes of the person whom I'd picked out in the audience for the Investment Banker's 'hot breath of a competitor' line. Here, however, the guy on the fourth row was as clear as daylight. And he was looking straight back at me. There was a true connection, and maybe the electrical currents of that connection overloaded my brain, giving me a moment of meltdown. Who knows? Whatever...

May 12th: First night at the Oxford Playhouse

I'm just so glad to be back in a bigger space. You'd think this verbatim play would be perfectly designed for intimate studio spaces, but I'm so much happier now that we're back in the big theatre of the Oxford Playhouse. Apart from anything else, I can't see the audience!

May 14th: Third night at the Oxford Playhouse

I don't believe it!

It's the last time Sir David Hare is going to see the play and I do it again! I fuck up! I'm shocked and appalled at myself. This time it was a stupid fluff, and again as the Investment Banker. What is it with that character? She's supposed to be calm and confident. Instead of saying, 'In fact, you can hardly get out of the country without using something I've had my finger in,' I say, 'In fact, you can hardly get your finger... out of... something I've had my finger in...!' In that split second, my brain does a million somersaults as I strain to bring

> everything back to the present tense. But what a load of bollocks came out of my mouth! And I know what Sir David is like! I know he won't let me off the hook!
>
> Sure enough, he's backstage after the show in the middle of a conversation – and suddenly he sees me. 'And as for you!' he booms down the corridor. 'Oh, no – could you tell?' I wince. 'Of course I could tell! It was a load of rubbish!...' And off we all troop into the Yorkshire night. And the knight goes off to the station to catch the last train back to London. And yes, yes – I'll never work in British theatre again...!

My stage fright grew worse in the final two weeks of the run. I came down with chronic laryngitis and could barely be heard. It was as if my body didn't want me to go out onto the stage and into the spotlight any more, but, with no understudies, I had no choice.

As it turned out, I wasn't alone in feeling performance anxiety so very late in this long run, and little by little some of the other actors spoke of how uneasy they were feeling. It was then I began to realise that sharing our fear-based stories brings with it a kind of talking cure.

The talking cure

It takes courage to be an actor. It takes even greater courage to admit how terrifying it can be. Yet the very act of admitting it can be transformative. Describing the actor as *An Acrobat of the Heart*, Stephen Wangh writes, 'It takes real courage to say, "I am afraid", so in the act of naming it you are already converting the fear into usable energy.'[4] Certainly sharing my 'shameful' secret with some of my fellow actors was an important part of dealing with the situation. That said, not all of them wanted to talk about their experiences. And it's true that the small amount of literature that exists about stage fright tends to stem from psychologists and theatre scholars, rather than the actors themselves. There's something of a conspiracy of silence. Which isn't surprising. We all know that stage fright is an irrational fear. After all, the audience and the performance situation can't (usually) harm us. So the damaging force has to be our own inner messages. In fact, all too easily stage fright can feel like some sort of mental illness, or what German scholar Adolph Kielblock (back in the 1890s) called, 'the result of a morbid state of the imagination'.[5] That's almost the scariest part of the fear: we're doing it to ourselves. And if we're not careful, we start perpetuating our own downfall. Our morbid imagination conjures up all sorts of catastrophic conclusions that wholly outweigh any rational assessment of the situation – like 'I'll never work in British theatre again...!'

The thing is that, whether we realise it or not, we're going to talk about our stage fright anyway. If we're not going to talk about it out loud to others, we're going to find ourselves talking about it over and over and over in our heads. In fact, there aren't many *healthy* options when it comes to dealing with stressful situations. Sometimes we pretend they don't bother us. Sometimes we try to avoid them. Yet both of these strategies (according to writer Taylor Clark) 'are destined to fail'.[6] Clark suggests that if we try to control our emotions or we try to avoid the stressful situation, we actually keep our fears alive – because then a significant part of our thoughts is taken up with worrying about *how* we're going to avoid it. It's a downward spiral. We'll look at worry in more detail in Chapter 1. For the moment let's acknowledge that worrying may have the *short-term* pay-off of making us less afraid, but in the *long term* it traps us in a cycle of anxiety.[7] This cycle of anxiety is perpetuated by the fact that the voice in our head ('the Fear Voice,' as sports psychologist Don Green calls it)[8] doesn't just talk – it literally poisons us. It leads our brain to create more stress chemicals such as cortisol. And these stress chemicals increase our physical state of alarm – and so the situation simply grows worse. Our inner Fear Voice is *chemically* – as well as psychologically – unhealthy. So we might as well talk about our stage fright out loud!

Yes, indeed, talking about our anxieties has been scientifically proven to help. It's known in psychology as 'flooding therapy'. Every time we confront, describe and relive our thoughts about a negative experience, we find that 'the very act of disclosure lessens these thoughts'.[9] So by putting our feelings into words, we actually *change* how our brain deals with the stressful information. (Not least because we're producing less cortisol.) It's also known as 'mindful noting'. And the very act of translating our stressful feelings into words (or *mindfully noting* them) is almost more therapeutic than *understanding* them. As we try to put the chaos of our feelings into logical sentences, we find ourselves unpicking that chaos, like knots in a string. And then we can be more objective about what we're feeling, whether or not we actually understand it.[10] ('I feel afraid – though I've no idea why – but at least I feel better for naming it "fear".')

Of course, it's very difficult for us as actors to confess that we're experiencing *anything* that might in any way impede our work as professionals. Jobs are hard enough to come by without directors or casting directors getting a whiff that we might be afraid of what we do. Yet if we don't talk about it, our Fear Voice keeps us *alone* with our fear, and coping with a fear alone can be difficult and distressing. As biophysicist Stefan Klein puts it: 'Loneliness is a burden for spirit and body. Getting support is normally one of the best ways of dealing with stress.'[11] So rather than churning our anxieties over in our heads, we should share our fears out loud. That way, we can change our damaging inner monologue and, thus, reduce our stress hormones. This is pretty important for us as actors, as stress hormones do two unhelpful things. They undermine our immune system (and no actor can afford to be ill) and they affect our memory (and absolutely no actor can afford to lose their memory!). As we'll see throughout this book, loss of memory and stage fright are intricately interwoven. So talking about our fear might actually improve our memory, which in turn will reduce our stage fright. Seems like a no-brainer to me!

So let's put the talking cure straight into practice with two more stories about stage fright. Both of the actors who share their experiences here were open and generous in their vivid descriptions. And they pinpoint some of the powerful factors that can trigger our feelings of stage fright.

'The embodiment of evil': losing faith in our performance

Richard Seer is an award-winning actor and director, as well as running the MFA Theatre programme at the University of San Diego. His story highlights what can happen to us when we lose our faith in our performance:

> I was in a pretty terrible production of *Richard III* which had started at Stratford, Connecticut, where the New York critics had seen it – and they hated it. Then we moved to the Kennedy Center in Washington, DC, which is a very high-profile venue. I was playing Tyrell, but it was actually six roles all put together to make me sort of 'the embodiment of evil'. And I'd already been told by the critics that I wasn't any good. But it wasn't just me. The disdain for the production was universal – we were all equally hated. So each night, I had to go out there with a kind of bravery and say, 'No, it's just fine.' But in the back of my mind, I knew it wasn't just fine.
>
> Then, during one particular night's performance, I had the most trouble...
>
> The incident happened quite far into the play – in a moment when King Richard summons Tyrell to his presence. The director had staged it so that every time I made an entrance, the rest of the cast would freeze. The wind would sound and the lighting would change, and I would make a slow entrance onto the stage – after all, I was the Embodiment of Evil. The

other characters would make a big deal about it for a moment and then everything would return to normal. The audience, of course, was utterly perplexed as to why I was doing it – which made it worse. Since I was essentially playing the servant's role, the audience must have thought, 'Who *is* that guy?'

Anticipating this particular entrance on this one particular evening, I started to panic – really panic. I thought, 'I can't go on. I don't know my lines. I don't know what I'm going to say.' And this was unusual, as I'd never had a problem learning lines in the past. I went straight to the stage manager and I said, 'I don't think I can go on.' I was having trouble breathing. Incredible heart palpitations were happening. My costume was very constricting. So I kept trying to open it up, to loosen it, because I thought, 'Am I going to faint? Am I going to black out?' All I knew was that I was panicking.

The stage manager didn't know what to do. There was no way of notifying my understudy as he was already on stage in an ensemble role. So the stage manager kept saying, 'No, I think you can try. Just get through this scene.' And finally – I simply couldn't. I went to my dressing room and they rang the hospital. Meanwhile, King Richard called several times for Tyrell to come onto the stage. Fortunately my understudy figured out that I wasn't coming on, so he stepped forward and started saying my lines.

At the time, I thought I was having a heart attack because my heart was going like crazy and I couldn't breathe. So, sure enough, they sent an ambulance, I was taken to the hospital, they did all the appropriate tests for an emergency, and the doctor said, 'No, there's nothing wrong with you. You seem to be fine.' But I didn't quite believe it...

A couple of days later, sure enough – the same things were happening. They called the ambulance again and I went to the hospital again. Thank God the same doctor was there in ER. And after they'd finished the tests, she said, 'I think this is psychological. I'm not saying it's not real, but it's different. These are panic attacks that you're having.'[12]

> Over the course of the next few days, the panic attacks grew quite severe. I was no longer sleeping. I had extreme muscle contractions in my back and my neck, which were *gripping* me. I would wake up in the middle of the night with intense pains that would last most of the day. And there didn't seem to be anything I could do to solve it. I tried exercising. I tried all sorts of things. Nothing worked.
>
> I was still performing every night and it was miserable – because I felt as if I'd caused a big scene and let everyone down. So it took hours of mental and physical preparation to go through all this. It was as if I were preparing for death in a way, which made the panic even greater: 'Is it going to happen now? Am I going to feel this way again?' And I began to understand by the end of the run that in some way I was creating this.[13]

Richard Seer's overwhelming sense of self-sabotage is no doubt shared by many of us who have suffered acute stage fright. We'll explore this more in the course of *Facing the Fear*, as well as the idea of the power of the critics. But for the moment, let's have some more talking cure.

'Rejecting the play like a failed organ transplant': losing faith in the material

Tim Orr – Producing Artistic Director at the Colorado Shakespeare Festival – vividly conjures up in his story the panic that can arise when we lose faith, both in a play and in our actual, creative existence. Again, his words speak for themselves:

> A few years ago, I was in a production where I had a near panic attack in the middle of a performance, and it scared the hell out of me. In my mind, I was gripped by this overwhelming panic for five to ten minutes. In actuality, it was probably under a minute. It had never happened before and it has never happened since.

The play was a two-hander comedy from the early 1960s. It's horribly dated and hugely insensitive to women, it's not very funny, and it makes light of suicide. We were doing eight shows a week and I just hated doing it. My *body* didn't want to do the play. I had to drag myself to the theatre, put on that costume, and throw myself onto the stage. Not out of stage fright: it was just worse than digging a ditch. Because the play was a two-hander, I knew that as soon as I stepped out on stage, I wasn't leaving it for two hours. Two hours of having to speak the most awful dreck with no escape... The director and I had locked horns a couple of times during rehearsal because he wanted me to have twice the energy – but I just couldn't find it.

It's a Thursday matinee. There are seven people in the audience. I'm out there on the stage with the woman playing the other part. We're on page two of this play and she's talking. I know that she's about to finish talking *any second now...* and I suddenly realise that I just don't know what's going to come out of my mouth. I've had that feeling before on stage and I know that as soon as I inhale, something will come out – and nobody's going to die if I say the wrong thing or get lost for a moment. But usually I'm in a play with eight, nine, ten, fifteen people: there are places to hide, there are people to help.

She's still talking and I still have no idea what I'm going to say. And I realise that I'm blank about *the rest of the whole play*. That my body is about to say, 'No!' to doing it. That my body is going to reject doing the next hour and fifty-eight minutes of *this* play for *these* seven people in *this* auditorium. And I'm not going to be able to *will* my body. The whole play has just flown out of my head, and I don't think I'll be able to call it up right now – because I just don't want to do it! I suddenly break into a very cold sweat. And I think, 'I'm going to have to turn to the audience and apologise to them and leave the stage. I think I'm about to call the show! Yes, I think I'm about to do that!'

So the actress stops talking and I take a deep breath. And that's when I have the panic attack. I have a moment of doing absolutely nothing. Then I just start moving all over the stage, picking up all the books I can find and piling all these books into my arms – while blathering, babbling some words in the moment. Somehow it feels natural to start picking up props. I think, 'If I just start moving, the audience won't know that there's nothing happening in my head. If I'm moving, it'll look as though it's part of the action of the show – and I'll eventually get out of this silence in my head.' I knew my character's intention at this point in the play, so I improvised there for a second – and actually I was pretty darn close to the text. But it was as if I was on the outside, looking down – and it was terrifying!

At the same time, I was angry. I was angry about having to do this awful play. Angry that this was what I was doing for a living right now – in a terrible, terrible contract for a terrible, terrible wage. Doing this eight times a week was absolutely meaningless. And that anger suddenly gave me adrenalin. Adrenalin was leaking out of my ears and out of the corners of my eyes and I had more energy than I ever thought possible. And it launched me into the play. I was back on track. I got on a roll and I reached the finish line. Maybe the fear of the fear returning is what kept me going. I probably did the show at twice the speed – probably the speed that the director had wanted all along!

For the rest of the production run, I got through each performance on sheer willpower. The memory of that experience didn't leave me: it was always lurking in the back of my mind. Success for me was just getting through a show. I never felt as if I owned my performance: my body rejected that play like a failed organ transplant.[14]

From the inside out

What these vivid stories encourage – apart from the easeful cure of talking – is a curiosity about what causes stage fright in the first place. After all, few actors are the same again after they've experienced it. To begin answering these questions, *Facing the Fear* uses what's known as 'practice-based research'. Practice-based research is really just research based in *action* rather than *theory* to solve a problem. It operates from the inside out, in the sense that, as the writer of this book, I'm not a scholar or a critic or a psychologist. I'm an actor steeped in the experience of stage fright and I have a clear intention of finding some answers for that problem. Usually, in the creative arts, practice-based research is 'motivated by emotional, personal and subjective concerns'[15] – and that's exactly what stage fright is. It's emotional. It's very personal. And it's highly subjective. In the pages of this book, we analyse the personal, emotional, subjective experiences of stage fright to see how we can diminish the power of this otherwise crippling Fear – working from *inside* the problem and reaching *out* to our fellow actors.

The first half of *Facing the Fear* looks at the very nature of stage fright from various perspectives and we ask a series of questions. We start in Chapter 1 by asking, 'What is stage fright?' (And we'll look at it physiologically and psychologically.) In Chapter 2, we ask, 'How did we get here?' (And we look at the power of the audience itself.) Since most actors' biggest stage-fright fear is forgetting their lines (as we've seen in the three personal accounts so far), we address in Chapter 3 the question audiences ask us all the time: 'How do you remember all those lines?' (And we look at the neuroscience of memory and learning.)

Then in the second part of the book, we move into a practical terrain. In Chapter 4, we ask, 'What goes on in the rehearsal room?' (And we look at the immensely powerful actor-director relationship.) And finally in Chapter 5, we ask,

'How do we develop good practices?' (And we'll see how we can formulate our own anti-fear strategies.) The intention is that, by the end of *Facing the Fear*, we'll have torn stage fright to shreds – like a terrier with a rabbit in its jaws – till there's not much left to scare us.

The important thing to remember is that many actors never suffer bad stage fright. Most of us experience a lively adrenalin buzz – and that's perfectly normal, if not actually rather helpful. The point of this book is to dispel the *un*helpful nerves. If you've never suffered from stage fright, it's a chance for you to get to know what your fellow actors might be going through. And there's no need to worry that by knowing all the ins and outs of stage fright, you're somehow going to provoke it. In fact, the opposite is true. By the end of this book, you'll see that not only is a certain performance buzz a benefit, but that any unnecessary stage fright can ultimately be overcome. In fact, the monster is rather funny when you look it in the eye. It need be no more frightening than Shrek!

Fighting or facing?

When I originally conceived of this book, I was going to call it *Fighting the Fear*. Like Olivier in the quotation on the frontispiece, I saw it as a battle. As the quest has unfolded, though, I've become more and more convinced that if we *fight* against the fear, we actually make it worse. If we can live with it, finding positive ways of facing it – even *embracing* it – we really can diminish its grip and in many ways overcome it. The poet Maya Angelou was very open about her own nervousness before every performance. Her advice was categorical: 'Accept it; don't fight it.'[16] Sound advice – but we can't accept it until we've faced it. And although we're not going to fight it per se, we're going to adopt some battle imagery in our first stage of facing the fear, since forewarned is forearmed. Once we get out onto the battlefield, however, our maneouvres will be more like t'ai chi and aikido than those involving armoured tanks and AK47s: we'll topple our enemy by using its own force. But first, let's head into the war room and begin to know the nature of that enemy.

1

What is Stage Fright?

The Role of the Fear

'It is… a monster which hides in its foul corner without revealing itself, but you know that it is there… He can come at any time, in any form. The dark shadow of fear.'[17]

Laurence Olivier

1. *What is Stage Fright?*

'Know the enemy'

Sun Tzu (the famous Chinese general from 6 BCE) was a fearsome military strategist. 'Know the enemy and know yourself,' he wrote, 'and in a hundred battles you will never be in peril.'[18] The last thing we want when we're on the stage is to feel as if we're in peril. So our task in this chapter is to get to know our enemy – and that inevitably involves us getting to know our self. After all, the enemy of stage fright lurks inside our own brain and body: we ourselves are its Trojan Horse. It's a mind-expanding journey that we're about to embark upon. The terrain is treacherous. The enemy cunning. So, like generals in a war room, we'd better lay out a battle plan as clearly as we can.

There are three key assessments that we need to make: (1) How is the war waged? (2) Who is our enemy? And (3) What are our own capabilities? The bulk of this chapter falls into three sections that deal with each of these assessments.

In the first section – *A Bird's Eye View of the Processes of Stage Fright* – we address how the war is waged. We lay out the battle plan and examine the enemy's tactics, asking the questions: how do we experience stage fright? What provokes it, given our DNA (i.e. the *evolutionary factors* that we might not know)? What provokes it, given our industry (i.e. the *external factors* that we can't control)? What provokes it, given our temperaments (i.e. the *internal factors* that we might be able to change)?

In the second section – *The Nature of Fear* – we study more closely who our enemy is. As if we're placing figures onto the battle plan, we encounter the 'fear family' of worry, anxiety, stress and depression. After all, once we get to know our enemy, we can start to know our self.

The third section – *The Nature of Us* – is all about getting to know our self and our own capabilities, so that in a hundred battles we shall never be in peril. This involves us unpacking the basic paradox of acting: i.e. how can we be fully engrossed in the role while at the same time being attentive to all the technical stuff? As actors, we need this level of 'dual consciousness': indeed, we can't do our work without it. We have to be able to lose ourselves in the passionate kiss with Antony, whilst also making sure that we're in the light, that we're facing downstage, and that our Cleopatra headdress doesn't fall off. Yet when stage fright hits us, it's like an ambush. It can take us by surprise and with such a force, that our consciousness is no longer dual: instead, it shatters into a thousand shards. So in *The Nature of Us*, we look at what *consciousness* really means, in terms of who are we, and what makes us who we are. Then we may be able to understand what's happening when our consciousness fragments during stage fright.

The very thought of facing our stage fright can be daunting. Human beings are complex and there's a lot in this chapter to understand. So we'll end the chapter with a note on courage. In fact, we focus on two people whose courage turned their stage fright into something that could benefit us all: the pioneering actor-trainers, Konstantin Stanislavsky and Lee Strasberg.

By the end of this chapter, we should have some clear knowledge about how the enemy operates, who exactly they are, and who *we* are as their opponents. We'll then be in a stronger position with the following chapters to create some strategies for facing the fear and embracing the foe.

Assessment 1: A Bird's Eye View of the Processes of Stage Fright

Our first battle tactic is to recognise the two ways in which our stage fright manifests itself: *physiologically* and *psychologically*.

Physiological manifestations of stage fright

It's not difficult to recognise when our body is suffering an attack of stage fright. Our muscles tense. Our knees tremble. Our heart pounds. Our hands grow clammy. Butterflies batter about our stomach and we think we need the loo. Then out we go onto the stage – and just when we need our spittle to speak, our mouth dries up like the Sahara Desert. We suddenly feel light-headed, maybe even to the point of vertigo. In fact, when Anthony Sher was playing Iago in Japan for the Royal Shakespeare Company, he suffered 'small but alarming losses of balance' which threatened to tip him off the stage and he thought he was in an earthquake![19]

All these physiological gymnastics are the body adapting to what it knows to be an important situation. The trouble is that our body doesn't actually need to do all that preparation: it's out of kilter with the task in hand. After all, it's not an earthquake and we're not really under attack. And what happens when our physiological response is out of kilter is that we find it hard to concentrate on what we're supposed to be doing. Indeed, fractured concentration is a large part of the other incarnation of stage fright: the *psychological manifestation*.

Psychological manifestations of stage fright

Which comes first: the physiological manifestations or the psychological manifestations? It's not always clear. My own stage fright in *The Permanent Way* began totally out of the blue with the physiological manifestations, and then – like an unstoppable avalanche – the psychological manifestations followed. Thereon in, the dialogue between the physical and the psychological was self-perpetuating. I'd *think* about getting nervous and my body would come up with the signs – and then I'd *feel* nervous, and my body would show more signs. And so it went on... Which is actually perfectly normal, given that as human beings we're psychophysical. In other words, whatever happens in our body inextricably impacts our psyche, and whatever's going on in our psyche inextricably affects our body. Perhaps the most unsettling aspect of psychological stage fright is that it's *in our heads*: it's *us* creating our own distress, and that makes us feel as if we're going crazy. So what triggers this strange self-sabotage?

The basic trigger for psychological stage fright is usually some kind of dislocation from the script. An interfering thought suddenly pops into our heads, and we find ourselves thinking about something other than just performing. And this can be the first warning sign of a more disruptive fracture in our consciousness. Here's how: in everyday life, we have two 'selves' which normally collaborate very effectively so that we can go about our daily business. These two selves are known as the 'functioning self' and the 'observing self'.[20]

The *functioning self* is the part of us that gets on with the task in hand. It enables us to live happily during a performance in our dual existence of kissing Antony while finding the light, facing downstage, and holding on to our headdress.

The *observing self* deals with any necessary adjustments. It responds with split-second timing to the coughing fit on the fifth row (if it's theatre); it adapts our performance from the long-shot to the mid-shot to the close-up (if it's film); it picks up the asp that just fell off the divan without interrupting the dialogue. And, at its best, our observing self is our invaluable ally. Yet at its worst, our observing self becomes a self-sabotaging demon, watching us objectively with an evil smirk. And, when psychological stage fright kicks in, that demon starts to create all kinds of unhelpful scenarios.

Sometimes in those scenarios we become overwhelmingly aware of our own body. Actions that we normally execute without even thinking – walking or sitting or picking up a cup – become trembly and self-conscious. As the beleaguered actress Nina bewails in Chekhov's *The Seagull*, 'I didn't know what to do with my hands. I didn't know how to stand, I couldn't control my voice.'[21] With psychological stage fright, we become 'helpless witnesses to our own malfunctioning'.[22]

*

Clearly, stage fright is not very pleasant – either physiologically or psychologically. Yet this is the first step in knowing our enemy: registering what it feels like when they've embarked on an attack. The next step is to look at why the attack happens in the first place. Why do we find the career that we love becoming the experience that we dread? One of the answers to this question lies in our *evolution*. So let's go right back some 200,000 years...

Evolutionary provokers of stage fright

Picture this for a moment. We're sitting in the mouth of our cave. Out there in the darkness, we see – or maybe only sense – blinking eyes staring back at us in silence. Far from being a rapt audience listening to our recounting of a brave day's hunting, those eyes belong to creatures fathoming out whether or not to eat us. And the thought of being devoured triggers the most ancient part of our brain to spring into survival-mode action. That ancient part is the tiny, almond-shaped amygdala. So – in the briefest of briefs – what does the amygdala do?

Well, picture this for a moment. It's another late-night scenario. A nervous young sentinel is sitting at the outpost, surrounded by darkness. With hyper-attentive vigilance, he suddenly sees a spark in the dark, and he rushes back to the camp shouting, 'Alert! Alert! We're under attack!' 'Nonsense,' says the commander, knowingly. 'That was just Carruthers lighting a cigarette.' That twitchy sentinel is a bit like our amygdala. ('The Vigilante', I call him in Chapter 3.) It responds more quickly to a potential threat than the brain regions that emerged later in our evolution (the regions connected to our more sophisticated consciousness). So whether or not we actually *need* to fear a situation, the amygdala sends fear signals to our body and brain. What this can mean if we're actors in the throes of performing a scene is that the amygdala senses all those eyes watching us ('devouringly') in the dark and it triggers our fear. Yet there's nothing to be afraid of: there's nothing out there to devour us. It's only the audience and the ushers, or the camera crew and the director, watching us supportively as we do our work. Strange as it may seem, the fear of being watched is hardwired into our brain. Which means that when it comes to keeping cool under pressure, 'Virtually by design, crowds are destined to make most of us want to flee the vicinity in terror.'[23]

But as actors we can't flee. We're trapped – in the wings just about to make an entrance. Or on the stage in the middle of a scene. Or in front of the cameras with vast amounts of money dependent on our performance. And we're not just trapped by the fact that we've got a job to do: the setting itself can hem us in. A traverse stage (with the audience on both sides), a thrust stage (with the audience on three sides), an arena (with the audience on *all* sides), or a film set (with crew, grips, floor managers, make-up teams and extras *everywhere*)... – You can see just how terrifying these environments can be when our primitive survival-mode kicks in. All eyes are on us and there's no place to shelter. But even if we could escape, our normal coping strategies are on hold, as we're *not* 'ourselves': we're in the given circumstances of a fictional character. And our job requires that we behave in ways appropriate to that character. It's the unavoidable 'schizophrenia' innate in our profession. And the very fact that, in the process of doing our job, we're consciously dislocated from our own, personal behaviour patterns can be pretty traumatic.

*

When you consider some of these innate, evolutionary fears that are built into our experience of public performance, stage fright is suddenly perfectly understandable and highly forgivable. And that's just the start. That's just the evolutionary stuff. What about the *external realities attached to our profession* that can potentially provoke our fear?

External provokers of stage fright

There are certain facts of the industry that can stir up our nerves. In fact, a degree of low-level anxiety underpins our whole profession, so we need to keep our wits about us. Here are just a couple of red flags.

Loss of control over our careers

When we sign up for a life as an actor, we essentially surrender our agency over our lives. (There's a reason why our agents are called 'agents'.) Unless we have a strong entrepreneurial streak – like Kenneth Branagh or Kevin Spacey – or the wherewithal to make our own work, we're dependent on our agents, managers, directors and casting directors, and a whole host of other figures in production, commerce and administration to determine our personal destiny. If we're not careful, we begin to feel like a leaf on a breeze, fluttering wherever the next gust takes us. We don't book a vacation – just in case the phone rings and we get an audition. We commit to a family reunion – and, sure enough, the phone rings and we've got an audition. And as researchers into happiness have found, when we lose autonomy over our lives, the feeling in extreme circumstances can be devastating.[24]

We might be able to deal with the loss of autonomy – of when, where and whether the jobs come up – if it weren't for the fact that there are so many variables in how the roles are actually cast. Which takes us to our second external provoker of stage fright: *the vagaries of casting.*

The vagaries of casting

The employment statistics in the acting industry have never been particularly encouraging. And it's not just a matter of money. Any of us who have endured bouts of unemployment know that an actor without a job is like a soul without a body. Not knowing what to do with ourselves or how to channel our creative instincts when we're out of work naturally makes us nervous and unhappy. 'Inactivity and the feeling of helplessness are the greatest enemies of happiness.'[25] And our helplessness is exacerbated by employers not necessarily knowing what type of person they want for a role until a particular actor walks through the casting-room door and they suddenly go, 'Yes – that's it!' We want to be versatile, so that we can make ourselves available for a wide range of jobs. Yet, at the same time, our agents – the major gatekeepers into our employment opportunities – have to categorise us in order to work most effectively for us. If your type is obvious – 'beautiful juve', 'funny fat friend', 'muscular tough guy' – then it's easier to market the product that is 'you'. As we become better known, the product that is 'us' can actually get us the work. The lucky few become a kind of brand

– be it the 'Eddie Redmayne' or the 'Carey Mulligan' or the 'George Clooney', etc. But for many of us, it's really not so clear.

*

For some actors, the uncertainty of the industry is part of the kick. They don't want to know what they're doing next week, let alone next month or next year. They shy away from the restrictions of a 'proper' job. And they're quite happy for their agents to deal with all their financial concerns. Yet it's a hardened soul that isn't at all affected by the loss of control and the vagaries of casting. And then these external factors can arouse *internal feelings* that also trigger our stage fright.

Internal provokers of stage fright

As Newton's third law in physics tells us: for every action, there's an equal and opposite reaction. It's just the same with creativity. Anyone who has the capacity to be highly creative also has the capacity to be deeply destructive. And most of us as creative artists pendulum-swing somewhere between the two extremes. Sometimes we can control it, sometimes we can't. So what are the inner, temperamental tendencies that can nudge us towards stage fright? If we know that they're there, we can be on our guard...

Perfectionism

Every musician knows that a B flat can only be a B flat. It can't be a B. It can't be an A. There's a precision to it, a perfection. Just so for the ballerina, as she drills the technicality of a pas de chat. Just so for the skater, as he executes a triple Salchow. But acting? Acting is messy. It's an imperfect craft. It's about expressing human behaviour. And human beings are chaotic – they're unpredictable and contradictory. And, therefore, so is acting. Added to which, the *technique* of acting is endlessly variable because each of us has such an individual instrument. *My* voice, *your* anatomy, *his* emotional palette is entirely unique, so there can never be a definitive way of honing an actor's instrument or interpreting a character. As a young Antony Sher discovered, 'I had yet to learn the golden rule about acting – there isn't one. No blueprint. No single technique.'[26] It's a reality we have to deal with: there *is* no blueprint, ergo there can be no perfect performance. Yet, so often as actors we ignore that reality. We're high achievers. Ambition drives us. So we aspire to artistic *perfectionism.*

However, perfectionism and creativity are highly incompatible. In fact, psychologists Hewitt and Flett go so far as to say that perfectionism is a neurosis. A perfectionist personality (they suggest) *subverts* the very act of performance and '*nothing* good can ever come of perfectionism'.[27]

In and of itself, aspiring to our best isn't bad. The tricky thing with perfectionism, though – besides being impossible in acting – is that it can also tip us into *self-sabotage.* And that's when stage fright can really make us feel as if we're sending ourselves crazy.

Self-sabotage

Steve Blass was an ace pitcher for the Pittsburgh Pirates – until performance anxiety threatened his professional career. He described it as an imp hiding inside his body, sabotaging his every throw: 'I could start the wind-up the way I wanted to, but then at the point of release it just *froze.* Way down deep, I'd say to myself, *This is not going to work.*'[28] And sure enough – he'd screw it up! Although this is a sports tale, any of us who have experienced severe stage fright will probably recognise the same inner imp. Our very own mind turns into our nemesis, our own inner terrorist, sabotaging our performance joy. Musician Stephen Nachmanovitch describes it as 'a petty tyrant who has entered our lives' and starts taunting us with judging inner voices that 'throw doubt on whether we are good enough, smart enough, the right size or shape'.[29]

There's a name for our inner imp's judgemental voices. Psychopathologists call them 'toxic introjects', and they're self-interruptions in the flow of our lives. Basically, there are two components to a toxic introject. First of all, there's a *content* (i.e. a subject which is specifically forbidden). Then, allied to that content, there's a *catastrophic expectation* (i.e. a threat that something awful will happen if we disobey the voice).[30] Unfortunately, our dialogue between the 'forbidden content' and the 'catastrophic expectation' can be woefully compelling: it can hook us in its thrall. And when we're suffering stage fright, our toxic introjects can go in one of two equally compelling (though equally distressing) directions.

The first direction involves our judgemental, parental voice, warning us, 'You'd better not screw up. You'd better not forget your lines. It'll end your career.' In this case, the 'forbidden content' is forgetting our lines. (After all, knowing the lines is the very least we'd expect of a professional actor.) The 'catastrophic expectation' is that we'll ruin our career if we do forget them. (After all, if knowing the lines is the least we'd expect of a professional actor, then surely we don't deserve to be called a professional actor if we *do* forget them!)

The other direction that our toxic introject can take is even more perplexing, as it's less like the judging parent and more like the wicked child – not so much forbidding us as goading us. The 'content' becomes, 'You're going to forget your lines. You're going to screw up. You're going to humiliate yourself in front of this audience!' (It really is the imp in our head.) The 'catastrophic expectation' becomes, 'I knew you'd screw up. I knew I could wreck your performance. I knew you were nuts!!' And this is the most toxic part of it: something in our brain knows that sabotaging ourselves so acutely – turning something that we love (i.e. acting) into something that we dread – is just plain crazy. Why would *anybody* do that to themselves?

And yet we *do*. But even more perversely (and this shows how cunning the Fear can be), *any* self-interruption can throw a spanner in the works. It doesn't need to be a 'negative' thought. A 'positive' distraction can be just as self-sabotaging. How many times have we been onstage in the full swing of our acting and we've momentarily thought, 'Hey, this is going well!' only to find that this very thought seizes our attention away from the stage narrative, and we suddenly have no idea what we say next? It's known as 'self-enthrallment'.[31] And in that moment of naive, narcissistic awareness of 'Aren't I good?', we're so pleased with what we just did that we forget what we're supposed to do next. And that momentary lapse – even though it's a 'positive' one – can just as easily bring on stage fright. In other words, we don't have to be feeling anxious for stage fright to ambush us; on the contrary, we can be feeling just great. Yes, that's how sneaky the Fear can be – all the more reason to 'know the enemy'.

The truth of the matter is that these inner monologues merrily chatter away in our heads all the time in our everyday life, and yet we usually manage to function perfectly well. But when it comes to performing, we have to rein them in like wild mustangs. If those inner monologues become self-sabotaging, we also run the risk of (what's known in performance psychology and sports psychology as) *choking*.

Choking

Choking is a little different from self-sabotage. With the inner monologue of *self-sabotage*, the audience may barely notice anything is amiss. With *choking*, it's bloody obvious to everyone! The word *anxiety* actually 'comes from the French *anguere*, meaning to choke, constrict, strangle, or cut off at the airway.'[32] And the term 'choking' is used to describe what's known in psychology as a 'sub-optimal performance'. A sub-optimal performance is one in which we do worse than what we know we're capable of doing, worse than we've done in the past, and worse than everyone – including ourselves – expects us to do now.[33] It can only really happen in a stressful situation when the stakes are personally and professionally high. (It's hardly likely to happen if we're pootling through a practice of a performance alone in the back garden. No 'devouring' eyes are watching and there's little to prove.) Whereas self-sabotage tends to manifest as an unseen, psychological phenomenon in our heads, choking tends to focus on our body and our movement. It might even bring us to a grinding halt. That's why it's so bloody obvious to everyone when it's happening (as we'll see in Chapter 2 with the tale of Paul Greenwood). So how does choking come to pass?

Whenever we learn a new task – such as a new song-and-dance routine or stage fight – we have to think about it consciously at first so that we can coordinate the various parts of our body. To do this, we use what's known as our 'short-term memory' (also known as our 'recent' or 'working' memory). We're actively thinking, 'Where do my arms go? Where do my feet go? Is this a thrust or a parry?' The more we rehearse the activity, the more accomplished we become. And maybe by the tenth time of doing the dance routine or the fight, we can integrate all of these coordinated actions without even thinking about them. This is because we've now lodged them in our 'long-term memory' (also known as our 'implicit' or 'explicit' memory, depending on the nature of the memory). (Just note for the moment that our long-term memory is housed in the region of our brain known as the 'prefrontal cortex'. We'll look at all this in greater detail in Chapter 3 when we unpack the processes of learning.)

What happens with choking is that the information we've lodged in our implicit long-term memory – through all those hours of practice and endless repetitions – suddenly becomes yanked out of that implicit (unconscious) memory and plonked back into our explicit (conscious) memory. The result is that we start to think about it too much – and so we screw it up. We choke. We suffer from what psychologists call *paralysis by analysis* – because now we're overthinking what our brain already knows. What this means when we're acting is that we may suddenly become overly aware of our movements. ('Is this where I normally do the shuffle-step-ball-change? Is this where I parry his attack?') Or we may start to question the words of the text. ('Is that the right word? Does that sound right?') And actively questioning what we already know scares the bejesus out of us.

We worsen our paralysis if we start presuming that the audience knows how afraid we are. We think they can see right through our mask of confidence. We imagine that they're judging how well we're managing to keep our demons at bay. 'Or will tonight be the night when we screw it all up? Oh, the audience will love that, won't they? They'd love to see us fail!' We unwittingly turn the audience into our adversaries. And, as these negative thoughts thicken, every waking moment – even when we're not on stage – becomes a living nightmare (as we saw with Richard Seer in the Introduction). We can't just go about our usual routines because we're too busy anticipating what we're afraid might happen in tonight's performance. This anticipation in and of itself can put us into choke-mode hours before the actual show. It's those pesky imps in our brain again. And when those imps are let loose on stage, they don't just cause us to screw up our well-rehearsed words and actions: they can actually make us believe that we're going to do something way more inappropriate...

Loss of inhibition

It was the second night of Nell Dunn's *Steaming* at the Swan Theatre, Worcester, and I was playing Josie, the foul-mouthed hooker. The build-up to the production had been quite intense, as the play involved several of us stripping down to our Naughty Naked Nude. Consequently, the adrenalin rush at the first performance had been pretty huge. To my great surprise, however, I'd actually loved the experience – and the second night promised to be a breeze.

So, on that second night – as I came launching in for the scene in which I take off all my clothes – I delivered the first sentence of a highly strung rant of a speech and… Instead of saying the playwright's text, out of my mouth came words of dubious origin. I think I might even have said (though I can't actually remember), 'I've no idea what I'm talking about…' It was the only other time in my life that I've suffered sudden and unexpected stage fright.

I must have finished the speech all right, as my onstage partner continued with her cue as if everything were perfectly fine. Yet, in the moment of screwing up my lines, I had to rein myself in like a wild horse to stop myself from turning to the audience and saying, 'What are you all looking at? Have you any idea of the hell I'm going through up here?' This kind of temporary sense of *loss of inhibition* – this dreamlike quality of 'What the fuck?!' – is a real shock to the system. And it can lead us to believe that we're going seriously nuts.

Mercifully, it's actually a very common experience. In fact, psychotherapist Alvin R. Mahrer describes its many facets: 'There is a fear of losing control, of giving up that moment-by-moment control that is almost always there. There is a fear of becoming uncivilised, out of control, wild, animal-like. There is a fear of craziness, lunacy, derangement, losing your mind.'[34] And there are some reassuring explanations for why we suddenly find ourselves in this uncivilised derangement. 'When the stress is on,' explains cognitive scientist Sian Beilock, 'working memory and the prefrontal cortex can be compromised and our *inhibition* is one of the first things to go.'[35] Not only does the prefrontal cortex house our long-term memory (as I noted earlier), it's also the seat of our ability to *appraise* a situation. So when stage fright attacks us, our ability to appraise what we're doing becomes compromised: 'Handling yourself appropriately under pressure involves recognizing when your prefrontal cortex is most likely to resemble that of a *teenage brain* and applying effective techniques to deal with the regression.'[36]

So that's what's happening! We momentarily regress into a 'What the fuck?!' teenager! It's a blessed relief to discover that we're not alone in feeling these sudden unleashings of primitive, chaotic voices in our head. What's more, we're not going mad. We're just experiencing one of the effects of the chemicals released in our brain when our body is under stress. In fact, an actor once told me of his stage fright during a schools tour, which manifested as a barely controllable desire to face the nine-year-old audience and yell, 'Fuck the lot of you!' He was so worried about this maniacal voice in his head that he decided to go for therapy. For any of us who have grappled with that anarchic inner monologue, it's such a relief to know that we're not crazy. We're perfectly normal. We're just dealing with our brain's complex hard-wiring. A deep breath, a moment of reappraisal – and that teenage brain will sober up.

*

So there we have it. Assessment 1 complete. We've laid out the battle plan. We've studied how the war is waged. We've seen how stage fright manifests itself both physiologically and psychologically. We've looked at some of the evolutionary, external, and internal provokers of stage fright. So now Assessment 2 involves us analysing *The Nature of Fear* itself. As we encounter the enemy, we see it has various subdivisions – which I'm going to call the 'Fear Family'. They include worry, anxiety, stress and (even) depression. That may sound like a grim cohort of adversaries. Yet, as ever, forewarned is forearmed. If we can lay these adversaries out on the map in the war room, we can understand them better and diminish their potential threat. Onwards...

Assessment 2: The Nature of Fear

Let's start by getting a few things straight. Who *is* this enemy? And what do we need to know about the Fear? Here are four quick insights into how it generally operates.

Four things we need to know about fear

First of all, *we're conditioned as human beings to be afraid of fear.* It's one of our six fundamental emotions (along with anger, disgust, happiness, sadness and surprise) – and much of the world runs on our fear of fear. Burglar alarms, insurance policies, medications, airport security systems, Ebola-avoidance tactics, earthquake drills – you name it. But fear befuddles us. 'No passion so effectively robs the mind of all its powers of acting and reasoning as fear.'[37] (So said philosopher Edmund Burke back in the 1700s.) Which is why we're conditioned to be afraid – it can bypass much of our reason so that we don't question things too much!

Yet, the second point to note is that (despite our deliberate battle talk in this chapter) *fear itself has no sinister intentions.* How can it have? We know it's not really an ugly homunculus sitting inside our head – a pesky imp or a monster or a demon. In fact, fear is nothing but a series of physiological activities. And those activities are highly helpful. They're designed to equip us to deal with danger and get us to safety quickly, so we should be incredibly grateful for fear. It makes all our major decisions for us. It gives particular meaning to our achievements. It makes us feel more alive.[38] It even improves our performance: we've known for more than a hundred years that human performance actually *peaks* when we hit an optimal nervous activation.[39] So, we shouldn't be afraid of fear. It's an albeit primitive means of ensuring that we don't just survive – we actually thrive.

But this is the third thing we have to note: *fear is primitive.* And that's part of the stage-fright problem. As we've already seen, it's triggered in the ancient part of our brain known as the amygdala. On one level, this tiny little security system is amazing. It's designed to automatically override every other conscious thought in our head so that – right this minute, in this danger – we survive. And we survive by doing one of three things: we freeze, flee or fight. That's great – but on another level, it's very primitive. It's primitive because this fear system is designed for hunter-gatherers – and obviously we're not hunter-gatherers any more. So, there are times when the amygdala makes us take a particular action – like freeze, flee or fight – when the circumstances don't require us to do anything quite so drastic. Certainly not as actors. And certainly not in the theatre. Let's be honest: our average audience is hardly going to harm us, let alone kill us.

And this is the fourth thing we need to note about fear: *it can't tell the difference between a real threat and an imagined threat.* For all our technological advancements in the twenty-first century, our subconscious is still too primitive to tell the difference between reality and imagination. In fact, sometimes we're even *more* scared of what we imagine than what we actually perceive.[40] Think of those vivid nightmares from which we awake with pounding heart and shallow breath and sweating body – as if we really *were* being chased by the Russian drug cartel even though we're snug in bed. And it's the same with our attitude towards an audience. If we *think* they're worth being afraid of, then that's exactly what we'll do. In fact, our fear response is so primitive that we can condition ourselves to be frightened of something that's absolutely neutral,[41] like a house spider, or going on stage. Neither of them is a *real* threat. They're both quite benign – if not rather magical.

So those are four quick insights into fear to help us understand how it operates. We know it affects our *mind.* And we know it fuels our *imagination*. So now let's get to the nitty-gritty of what it does to our *body*. Let's unpack those physiological manifestations that we listed at the start of this chapter.

What's going on in our body when our fear system revs up?

The answer is: a lot!

When our body thinks we're in danger, a huge amount of physiological activity immediately kicks in. After all, we might have to flee or fight, so we'd better be ready to respond. To which end, more blood pumps through our arteries and our breathing quickens, in order that a surge of adrenalin can send more glucose and oxygen straight to our large muscle groups. (That's good. Now our arms and legs are charged with energy ready for emergency action.) Then the blood vessels on the surface of our skin constrict so that our skin grows pale and slightly numb. (That's good. It's like a temporary layer of armour. Now we're less likely to hurt or bleed if we're injured in the possible fight or flight.) Arteries – lungs – blood – muscles – limbs – skin! That's a lot of instantaneous and all-consuming activity. No wonder fear makes us feel more alive. That's exactly what it's trying to do – keep us alive.

The downside of all this major preparation for action is that our more intricate motor skills are seriously impaired. And that's why stage fright is a major screw-up for us as actors. Suddenly we can't hold our props. Why not? Because the blood flow to our skin is constricted, so our hands have become shaky and clammy. Suddenly we've got a kaleidoscope of butterflies beating inside our queasy tummy. Why? Because eating isn't a priority at this moment, so our digestive processes are shutting down. Suddenly our mouth is as dry as cotton wool. Why? Because we're not eating, so we don't need saliva for breaking down food. But worst of worst: our bowels feel like they're going to explode and we seem to be dying for a pee all the time. *Why, oh why?* Because we might have to run away, so we need to keep ourselves as light as possible by jettisoning any extra weight.[42] ('Any extra weight? But I only had a banana for supper!') As if all that wasn't traumatic enough, now our pupils are dilating so that our vision is heightened in case we have to see our passage of escape. But the only thing it's doing in the end is making us see more clearly those audience members – sitting out there, ravenously gazing from the cavernous darkness of the auditorium!

But it doesn't stop there! This survival activity isn't just physical – it's profoundly neurological. So our conscious mind gets hauled into the action, too. If we're seriously under threat, our mind needs to keep things as simple as possible, so that we only have to make one basic choice: flee or fight? Anything more complex and we could be dead by the time we've thought it through. In other words, our ability to process any complex, neurological challenges totally plummets. This is a disaster if we're trying to act. How on earth can we do our job if we can't process complex, neurological challenges – like remembering our lines and engaging with the script's emotional nuances?

And it doesn't stop *there*. If you've ever felt light-headed when you've been attacked by stage fright (as I certainly did in *The Permanent Way*), it's because in big-fear, real-life, stress situations, our neural framework often maxes out. It's almost as if the whole fear experience is far too monumental for our brain to compute.[43] So instead of trying to process whatever's going on, our brain ensures that we don't have to process *anything*. And so we faint – or freeze – or at least, we come close to it. (Which, I suppose, is why I felt in *The Permanent Way* that I was in a strange floating-away place.)

With so much going on chemically and neurologically in our bodies and brains, it's no wonder we experience stage fright like some massive, inner earthquake. Because it is! Which is why we have to seek ways of befriending the Fear so that we can lessen its grip. If we don't, its long-term effect on our lives can be very destructive – both physically and mentally. On the subject of which, it's time to encounter some of the members of the Fear Family, as they can play a major role in how we deal with stage fright. We start with *worry* – as he's the kind of kid brother, the easiest to handle.

Worry

Worry is the result of our imagination going haywire. It grabs onto an event that might hold some potential threat, and it starts up a Fear Voice, conjuring up all kinds of things that *might* happen in some imaginary future. And thus it morphs that event into something way out of proportion with reality. In other words, worry doesn't *process* fear: it *incubates* it.[44] And there are three main reasons for facing our worry – otherwise, it can be very unhelpful to us as actors.

First of all, *worry mutes our emotional expressiveness*. That's not a great thing for us as actors, either for interpreting characters or for our long-term career trajectories. If we let a worry-monologue burble away, we become afraid of putting ourselves into experiences that we might find unsettling, and then we don't give ourselves the chance to overcome those worries. So we don't take that bold choice in rehearsals, in case we look stupid. So we don't talk to that director in the bar, in case they think we're coming on to them for a job. So we don't call our agent and tell them about a casting that we've just heard about, in case they say we're not pretty enough/young enough/famous enough (delete as appropriate). And thus we restrict our chances to expand our self-expression.

Second, *worrying takes up our vital short-term memory* – memory that we could otherwise be using for relevant activities, such as learning our lines. After all, our brain is not so different from the storage system on our computers. We only have a certain amount of active memory available to us at any one time.

So we don't want to clog it up with useless ramblings about fantasised, apocalyptic futures. (Unlike our computers, we don't have pop-up blockers in our head to stop the junk coming in; therefore, we have to do it consciously.)

Third, *it's impossible for us to 'talk' with two voices at once.* This is especially important for us to remember when we're performing. Whether it's an inner worry-monologue or an actual spoken script, those voices are language-based and, therefore, they both use the same neural networks in our brain. It's a bit like a telephone connection: only one party can come through at a time. So if we've got a powerful, inner worry-monologue telling us that we just screwed up a scene, then it's taking up the 'telephone line' that we should be using to deliver our character's text. This is double-whammy self-sabotage. Not only are we sending ourselves criticising messages that are totally non-conducive to giving a great performance, but we're also draining our brain of vital horsepower to do the very job that we're supposed to be doing.

There's no denying that the worry-monologue can really screw us up as actors, which is why we have to keep an ear out for the kid brother. Otherwise, it can foment in the long term a more persistent *anxiety*.

Anxiety

A close cousin of worry, *anxiety* is way more pernicious: it's a busy activity that significantly affects our nervous system. In very simple terms, our nervous system has two sides. One is known as 'the sympathetic nervous system' and it's our *on*-switch (if we feel under threat, it switches us to 'alert', and makes us ready to fight or flee). The other is known as 'the parasympathetic nervous system' and it's our *off*-switch (it calms us down, relaxes us, and helps us go to sleep at night). As we go about our daily life, the actions of the sympathetic and parasympathetic systems 'are always in balance, one tending to dominate the other according to what we need to do.'[45] If something is worrying us – 'Did I finish my tax return?' – it's usually fairly easy to remedy the situation and turn the switch to *off*.

What happens when we're anxious is that our *on*-switch becomes stuck. And when we're stuck in *on*, our concerns start to snowball and the results soon manifest themselves. For example, suppose we're about to go on stage and we're suffering performance anxiety: that anxiety shows up in three different ways. We have a *mental* response (which only we can know as it's inside our head, but it's usually along the lines of, 'I'm going to screw up!'). We have a *behavioural* response (which other people can see as they notice us muttering our lines or pacing backstage like a tiger). And we have a *physiological* response (which are the changes we've talked about already: the sweating palms, the butterflies, and all the other reactions of our body to the fight-or-flight dilemma). So, like I say, anxiety is a pretty busy activity.

What's more, it's totally antithetical to acting. Most of us love acting because it gives us a heightened state of presence, a real *in-the-moment* aliveness. Anxiety, on the other hand, is all about the *future* – a future full of anticipated, negative outcomes. So it's impossible for us to be *present* and to be *anxious* at the same time. So which would we rather experience? Pleasurable engagement with the present-tense experience of the onstage storytelling? Or anxiety-drenched focus on an imagined, calamitous future? It's another no-brainer, isn't it? We'll uncover some strategies for 'tripping the switch' throughout this book, but for the moment our task in encountering the Fear Family is to understand how unhelpful they are. And not just unhelpful, but unhealthy.

Indeed, one of the most compelling reasons for confronting our anxiety is that it's closely related to long-term *stress* – and that can be very damaging to our body.

Stress

Stress is a bad boy in the family. Stress involves chemicals. And those chemicals can cause us real harm. So how does that come to pass?

As human beings, we need certain challenges to keep us motivated and excited. It's how we learn and grow. So we take on a Shakespeare role – or we feature in an action movie. Yet when a challenging situation overwhelms us and we can no longer meet that challenge, our system is chronically and repeatedly exposed to adrenalin and stress hormones (such as cortisol). In other words, stress is the chemical result that arises when we find a situation emotionally or physically challenging and we don't know how to deal with it. So stress doesn't just *affect* our brain (like the voices of worry and anxiety do), stress actually *changes* our brain. And most disruptively for us as actors, it causes serious, long-term memory problems. When we're stressed, various networks in our brain (that would normally work together to help us with our reasoning) stop cooperating with each other. And 'this can have dire consequences for our thinking and our memory capabilities.'[46] Obviously that's bad news for us as actors.

The reason that we have to be on our guard against stress is that it increases over time. Fear can actually come and go pretty quickly: it's acute and obvious. (Like the adrenalin rush as we slam on the brakes to avoid the plastic bag on the motorway that we momentarily thought was a dog – the fear arrives in a nanosecond and goes within minutes.) But stress is chronic and subtle. Over time, it floods our body with more and more toxins which impede our mental and physical efficiency. So we can't ignore it. In fact, if we don't face our stage fright, the stress that arises can be hugely detrimental to our brain. Stress and a healthy brain are incompatible. Stress and pleasure, likewise. Which is why we should talk about our stage fright and air our anxieties (as we discussed in the

Introduction). Because if we don't... our stress can worsen and then *depression* can darken our life.

Depression

Depression is like Masha in *The Seagull*. Always in black. In mourning for her life. Pinching snuff and swigging vodka and hiding in the shadows. So how does depression descend upon us? Basically, when stress builds up chronically and lasts for a long time, the stress hormones don't disappear from our body. They linger in our system, causing significant chemical imbalances. And when our brain becomes heavily imbalanced, depression can set in.

With depression, our brain loses its adaptability.[47] It's no longer nimble and curious and excitable. We don't want to seize new opportunities, face new challenges, learn new speeches, or meet new casting directors. Instead, a kind of melancholy state of rigidity sets in, paralysing all our va-va-voom and hardening our depressive condition like a rock. And in this ossified, depressive state, our brain continues to imagine and create threats that simply don't exist. The future can seem like an endless tunnel of unemployment or unfulfilling bit parts. We become increasingly despondent about our powerlessness to carve out a professional path. And, even when we're *in* a job, we talk ourselves into believing that the director doesn't think we're *up* to the job and so we look for ways to get *out* of the job. When we're stuck in these dark and ossified states, we just can't seem to shift the blackness.

*

Now you see the enemies that we're up against. And how important it is that we disempower them – especially given the nature of our industry where they could so easily and subtly claim terrain. We're the general in this war room, figuring out who's where and what they're doing, and – if they've already made inroads to our territory – how we can best stop them in their tracks. But before we draw close enough to face the foe through the rest of this book, we ought to consider the actual nature of the general in this war: i.e. us and our own capabilities. After all, 'Know the enemy and know yourself: and in a hundred battles you will never be in peril.'

But who exactly is 'us'? That's a hard enough question to answer in everyday life, let alone as actors. Let alone when we're suffering stage fright. We've already noted that when stage fright hits, it's like an ambush. It's a force so great that we can temporarily forget who we are. And our normal degree of professional dual consciousness can fragment into myriad pieces. Time, then, for Assessment 3: to take a look at who we are *before* we're fractured so that we can understand what to do if we *become* fractured.

Assessment 3: The Nature of Us

It's not surprising that, when we suffer stage fright, it can feel as though our whole sense of self is disintegrating. Our job is challenging enough under normal circumstances. In the throes of performance, we're multitasking like mad. We've got four identities that we're juggling simultaneously, and they're spread across all four points of our own inner compass.

First of all, we've got *our self* – our own personality. (This will determine how we interpret a part. So Ralph Fiennes will make different choices about Richard III from Antony Sher or Al Pacino. Mariah Gale will make different choices about Ophelia from Helena Bonham Carter or Kate Winslet. And directors often cast us specifically because they want the choices that come most naturally to our particular imagination.)

Second, we've got the *role* – the writer's creation. (This will bring out different aspects of our individual personality. For example, my Masha will be different from my Mad Margaret, which will be different from my Mrs Cratchit or my Maria Marten.)

So the 'self' and the 'role' form the north–south pole. And there's a kind of symbiotic relationship between the two of them: 'I'll bring out these qualities in the role, and the role will bring out these qualities in me.'

Third, we've got the *technician* – the actor. (This is one half of our dual consciousness: the half that knows we have to deliver the lines, hit the mark, find the prop, and tell the story.)

Finally, we've got the *character in performance*. (This is the other half of our dual consciousness: the half that immerses us in the flow of the show, finding the rhythms each night, feeling the emotions afresh, and connecting to our onstage partners.)

The 'technician' and the 'character in performance' form the east–west pole. (We referred to it earlier as the collaboration between the *observing self* and the *functioning self*.)

So you can see there's a lot going on here. And at the centre of the compass of these four points is just *us*: our body, our imagination, our emotional palette, and our voice. So, in the throes of performance, there's a complex balancing act that's taking place inside what's already a complex consciousness.

But what exactly *is* consciousness? And who exactly *are* we? To unlock this thorny issue, we're going to use a simple analogy. Just imagine for a moment that each one of us comprises all the generals in the war-room setting out to battle with stage fright. So we're not just one general – we're actually three.

General number 1: our protoself

At the centre of our war room stands the perfect general. The general who never gets flustered. His task isn't to think about the enemy or work out the strategy or worry over the consequences. His task is simply to make sure that everything is just fine. So simple is his task that it requires no conscious awareness. In fact, it may surprise you to know that 'who we are' actually starts at a place of *no* consciousness. Let's turn to the major pioneer of consciousness studies – psychologist and neuroscientist Antonio Damasio – to unpack this analogy...

Every moment (and usually without us thinking about it), our body is beavering away looking after us, making sure that we're doing okay as a living organism. ('Am I warm? Am I cool? Am I comfortable? Am I breathing?') And at the heart of this activity is our *protoself*. Our protoself is a kind of Zen master extraordinaire in a place of pure existence. It has no powers of perception. It holds no knowledge. It doesn't interpret anything. In other words, it actually has no consciousness of its own – because it doesn't *know* that it knows anything. It simply offers reference points, such as 'pain in rib' or 'light in eyes' or 'grumbling in tummy'. And it leaves it to another part of our brain to interpret that information and to act upon it accordingly: 'Loosen corset between acts.' 'Move out of partner's follow-spot.' 'Remember to eat in the interval.'

The protoself's only concern is our organism's physiological balance in the world (otherwise known as our 'homeostasis'). It just makes sure that we're doing fine. So our protoself (as Damasio proposes) is very stable, which is very reassuring. After all, when it comes to the chaos of stage fright, it's good to know that there's an innate, primordial, non-emotional, non-thinking aspect of our existing selves – let's call him 'General Protoself' – that gets on with keeping us safe. You could say that, however destabilised the ambush of stage fright may make us feel, it's actually extremely difficult for us to completely self-sabotage. Stage fright really *won't* kill us.

General number 2: our core self

Next we have the general whom we always send out into the battlefield, because he is totally instinctive and intuitive about the manoeuvres in the very moment they occur. Let's draw from Damasio's nomenclature and call him 'General Core Self'. Our *core self* is what we experience instantaneously here and now. It's that split-second awareness that we're *conscious* that we're conscious: we're not just feeling or doing something, we're *aware* that we're feeling or doing it. In that split second, three things happen. Through one of our senses (sight, sound, taste, touch or smell), we encounter an object in the environment (say, a skull). Instantaneously, through all of our brain's electro-chemical circuitry, it constructs a mental map of that object (an image of a skull). Automatically, we discover a relationship between the object and ourselves ('Oh! This is a skull! Must speak the Yorick line!'). And these three steps take place in the blink of an eye. When as actors we really feel we're 'in the moment' of a performance, you could say that in many ways it's our core self at work. It's unencumbered by any sense of past or future. Which is why we come off stage and we can't necessarily remember what we did – and we certainly didn't pre-plan it. It seemed to happen there and then, and it's a very exciting state to be in when we're acting because there's a real 'flow'.

That said, this state can only exist if we have a bigger picture sense of self to back up our courage to take these in-the-moment risks. Which leads us to our next level of consciousness, our next general in the war room...

General number 3: our autobiographical self

'Love is a battlefield,' belted Pat Benatar as she topped the charts in 1983. Well, life can be something of a battlefield, too. And the only way we can fully negotiate its twists and turns – its minefields and peace treaties – is to have a sense of the bigger picture. Arguably the most powerful general in our war room – in fact, he's probably a field marshall – is the one that truly understands battle strategy. That means he can recall what happened in the past, he can anticipate what might happen in the future, and he can draw everything together into a comprehensive, narrative sequence. That narrative sequence is what we experience as our life, and this state of conscious existence is what Damasio calls our *autobiographical self*.

Our autobiographical self is made up of all our actions, memories, desires, pleasures and pains. In other words, it's the total sum of our life experiences, including things that are still in our imagination, such as the plans we've made for the future.[48] With lightning speed, 'General Autobiographical Self' juggles past, present and future, configuring this vast mass of information and assessing how we might make sense of each and every moment. It's literally mind-boggling how, in a nanosecond, all this information and memory is coordinated on a multi-site network right across our brain – a bit like some central command station in a *Mission Impossible* movie.

What makes this process even more amazing is that our memories aren't static. They're constantly being modified and remodelled as we negotiate the world, even when we're dreaming. Every single moment of our lives, our brain is constructing and reconstructing who we are through an astonishing number of integrated, electrochemical operations. Half the time, we don't even know that we're remodelling ourselves. It depends on all kinds of things: where we are, what we've eaten, who we're with, and what we're drinking. This constant modifying and remodelling gives rise to an extraordinary mercurialness. We can 'vary and waver, succumb to vanity and betray, be malleable and voluble,' writes Damasio. 'The potential to create our own Hamlets, Iagos and Falstaffs is inside each of us.'[49] You can see that, the more we discover about our consciousness, the more astonishing it is that we ever keep a sense of 'who we are'! In fact, the only way we *can* keep a sense of who we are is by having some kind of stable core, or (as Damasio calls it) a 'home base' to come back to: 'We can be Hamlet for a week, or Falstaff for an evening, but we tend to return to home base. If we have the genius of Shakespeare, we can use the inner battles of the self to create the entire cast of characters in Western theater'.[50] So you see, we've *all* got multiple personalities – whether or not we're actors.

Suffice it to say, this whole interaction of the various generals – our protoself, our core self and our autobiographical self – is a staggering neurobiological process when we're just being ourselves in everyday life, let alone when we're working on a role. When our professional life is devoted to incarnating these multiple personalities – when we're professional 'schizophrenics', so to speak – we have to be mindful about where 'home base' is. No wonder our sense of self fragments when we're ambushed by the panic of stage fright: it's a mutable self in the first place. For us to really understand our capabilities as a warrior, we should take a quick look at what's happening when all is well and we're in a personal 'peacetime'. Then we can better understand how to handle the situation when all is *not* well and our stage fright backs us to the edge of an abyss...

When it's all going well: a healthy dual consciousness

As actors, we're consciously and deliberately shifting between the 'home base' of ourselves and the canon of global theatre. So, in the duration of an actual performance (as we've already established), we have to have a keen sense of *dual consciousness* (a key tool in Stanislavsky's toolkit). We have to be able to commit to the character's given circumstances (with our functioning self) while handling the technical demands of performance (with our observing self). As actor-director Joseph Chaikin pithily puts it, it's a 'balancing act of abandonment and control, of intelligence and innocence.'[51] And this balancing act is a crucial part of our craftsmanship as actors. We might be giving the most wonderful rendition of Hamlet, but if we keep turning our back to the audience, then no one will see what we're doing. We could be giving an Oscar-winning performance in the next Tarantino movie, but if we keep stepping out of the frame, then we wreck our chances. So we have to be absolutely clear that there's no contradiction between being conscious that we're on stage or in front of the camera, and being immersed in the role. Stanislavsky himself describes how he divided himself, as it were, into two personalities: 'One continued as an actor, the other was an observer. Strangely enough this duality not only did not impede, it actually promoted my creative work. It encouraged and lent impetus to it.'[52]

So what happens when it all goes wrong? What happens when our consciousness isn't just divided into two? When, instead, it fragments into pieces and we find ourselves teetering on the edge of an abyss?

Stage fright and the abyss of fragmented consciousness

As I mentioned at the start of this chapter, there's usually one reason why our consciousness fragments on stage. Some inner interference pops into our thoughts – and diverts the flow away from what we're doing in the role ('What shall I have for supper?' 'Did I just miss my cue?' 'She never says that line like that.' 'That sounded like my agent's laugh.' 'Oh, goodness, what do I say next?'). If the glitch is momentary and the threat to our performance isn't severe, then pretty quickly we can refocus our attention back to the task in hand. If, however, we allow the threat to throw us off-course – or worse, to explode in our imaginations like a bomb – then we're in deep trouble. Now 'some amount of attention will have to be mobilised to eliminate the danger, leaving less attention free' to deal with our acting.[53] So a kind of inner conflict-of-interests starts up in our head. Instead of getting on with our performance, we start to fixate on our screw-up and then on the audience. And (as we've seen) it doesn't take much for our fantasies about the audience to accelerate quickly into the 'rampantly (paranoid) delusional'[54] – and they become devouring wolves. The next thing is there's a quaking in our innards and there's chaos in our mind. And now suddenly we have an overwhelming sense of being on the edge of an abyss – a deep, alluring darkness – into which tumbling seems to be the inescapable end to this impasse.

The edge of that abyss between our self and the character – between our reality and the world of the play – can be truly terrifying. In fact, it's amazing how often the image of an abyss springs up in reference to stage fright. As psychologist Kirk J. Schneider describes it, stage fright 'opens us to the primal forces, emotions, blood, upheaval. Where safety once permeated, now we must fend for ourselves; where a smile once warmed us, now there is a cold abyss.'[55] Indeed, in a moment of awful stage fright at the National Theatre, Olympia Dukakis felt herself, 'actually pitch into a black hole. My body just jerked forward as if I was falling into a pit.'[56] A sense of vertigo – as Antony Sher experienced in Japan – is one of the most powerful symptoms of stage fright. And, for those of us who've experienced it, there's a kind of strange lure that almost urges us to fall into this place of unknowing… as if we're drunk or drugged or lost in a fantasy world. In defiance of that lure, Laurence Olivier famously said: 'I have been there, I have looked over the edge, and I have returned.'[57]

When we're standing on the edge of this abyss, it's curious how often we experience a gap in time. Yet what seems to last a lifetime for us is less than a moment in the audience's awareness. That moment's hesitation, that tiny gap (as director Ingemar Lindh points out) is the gap between what we intended to do and what we actually did.[58] We intended to say one word, but instead another word came out of our mouths. We intended to deliver our monologue, but instead another thought popped into our heads. That tiny gap between what we intended to do and what we actually did becomes this abyss full of self-evaluation, self-doubt, and self-consciousness. That's certainly a lot of 'self' filling up that abyss. Which could mean that it needn't be a terrifying image, after all. It could actually be a very useful one. Here's why...

We've already noted that our experience of life is the result of a lot of electrochemical activity going on in our brain. We'll look at this in greater detail in Chapter 3, but the main point to note here is that our sense of self – our consciousness – is actually *created in the gaps between our neurons...* That's an extraordinary thought, so let's take it slowly...

Our neurons are extremely communicative. They send tiny messages to each other via sites (or junctions) called 'synapses'. And it's through all those tiny electrochemical messages – those leaps across the synaptic dark – that we experience everything that makes us 'us'. Our memories, images, impulses to actions, feelings, sensations, and emotional activity. It has even been said that we *only* exist in the gaps within our brain: we are born in a synaptic cleft.

When you think of it like that, it's not surprising that stage fright can feel as if we're falling into an abyss. We've got all these millions of gaps with which we have to contend neurologically on a nanosecond-to-nanosecond basis – in order just to exist! And yet at the same time it's a very empowering image. After all, those gaps aren't dark and empty abysses in which we might lose ourselves – they're actually very full of 'us'. You could almost say that in those moments of stage-fright 'gap', we're most deeply connected to our selves. We're at our most true – most authentic – most honest. No mask, no funny voice or honed gait to disguise us.

If we look at the situation like this, there's potentially a way of turning 'The Gap' into something to welcome, rather than something to fear. We know those gaps are natural and necessary. Therefore, if we can't avoid them, we might as well face them – just as that tiny electrochemical message in our brain faces the gap as it leaps out into the synaptic dark. In fact, one of the most useful acting tools I know is David Mamet's 'terrifying unforeseen'.[59] Entering the terrifying unforeseen is the moment of stepping out on the stage or in front of the camera and not knowing exactly what will happen. Like the Fool in the tarot cards stepping off the mountain in the hopes that the ground will come up and meet him, let's have the foolish *courage* to step into the terrifying unforeseen.

Acting with Courage

Yes, indeed – acting takes *courage*. It takes hard work. It takes commitment and unremitting dedication. And it costs us a lot. When we pursue the life of an artist, 'illusions are stripped away,' writes Stephen Nachmanovitch, 'we confront difficult pieces of self-knowledge... we have to stretch our physical, emotional, intellectual stamina to the limits... our patience and our ability to persevere and transcend ourselves are tested.'[60] Acting requires all of our being and it consumes our whole life – and that can be scary. So, yes indeed – acting takes courage. And the natural pendulum-swing that counterbalances courage is – inevitably – fear.

Our fear and our courage coexist. They're two sides of the same coin. So they both need embracing. To which end, David Mamet's words on the subject are provocative and inspiring:

> The actor before the curtain, the soldier going into combat, the fighter into the arena, the athlete before the event, may have feelings of self-doubt, fear, or panic. These feelings will or will not appear, and no amount of 'work on the self' can eradicate them.
>
> The rational individual will, when the bell rings, go out there anyway to do the job she said she was going to do. This is called courage.[61]

As Mamet says, we won't eradicate our fears, but we can learn to live with them. We can even learn to live with the vulnerability of very public stage fright, as Olympia Dukakis found out: 'Pretty soon you get to the point where you realize that you can live with people knowing a lot of things about you that you thought you couldn't reveal.'[62] To which end, I finish this chapter with some thoughts about two actors who suffered terrible stage fright and yet lived with it and fought it with courage. So much so, they've become the major pioneers of contemporary Western acting: they were *Konstantin Stanislavsky* and *Lee Strasberg*. While I was preparing this book, I took another look at each of their works and realised with renewed insight that maybe the very reason they formulated their acting methods was that they were both acute sufferers of stage fright. Had they not been, they might never have needed to come up with their revolutionary systems in the first place. So, clearly, there are some highly productive benefits to stage fright.

Konstantin Stanislavsky and stage fright

This may come as a surprise to know, but, throughout his acting life, Stanislavsky experienced an uncomfortable dialogue between himself as an actor and his audience. Early on in his career, he realised that he was (what he called) a character actor, not a personality actor. As long as he could create characters that were very different from himself – big noses, altered voices, unusual gaits – he felt confident on stage. To base a character on *himself* – to be 'truthful' to his own personality – required far more faith in himself than he felt he possessed. He was actually a remarkably reserved person, and in biographer Jean Benedetti's words, 'He needed the protection of another individual's identity and mask of make-up'.[63] Over time, however, he became increasingly frustrated with his own strutting and posturing on stage. You get the sense from his writings and photographs that he wasn't always the subtlest of actors. And maybe he knew it. Maybe that's why he devoted himself to figuring out ways in which an actor *could* use their own self to build a character without feeling coy or egotistical.

Nonetheless, that complicated relationship with the audience dogged him. Using the mask of the fictional student Kostya, he writes: 'I went out to the front of the stage and stared into the awful hole beyond the footlights, trying to become accustomed to it, and to free myself from its pull; but the more I tried not to notice the place the more I thought about it.'[64] His perplexed relationship with the audience and his lack of confidence in his own skin manifested itself in chronic stage fright – and often he just couldn't remember his lines.

He had always found learning lines difficult. He wasn't one of those actors who could learn scripts parrot-fashion, and so he really benefitted from longer rehearsal periods. Yet as early as 1899, just one year after the creation of the Moscow Art Theatre, his co-founder and director Nemirovich-Danchenko grew so frustrated with Stanislavsky not knowing his lines as Astrov in *Uncle Vanya*, that he wondered what the point of disciplining the other actors was if the leading man set such a bad example! Stanislavsky's trouble with line-learning continued for years, as he himself describes in 1915 when he was trying to memorise his role in *Mozart and Salieri*:

> I acted the part all night, tormented by insomnia and the more I went through the lines the more I forgot them. During the day, in the street and in the carriage, I wore myself out with the same relentless, stupid repetition of the lines.[65]

Fortunately and luckily, Stanislavsky was more than fine in his performance of Salieri and his stage fright actually motored him:

> With my inner plan in pieces I decided, in actors' jargon, to pull out all the stops, let fly physically and vocally. And did I not!! It

> was so easy but I knew that only sheer desperation could push me to such shameful lengths. The audience listened to me as never before. They even tried to applaud after the first scene. Moskvin rushed round during the interval and said that this was the only way to play it. I don't understand a thing.[66]

By pulling out all the stops, and letting fly physically and vocally, Stanislavsky stepped out into the terrifying unforeseen.

Only two years later, though, Stanislavsky was truly crippled by stage fright as Rostanev in Nemirovich-Danchenko's production of *The Village of Stepanchikovo.* He just couldn't get what the director wanted. After 156 rehearsals, he was replaced at the dress rehearsal, and the experience shattered his confidence.[67] There were performances during his career in which Stanislavsky's nerves were so stretched that he would constantly call for prompts and, even when he received them, still managed to fluff his lines. Theatre scholar Nicholas Ridout even goes so far as to say that Stanislavsky makes stage fright the *precondition of theatrical success.*[68] Whether or not that's true, I've absolutely no doubt that if Stanislavsky hadn't suffered such catastrophic performance anxiety, he would never have taken the time and deliberation to process and analyse acting. Thank goodness he could be such a wreck – because he went on create such a legacy.

While Stanislavsky might have believed that stage fright was an essential part of acting, his American successor, Lee Strasberg, felt exactly the opposite – possibly due to his own embarrassment at suffering from so much fear.

Lee Strasberg and stage fright

It's not uncommon for interpreters of Lee Strasberg's Method to fixate on his desire for 'real emotion' in actors' performances. Some people argue that he was obsessed with emotional truth because he himself was emotionally very contained, and so his Method was geared towards emotional accessibility as a way of getting past his own restrictions as an actor. Whether or not this is really the case, I'd argue that – like Stanislavsky – Strasberg would never have spent so much time evolving the Method, if he'd been a confident actor from the get-go. His own frustrations with his instrument – possibly his own shyness, and even more possibly the fear he experienced if he couldn't access what he wanted for a character – proved to be invaluable stimuli that we've all been able to benefit from as actors in theatre and film.

That said, Strasberg was far less sympathetic than Stanislavsky towards stage fright. As strict with himself as he was with his students, Strasberg dismissed stage fright as 'the most vulgar preoccupation of them all.'[69] (Interestingly enough, this quotation comes from his discussion of Stanislavsky's issues with stage fright.) Yet Strasberg's own fear of forgetting his lines is particularly powerful and revealing.

It happened to him during the filming of *The Godfather Part III* and the stakes were very high. Here he was, a world-renowned actor-trainer who hadn't acted for quite some time, now invited by Al Pacino to make his movie debut. He knew the world would be watching him. And that pressure in itself was enough to prove that performance anxiety is not specific to live theatre. It can plague movie actors just as doggedly as theatre performers – even when we know we don't have to sustain a performance for more than a few minutes. Even when we know that if we screw up, we can just go back and re-record. Nonetheless, Strasberg reveals something very telling in the following quotation, which gives us huge insights into why he spent years creating a Method. And curiously his motivation seems to be exactly the same as Stanislavsky's:

> What troubled me most was not any concern about my acting, but would I remember my lines? Would I hit the marks? This anxiety was something that I have always suffered from. When I was a young actor I had an excellent memory – I still do. I memorized lines very easily, and yet, whether in

> rehearsal or in performance, I would always go through attacks of anxiety. Before uttering the first line, I would repeat it again and again. Then, afraid I would forget it, I would whisper it over and over to myself until I entered the scene. Once I was there, my fear of forgetting disappeared. My concentration was always firmly on what I was doing. Yet for many actors this anxiety can often impede expressiveness.[70]

What a relief to know that both Stanislavsky and Strasberg suffered *throughout their professional lives* from the exactly same fears that haunt the rest of us! Along with Jacobi and Gambon, Olympia Dukakis, and Vivien Leigh (to name but a handful), we're certainly in very good company and we needn't be ashamed.

Overview

In this chapter, we've seen that stage fright is a natural response to an important event. We've undertaken three specific assessments. First, we've taken a bird's-eye view of fear: we've looked at the *physiological* and *psychological* manifestations. We've looked at the *evolutionary roots* of stage fright and why it's perfectly normal to be afraid of silent watchers in the dark. We've looked at some *external factors* and some *internal factors*. Second, we've assessed the nature of fear and met the *Fear Family*. Third, we've assessed the nature of 'who we are' in terms of our states of *consciousness* – as well as what happens *when our consciousness fragments* and we teeter on the edge of the abyss. Finally, we've looked at just how productive stage fright can be, inspiring two of the greatest acting gurus in contemporary history to come up with a 'system' (Stanislavsky) and a Method (Strasberg) to help us all get over it.

*

Having put the actual phenomenon of stage fright under the microscope, let's head out into the battlefield and meet the foe. Let's see how – beyond the obvious fear engendered by a crowd of strangers in the dark – an audience became the enemy. How did it all begin? And how can the thought of stepping out in front of an audience make us want to run away from the profession that we love?

2

How Did We Get Here?

The Role of the Audience

'I've always been frightened by an audience – any audience. My stomach pounds, my head gets dizzy – and I'm sure my voice has left me.'[71]

Marilyn Monroe

2. *How Did We Get Here?*

What's to be afraid of?

Boiled down to the basics, fear is our *internal response* to an *external stimulus.* Simple as that. Something in the outside world gets our gut going. And with stage fright, it's the audience. For all the physiological and psychological chaos that churns around *inside* us, it's the *outer* circumstance – a group of people watching us – that kick-starts our anxiety. Especially when it comes to live theatre.

This is actually rather puzzling. After all, no one makes us become actors. It's not as if it's financially secure with a Clear Path to Guaranteed Success. Nor is it a national necessity – like fighting for one's country or becoming a doctor. We know that there's going to be an audience – there'd be no point in doing our job if there wasn't. So why on earth would we choose a profession and then become afraid of the very people for whom we're doing it?

In this chapter, we'll look at some of the reasons why antagonism – real or imagined – might have evolved between actors and audiences. In the first half, we consider some Reasons to be Fearful. And we start briefly with one of the main prompts to stage fright in the theatre: the *close encounter* between the consumer (the audience) and the producer (us), which takes us to the intimate power of the *theatre architecture* itself. We then focus on the inner dynamics of that *shared space* and *live audience*, as well as the power of the *theatre critic* (both professional and amateur). In the latter part, we turn to some Reasons to be Cheerful, and the nature of *human empathy*. In fact, we end with a couple of tales about how empathy or compassion can ease us away from the catastrophic fallout of the Fear. As ever in our probing of stage fright, our goal is to face it, embrace it, and to thereby overcome it.

Reasons to be Fearful

The close encounter between producer and consumer

When you think about it, the relationship between actor and audience is very unusual. One group of people is at work (the actors), while another group of people pays to watch them do their work (the audience). It's not often that the makers of a product and the consumers of that product come so intimately face to face.[72] After all, I don't pay to watch the man who bakes my bread – I just put it in my toaster. I don't pay to watch the plumber fix my shower – I simply pay him to fix it. Yet if there weren't people watching our work as actors, we wouldn't have any reason to do it. And that fact in and of itself instills the relationship with a very particular power balance. Not least because the audience (certainly in live theatre) lets us know directly to our faces whether or not we've done a good job (as we'll see in more detail anon).

The container for this face-to-face encounter is of course the *theatre space* itself – be it a permanent piece of architecture or a temporary structure. And that space has a mysterious and mercurial adaptability, which in its own way can affect our performance nerves.

The power of the theatre space

A *theatre space* is loaded with expectations. It's a space that transforms – subtly, unexpectedly, and provocatively.

Let's take the audience's arrival. If we're in a conventional theatre, the audience expects the buzz of the lobby, the plush of the seats, the gilt of the auditorium, maybe an ornate curtain that hides the world of the play from them and injects them with anticipation. If we're in a fringe venue, the audience shares the space with the pre-show atmosphere: maybe they have to walk across the set to get to their seats and maybe they're smelling the dust motes burning on the PAR cans at their feet. If it's Shakespeare in the park, they're unfolding their picnic blankets or watching the dusk fall or hearing the aeroplanes overhead. If we're in a site-specific venue, they're breathing in the library or the disused asylum or the arboretum or the custard factory, and they're filled with curiosity as to how it's about to be transformed into a performance event.

Then the performance starts and suddenly the space morphs for the audience. They may be plunged into darkness. They may be blasted with music or sound effects or singing. For an hour or three, they may find the magic of the theatre turns the most mundane of objects and commonplace of phrases into things of mystery and poetry and beauty. Maybe the audience finds themselves transported in their imaginations and transcended in their emotions and transfixed by new thoughts. These myriad possibilities make for a pretty powerful space.

Then the performance stops and suddenly the space morphs again for the audience. And something strange happens. For all the collective community that the theatre architecture has just created, suddenly it's dispersed and everyone is back to their individuality. Have you noticed how quickly an audience tries to leave an auditorium, even if they haven't got to catch the last bus or race to the car park? With a description that sounds more like disembarking from an aeroplane than exiting a place of entertainment, the Nobel prize-winning writer Elias Canetti describes how the theatre crowd 'inevitably disintegrates in the most violent manner. Only one or two persons can get through each exit at a time and thus the energy of flight turns into an energy of struggle to push others back. Only one man at a time can pass between the rows of seats and each seat is neatly separated from the rest. Each man has his place and sits or stands by himself.'[73] That sounds like a scary place...

How strange that the same space can take on so many atmospheres for an audience in such a short time! Any space that can change so much holds within it a certain titillation, a certain palpitation – if not a certain fear. And it's the same for us as actors. A theatre's architecture can morph into various different atmospheres in the course of a working day, and that mutability can be both exciting and unsettling. The stage door, the green room, the dressing room – each space has its unique qualities. Perhaps the most magical places in the theatre are the backstage area and wings. They're the threshold between the privacy of our preparation and the public-ness of our performance. Standing in the blue light... waiting to go on stage... we experience that pulsing liminal space between the *reality* of plywood and LX cables and the *hyperreality* of the onstage castle or living room or lower depth. Ian McKellen describes how he 'stood in the dust and dark backstage, comparing the tawdry reality with the glamorous illusion onstage. It's a contrast that still absorbs me. It holds a secret and a mystery that I never hope to solve.'[74]

Perhaps the most potent hyperreality of the theatre space is the living, breathing presence of the audience. The actual moment of stepping out in front of that darkened auditorium with its nameless, faceless crowd can be a double-edged sword. It teases us in equal measure with confidence and uncertainty. Using the voice of the novice actor Kostya, Stanislavsky writes:

> When I stepped away from the darkness of the wings to the full illumination of the footlights, headlights and spotlights, I felt blinded. The brightness was so intense that it seemed to form a curtain of light between me and the auditorium. I felt protected from the public, and for a moment I breathed freely, but soon my eyes became accustomed to the light, I could see into the darkness, and the fear and attraction of the public seemed stronger than ever. I was ready to turn myself inside out, to give them everything I had; yet inside of me I had never felt so empty.[75]

Stanislavsky absolutely sums up the ambivalent relationship that we have with the darkness and light – the fear and attraction of the public – not seeing the audience while all the time knowing that they're there.

Yet this trigger for our stage fright is a fairly recent phenomenon. It's only since the advent of gas lamps and electricity that we've experienced this strange state of amorphous reality in the theatre. When the actors and the audience could all see each other, their relationship was obviously more equal. When only one side can see the other, there's suddenly an awful lot of pretending going on. We're pretending that the audience isn't really there – when we know that there'd be no point in performing if they *weren't*. We're pretending that we're being intimate with our onstage partners – when we know that there's a dark space out there with hundreds of people watching. You could say that electricity has a lot to answer for when it comes to stage fright. Bertolt Brecht probably did his actors a huge favour when he turned up the lights in the auditorium as well as on the stage, so that everyone could stop pretending.

Yet – do we want to see our audience? Or don't we? I can't deny that when I was suffering from stage fright in *The Permanent Way*, I found it much more liberating to move from the intimate studio theatres to the big darkened auditoria, where I could fake looking people in the eye during my direct-address speeches. Actually, it was the French director André Antoine who first thought to make the darkened theatre feel more like a regular space. He invented 'the fourth wall' – the imaginary wall that separates the stage from the auditorium. This was a device that Stanislavsky seized on – probably as he tried to overcome his own stage fright. Combining the fourth wall with some of his meditational practices, he came up with the four 'circles of attention'. The smallest circle of attention focuses on our self, our props and the immediate set. The middle-sized circle takes in our onstage partner. A big circle takes in the rest of the stage. And the largest circle encompasses the whole auditorium. When his own wife, Lilina, was almost crippled with stage fright – and had to be fed with bromides and tranquillisers – she found the fourth wall and the circles of attention very helpful: 'I played Varya in a big circle of attention, and was not nervous for a single minute, and did not think about the public... and did not forget a single line.'[76]

Obviously it depends on the style and the piece – and with site-specific performances, the fluidity between us actors and the people watching us is often part of the show. In fact, the lure – and the fear – of live performance is indeed that shared space, and the possibility that we might actually change each other. Yes, we might just experience a collective transformation. That's why, when it comes to stage fright, the *shared space* can be tantalising.

The power of the shared space

The basic tenets of live performance are pretty simple. Two groups of people implicitly agree to come together in a *shared space* at a predetermined time. During that time, each group is subtly aware of its capacity to influence the other. And in this capacity, theatre is unlike any other art form. Unlike a poem or a painting, a pot or a piano concerto, a live theatre audience can affect the actual performance in its moment of delivery. And *vice versa*. It's not surprising, therefore, that this incredibly active and mutable relationship – in a space that's shared by all of us – alters the extent to which we feel afraid of our audience or not. Likewise, it can influence their feelings towards us. How so?

Well, generally, as human beings we tend to feel afraid when we don't feel safe. So, on a very practical level, what makes a space feel safe for an audience? They want to know that they've got the seat they paid for. They want to know where the emergency exits are. They want to know that their belongings are safe in the cloakroom. They want to be sure the piece will finish at the advertised time so that they can get home easily.

On a more intangible level, they want to be sure that the rules of engagement are clear. And unless a performance is advertised as 'participatory', those rules for an audience tend to be: 'You're on the stage, I'm in the dark: you do the talking, and leave me alone.' Yet sometimes those rules are tested – deliberately and playfully – for example, in the flurry of direct-address verbatim dramas over the last couple of decades. Our theatre ancestors in Shakespeare's day or in the Restoration would have been perfectly comfortable with actors engaging in some kind of banter with them. Not so any more. We're all far more ambivalent towards direct address in the twenty-first-century theatre. And that's because – unlike our Shakespearean or Restoration predecessors – as actors we don't really expect the audience to answer back. In fact, as Nicholas Ridout points out, twenty-first-century direct address is pretty disingenuous.[77] It *implies* that the audience is being offered the possibility of an actual response. (As was the case with the line I screwed up in *The Permanent Way*: 'Well, I don't know about you, but I can only work if I feel the hot breath of a competitor down my neck.') Yet we know that we're not *actually* offering them the chance to answer back. In fact, outside of pantomime, stand-up comedy or deliberately interactive performance, the rules of engagement in the shared space of conventional theatre really only encourage the audience to interject by laughing and maybe applauding at the end. However...

When those rules of engagement are bent, there can be a real frisson – even if the bending is *intentional*, as was the case with Rufus Norris's production of David Hare's *Behind the Beautiful Forevers* at the National Theatre in 2014. The actors (in character) directly addressed the audience, and the audience was invited to answer back. I've no doubt some audiences in the smart and usually polite auditorium of the Olivier Theatre were muted – and others were excited (like the night I was there, though I admit I was actually a bit timid). Either way, the rules of engagement were playfully expanded, as each night's audience tested out how far or not they could go.

When those rules of engagement are *unintentionally* broken, the space can start to feel decidedly *un*safe. We feel unsafe as actors when mobile phones go off or if cameras are used (we'll look at that in more detail later). And the audience feels unsafe if the production somehow doesn't fulfill its professional conditions – such as when an actor forgets their lines. Then the spectators may swing between one of two polar directions: towards judgement and disappointment or towards empathy and understanding. And of course it's the first one – the judgemental option – that's the scary one for us as actors. So let's look at that one first.

The power of the live audience

Growing up in the Midlands, I regularly went on school trips to the Royal Shakespeare Theatre in Stratford. One night, an incident took place during a performance of *The Comedy of Errors* which struck me so forcibly that it has remained part of my stage-fright hubris ever since. Part way through the performance, the well-known television actor Paul Greenwood stumbled through his lines, forgot them completely, and then turned to the audience saying (words to the effect of), 'I'm sorry, everybody, I've forgotten my lines.' He then walked off stage, received a prompt, came back on stage, and the play continued. As a perfectionist teenager aspiring to be an actress, I was horrified. In that moment, I turned into the worst kind of spectator that any actor fears to have. I thought, 'This is absolutely disgraceful! This is the RSC! The least one can expect is that the actors will know their lines!' Of course Paul Greenwood would've had no idea of my thoughts at the time. Yet my acute reaction left some lingering considerations in my head, and from my fourteen-year-old's pedestal I have subsequently – and very humbly – stepped down.

As actors we constantly put ourselves on the line. Emotionally. Physically. Psychologically. That's the nature of the job. And with that comes the matter of some very public critiquing of our work – from professional reviewers and The Public At Large. Some of that critique is immediate and face to face. And usually it's positive. A live performance tends to end with applause: that's the cultural and social expectation. We bow to the audience and the audience claps: it's a reciprocal ritual of mutual thanks and appreciation. Yet this it isn't always the case. Rare as it may sound, an auditorium of comparative strangers can (in the words of anthropologist Jane Goodall) 'devastate the performer with a range of strategies, from silence and walk-outs up through the scale of yawning, heckling, slow clapping, hissing and booing, throwing missiles to full-scale homicidal eruption.'[78]

Sometimes, the audience's actions are much subtler than that – and yet those actions can instantly arouse our stage fright because they so instantly disrupt our focus. What I'm referring to here is the audience's use of mobile devices! At first, as actors, we had to contend with things that bleeped, rang or vibrated. Now it's screens that light up and cameras that blink. (But more of that anon…) For some years now, prominent actors have been publicly perplexed by the proliferation of phones during their performances. 'In 2009, Hugh Jackman and Daniel Craig, still in character, berated one viewer whose phone rang out loud twice during their scene in *A Steady Rain* on Broadway. And in 2013, a usually cool James McAvoy stopped his *Macbeth* performance to tell a patron to put his phone away.'[79] In 2015, Patti LuPone was so perplexed by texting and phone calls during her performances in *Show of Days* at the Lincoln Centre, she issued a statement: 'I am so defeated by this issue that I seriously question whether I want to work on stage any more. Now I'm putting battle gear on over my costume to marshall the audience as well as perform.'[80] (She really did see the audience as the enemy.) Whether it's intentional or not, the very fact that audience members don't take a few seconds just to switch off their phones (especially if there's a public announcement before each performance asking them to do just that or there are notices around the theatre and in the programme) is a kind of brutal criticism in its own right. Those culprits don't think (carefully or highly) enough about what we're doing as actors to take this simple step.

Subtle or brutal – deliberate or unintentional – we can't escape the fact that audiences have been powerful critics for centuries. If we were to travel back in time to the seventeenth and eighteenth centuries, we'd find that audiences were literally judge and jury over the success (or otherwise) of a production. In fact, the first performance of a play was even called the 'tryall', and if the audience enjoyed a play and it passed its 'tryall', it could go on to a longer run. And if it didn't? Well, it was immediately pulled from the repertoire, and the playwright wouldn't get paid.[81] No wonder so many characters appear in epilogues pleading for leniency. In fact, the bow itself is a gesture of respect and humility: 'I offer the nape of my neck to you, so that if my performance didn't please you, you can strike off my head. So please be kind to me and show your appreciation.'

Symbolic beheadings or otherwise, it's really quite remarkable what kind of critical authority audiences have over actors and productions – especially as they don't always get it right. The Petersburg audience at the debut of Chekhov's *The Seagull* booed so angrily that Chekhov scurried from the theatre vowing never to write plays again. Likewise, Peter Hall's British premiere of Beckett's *Waiting for Godot* was greeted with (what he euphemistically called) 'counter-cheers'.[82] In each case, the audience had no idea that they'd just witnessed the birth of a classic. After centuries of audiences being more or less 'the ultimate arbiters of a performance's quality',[83] the pioneering director George Devine sought to create a new kind of theatre in 1950s' London. He wanted an environment that would nurture more intelligent, discerning spectators, so he co-founded the English Stage Company at the Royal Court. Did he feel he'd succeeded? Peering through the curtain on the first night of *The Entertainer*, he muttered to writer John Osborne: 'There you are, dear boy, take a look out there... What do you think of them, eh? Same old pack of cunts, fashionable arseholes. Just more of them than usual, that's all!'[84] It's both funny and startling that such a strong sense of antagonism can exist across the footlights. And as actors we know just how affecting that energetic communication can be from an amassed group of people watching us at work. That's why we have previews. It gives us the chance to 'tryall' the play before press night, so that we can sense what the collective energy, response, and approbation (or otherwise) might be from the audience – and adjust the production accordingly. (Though this isn't always the case, as we'll see in Chapter 4, when we look at the changing nature of previews.)

While, of course, we want a live audience to appreciate our work and while, of course, we fear their judgement, it's the individual voices of *the critics* – committed to word for all to see (online or in print; constructed argument or casual comment) – that can really set our nerves a-jangling.

The power of the critic – professional and amateur

A swathe of lights ignites the theatre. The fictional director Tortsov (in Stanislavsky's *An Actor Prepares*) is pointing out to his students how an actor's attention becomes split on stage between various different places. 'What's that bright light in the stalls?' asks one of them. 'That's the Severe Dramatic Critic,' replies Tortsov. 'He comes in for a lot of attention at the opening.'[85]

There's no denying that the professional critics' reviews have been known to make or break a production. And it's not just the production: they can make or break us as actors. Thinking about the critics' influence can send us crashing towards stage fright on a first night, as our attention swings like an unleashed bungee straight out into the stalls. The professional critic is a person to be respected. These people see *a lot* of theatre. We know their response will (usually) come from an informed, considered, and (hopefully) impartial perspective. Naturally we want to see their positive opinions in print – of course we do! And ideally in a high-profile place. A rave in *The Stage* has much more oomph than in the *Glastonbury Gazette*. And yet that's exactly what can arouse our angst: the *public arena* of the critics' opinions. Particularly if their reviews are bad. The impact of bad reviews can be devastating, as evidenced by Stephen Fry in 1995. When the *Financial Times* review of his West End appearance in *Cell Mates* by Simon Gray appeared, the negative opinion caused him to flee the production, flee the country and nearly flee his own life. To go back out on stage after receiving a panning takes immense chutzpah – and it's not always easy. Fry's plight prompted widespread outpourings of compassion from fellow actors, including Sir Ian McKellen.

Indeed, McKellen was keen to point out that cut-throat criticism can be just as painful when it comes from the casual observer. In his article, 'The Awful Hell of Stage Fright', he describes how some twenty years earlier, he'd overheard two actors discussing his performance in a successful West End show. They were attacking his diction and physique, and opining about his total failure as an actor. 'I thought I was impervious,' writes McKellen, 'but the next night, in the second act, I stopped in mid-flow, certain that every member of that night's audience agreed with my critics. Unable to say the lines, unable even to walk off stage, I longed for the proverbial trapdoor to open and release me from the hell of being a failed actor.'[86] Even though this critique was unintentionally overheard by a lone person, it was still painful. How much more painful is the critique when it's intentionally committed to print and read by thousands?

Curiously, there has been a gradual erosion of the professional theatre critic in the last few years, as printed publications diminish. Yet that hasn't made it any easier for us to escape being 'judged'. In fact, the rapid proliferation of online blogs and amateur reviewers (however partial) are rendering the relationship between us and our audiences increasingly complex. You could say that social media in the twenty-first century is returning the power to the people in the way that the seventeenth-century audiences experienced. I became all too aware of this shift in 'critical authority' at the burgeoning Hollywood Fringe Festival in the summer of 2015. An initiative had been created by the powerful online website – Bitter Lemons – whereby fringe participants could pay for an established LA theatre critic to review their production. The ire surrounding this initiative was startlingly hot, raising debate across the globe from the *American Theater Critics Association* to *American Theatre* journal to a blogger in Scotland to a multitude of festival participants and spectators: 'Was this initiative ethical? Should we trust the paid-for reviews?' Yet, curiously, it was not so much the professional reviews as the tweets, Facebook posts and the audience's web reviews that filled the houses – regardless of the established critics' opinions.

What all this means is that press nights are no longer the performances we should fret over. Every night is a press night, in the sense that every single audience member is a critic – just as they were back in the seventeenth century. Every spectator can get online and post a review for all to see – and it may not be informed and it may not be impartial – but it's there, nonetheless. And they may be quite rude about us. Or they may think we're great. Either way, the populus really can influence the fate of our work these days – and with an immediacy that's almost overwhelming. Indeed, in 2009, the Lyric Opera in Kansas officially introduced 'tweet seats', so that audiences could respond to productions as they were happening.[87] At least the Lyric Opera made it official – half the time, audiences will do it anyway. This is incredibly daunting. If we screw up a performance on a film set (which tends to be 'closed'), the director can re-take: it's in their interest to make sure only our best results are seen. If we screw up a performance on stage, it may be tweeted and retweeted in an instant: after all, everyone wants a nibble of the newsfeed pie. Many actors are striving to address this head-on, not least with Benedict Cumberbatch's stage-door plea to the audience for *Hamlet* at the Barbican in August 2015. But more on that, too, in Chapter 4, when we look at the nature of previews...

So, what can we do in the face of so many avenues of critique? Short of addressing our audiences directly, we have to take back some control – and that requires *mindset* as much as than any tangible *action*.

Responding to critiques

'To read or not to read? That's often the question...' mulls Antony Sher.[88] And a question it certainly is. Some actors choose not to read reviews. Some are curious as to what others are saying about our work, not to mention what others are reading about our work. Some, including Sher, find them strangely addictive – even if reading the reviewers' opinions of our own shows 'are never useful':

> Whether positive or negative, the printed word makes you self-conscious and it's better to retain your own sense of what you're trying to do; your innocence, in a way. If you've got a long run ahead of you, you simply have to believe in the show one hundred per cent or you're going to be very miserable. That's the theory. But reviews are like cigarettes. They can give you a buzz, they can also make you feel sick – either way, they're not good for you, yet they're addictive. You give them up, you start again, you stop, you tell yourself just one can't hurt. I've gone through various phases: reading, not reading, reading and not reading at the same time (it's done through the fingers, like watching TV when they're showing testicle surgery)...[89]

That pretty much sums it up. But, given that there are so many outlets for public plaudits and pans these days, it's increasingly hard to avoid reviews. And so we need to be realistic about their content, and at the same time monitor the fear-factor. If we give away too much agency to the critics (both professional and amateur), we experience what clinical psychologist Stephen Aaron notes as 'impotence in front of this crowd of a thousand strangers',[90] and that impotence increases our fear. Indeed, veteran theatre critic Michael Billington himself advocates that we should keep a realistic assessment of the professional reviewers' praise and critique. 'We are not there as audience representatives or spokespersons,' he declares. 'We are there to describe, analyse and evaluate what we see. We may be right or wrong, according to taste, but we are individuals expressing an opinion rather than tribunes of the people.'[91] Nobody is a tribune of the people when it comes to something as personal as artistic taste. Even the 'audience representatives' are only individuals – and half of them may be the actors' mums, dads, significant others, friends, foes, or paid publicists. Since there are so many opportunities these days for reviews and feedback, it all has to be taken with a healthy pinch of salt.

Instead of investing energy in the critics' and public opinions, we can just get on with the task of performing. After all, Billington is right: it *is* just a question of taste. And we won't please everyone. Besides, who says everyone's out to judge us in the first place? That is absolutely not the case. The trouble is that when we're suffering stage fright, we tend to fixate on the imagined negative judgements that our audiences will have of us. (We noted this when we looked at the Nature of Fear in Chapter 1.) So an important reconfiguring of our mindset is to be kind to ourselves. To acknowledge that the audiences are far more forgiving than our stage-frighted anxiety can cause us to believe. In fact, in the final part of this chapter, I want to turn to the positive aspects of the unique actor-audience relationship and its amazing potential for *empathy*.

Reasons to be Cheerful

Actor-audience empathy

Who are those people out there? 'Are they just viewers,' asks theatre scholar Helen Freshwater, 'or accomplices, witnesses, participants? Are they a crowd, a mass, a mob, or critics and connoisseurs?'[92] An audience is never a shapeless mass of people for any of us. As Joseph Chaikin suggests, every actor 'makes some decision about the audience in his own mind; personalizing, making specific the anonymous. He makes a secret choice, in the course of events, as to "who" the audience is... Who is he secretly addressing?'[93] And in this strange, secretive relationship, our audiences take on many of the identities above. They are *viewers* of our work. *Accomplices* in our shared experience. *Witnesses* of humankind's stories. And *participants* in an extremely powerful, emotional connection. Rather than fixating on our stage fright as actors, we should understand the nuances of our emotional connection with our audiences.

Emotions are infectious, especially in a theatre space where people have deliberately come together in order to share an experience. If we've ever come out of a low comedy laughing or a high drama weeping, then we know just how infectious emotions can be. And this emotional infection isn't anecdotal: it's scientifically proven. It occurs as electrochemical activity in our brains, which we experience as *empathy*.

Empathy, in the words of theatre researcher Bruce McConachie, is 'a kind of mindreading that allows one person to step into the shoes of another and experience that person's world from his or her point of view.'[94] This act of stepping into someone's shoes is actually our professional task as actors when we incarnate a role: we try to see the world from our character's point of view. More importantly for us here as we probe the Fear, it's the kind of mindreading that happens between us and our audiences. In fact, the powerful sharing of stories is even more interactive than we think: our collective brains are *actually connecting* across the darkness of the auditorium. Audiences are not *passive recipients* of our stories – they're *active participants* in our experiences. Here's what I mean...

In recent years, scientists have discovered that our experience of empathy takes place in (what are now called) 'mirror neurons'. Mirror neurons are brain cells that 'light up' in one person's brain in response to particular physical actions that *someone else* intentionally carries out. 'Significantly, these networks in your brain respond in the same way whether *you perform the action for yourself* or *see someone else do it*.'[95] To put it in (very basic) layman's terms: I see you crying. Automatically my own mirror neurons are triggered. Instantaneously my imagination comes up with some hypothetical reasons as to why you're crying given the circumstances that you're in. And I find myself experiencing your emotion as if it were my own – I may even find myself crying. All this interconnective activity takes place within a matter of milliseconds. In neuroscience, the process is known as 'imaginary transposition', as I imaginatively transpose myself into your shoes.[96]

The discovery of mirror neurons is really quite extraordinary. And the whole cognitive process of empathy is very relevant for us here as we explore the actor-audience relationship. We often talk about the fact that, as actors and audiences, we breathe each other in by sharing the same atoms in the same space at the same time. Now – through the discovery of mirror neurons – we really can say that we're getting inside each other's heads and hearts. The fact that the same neurons fire – whether we're actually doing something or simply watching it (or even imagining it) – means that an audience is far from inactive. When we're telling a good story in a compelling manner, they're grasping the contents of our minds – not through *thinking*, but through *feeling*. Not through *passive observation*, but through *active, psychophysical simulation*. And so, within the safe container of the theatre – where the terms of time, space, and social conventions are all pretty much predetermined – an audience has the chance to experience a whole panoply of emotions. They can enter vast realms of pleasure and pain that they might never otherwise have entered. Yet they can do so without any unexpected consequences. They can experience great joy – great sorrow – great excitement – great despair. And they can still get into their cars at the end of the evening and drive safely back home to their lives.

It really is quite amazing. But what does it have to do with stage fright? Well, increasingly through this book we'll see that a fundamental approach to overcoming stage fright is to reframe the distressing situation. And this is what I propose here: if our mirror neurons fire when we *imagine* going through something fictive that the character might experience – and if mirror neurons fire when the audience *watches* us re-enact those fictive circumstances – then isn't it possible that the same process happens when we *actually* experience something? Such as stage fright? In other words, isn't it possible that at least some members of the audience will experience true empathy at our glitch or our stumble or our complete memory breakdown? Of course, there's always going to be the collective, in-the-moment, breath-hold as the audience wills us back onto the track of the rehearsed script and staging – urging our unrehearsed agony to be over so that we can all return to a place of safety. But they're not out for our blood. They're not devouring wolves. They're human beings – like us.

It's probably a little inevitable that, if we've hit the big time, there may be a handful of Would-Be Hopefuls or Should-Have-Been Cynics wondering what's so special about us that we have the careers we have and not them... yet? But again it's a question of changing the mindset: it's *their* problem, not ours, as we're just here to tell a story and work our craft. Is it not entirely possible – if not probable – that if something goes wrong, if we really screw things up, empathy and compassion from the vast majority might quickly kick in after that momentary breath-hold? After all, everyone has experienced some moment of falter in their own lives – publicly or privately, professionally or domestically. And if the Would-Be Hopefuls and the Should-Have-Been Cynics smirk into their programmes with some temporary pleasure, then it could be that they have their own complexities to sort out – and that's not a burden for us to carry.

Many years after my fourteen-year-old self had been outraged at the RSC, I discovered that Paul Greenwood had been suffering chronic stage fright at that period in his life, forgetting his lines on one particular occasion on a monumental scale (as we'll see shortly). Live performances became a living nightmare for him. To be honest, I don't really know which was more shocking for me at the time: the fact that an RSC actor could forget his lines, or the absolute honesty shown by Greenwood in breaking the illusion of the fourth wall, and sharing his personal and actual reality with a packed auditorium. If I could travel back in time and revisit that evening, I'm sure I would find that in the moment of pure, shared experience and – with the exception of an uppity schoolgirl or two – the empathy and compassion in the audience were probably profound. Indeed, from my wiser perspective now, I would say, 'There but for the grace of God go we all…' If we don't actually experience mirror-neuronal empathy *at the time*, we may very likely experience deep compassion *in the time thereafter*. As indeed I do now, decades later, for Paul Greenwood.

In fact, performers whose stage fright is most notorious – such as Barbra Streisand, Laurence Olivier, Adele, and Ian Holm – have aroused immense public understanding and compassion. Fallibility in the famous is resoundingly reassuring. If facing the fear involves us reframing the situation, then knowing that someone out there in that darkness is rooting for us (rather than focusing our fear on the ravenous wolves), we can ease up on ourselves and trust to human empathy. In the years since my own experience of stage fright, I've witnessed several actors bluster, stumble, or scurry into the wings to check their lines, and it couldn't worry me less. My empathy for them is acute. My compassion for them is complete. My forgiveness (should it be necessary) is instant.

And so I finish this chapter with two tales that illustrate the audience's empathy and compassion when they witness stage fright. The first is part fiction and the second is full fact.

Tilly No-Body *and the journey to the brink*

It was some years after *The Permanent Way* ambush and I was battling with my stage fright. Although in the meantime I'd had numerous television, radio and theatre jobs – not least a remounting of *The Permanent Way* at the Sydney Theatre in Australia – my overall comfort as an actor had seemingly left me. I was wondering how to fight it. How to battle it and overcome it? Was the answer to quit acting completely? No –

that would be soul-suicide. So I decided to go to the other extreme. The Warrior Within wanted the Ultimate Challenge. A one-person play involving a range of comfort-zone-expanding activities and a conscious moment of stage fright to be shared directly with the audience. If I could let them know exactly how it feels, maybe I could face the fear in a creatively constructive way. I could take them with me on a kind of Trial by Fire.

Tilly No-Body: Catastrophes of Love is a solo play about the lives and loves of iconic German writer Frank Wedekind and his muse-wife Tilly. Set in a circus ring, it explores the notion of the actor's identity. Who are we when we strip away the layers of the onion that make up our fictional characters and our public personae? Who are we as actors when we don't have a role? Do we ever reveal our 'authentic' selves? And what does 'authentic' mean anyway? Frank Wedekind had spent years manipulating Tilly's identity through the roles that he wrote for her, and little by little she'd lost all sense of self and she began to suffer terrible stage fright.

Rather than sharing this biographical detail in some kind of objective way with my audience, I wanted to invite them to experience it subjectively along with me and the character. To which end, I scripted a sequence into the play that echoed Paul Greenwood at the RSC. At a moment relevant to Tilly's own personal anguish and loss of identity, I dropped all pretence at playing the character. Instead, I turned to the audience and stuttered, 'I am so sorry, ladies and gentlemen. I have absolutely no idea what I say next.'

I called for a line from the stage manager.

Silence.

I called again.

Silence.

I saw members of the audience turn towards the lighting box as if they were appealing to someone to help me out.

Silence.

What was delicious for me as an actor was that, from the moment I dropped out of character, I could hear a pin drop. The audience drew together tightly, like vacuum-packed bacon. It was as if they were sharing my anxiety (or was it Tilly's?), sharing my vulnerability (or was it Tilly's?). We were all in this together and the atmosphere was dense.

Little by little in the lines that followed, I shepherded the spectators back to a place of safety. The script morphed back into the character of Tilly, as she stood on the brink of her own insanity, facing the abyss of her own fear, confronting the darkness of her lost identity – and we were all back on track together.

To be honest, I was never *off*-track. Every pause, every hiatus, every stutter was tightly scripted. In playing a moment in which the actor seemed to have lost control of the performance, I was actually in total control. The reason for scripting the moment of stage fright was because I wanted everyone in the shared space to feel the connection between actor and audience. Whenever we suffer performance anxiety, we can all too easily default to assuming the wolves are baying for blood. They're not. We really have to remember that there's a tangible 'willing to succeed' that most audiences want for us as actors. As Peter Coyote stresses, 'When audiences to go to the theatre, they want you to succeed. And the last thing an audience wants to see is someone really frightened up on stage, really humiliated. Because it embarrasses them.'[97] If we can show them that if something goes wrong, we're not embarrassed, we're not humiliated – it's just part of the fabric of live theatre – then the audience can savour the aliveness and not feel embarrassed either. Although nothing really 'went wrong' in *Tilly*, I wanted to explore the experience of going on a potent journey with an audience. I wanted us all to go to the edge, take a peek over, and then all return in safety – a little bit like in a fairy story. From the responses after each performance and the critical reviews, we all seemed to return quite joyously.

This kind of playfulness – taking the audience on a particular journey of seeming screw-ups to lure them into another place of assured accomplishment – has been used to huge comic effect by many performers. Take the comedian Les Dawson playing the piano 'badly'. Or the magician Tommy Cooper 'flunking' the magic tricks. Or the characters in Michael Frayn's *Noises Off* forgetting their lines or falling down stairs or being sabotaged by the other actors. There can be the same agonising pleasure for the audience in these moments as those fairground rides that rob us of our gravity for a moment before plunging us (safely) to the ground. Of course these deliberate screw-ups are quite different in their dramaturgical effect than any unintentional moments of genuine stage fright. But what I'm suggesting here is that as actors we can aim to develop that same quality of ease within *ourselves*. We can develop our own playful awareness that there are times when live performance can herald the unexpected. Okay, so we accidentally derail on occasion. No big deal. We can get back on track fairly swiftly and keep the audience on the journey of the play. And if the audience can witness that it really is no big deal for us, we can hold them in a place of safety. Nobody need be embarrassed. Nobody need be ashamed. And this 'return to safety' is what *Noises Off* and *Tilly No-Body*, in their different ways, have woven into their dramaturgical fabric.

So from the semi-fictional to the solid actual...

The Happiest Days *or the darkest of nights?*

There are all sorts of stories about performers screwing up and the audiences love them all the more for it – as evidenced by Paul Greenwood's *ultimate* actor's nightmare, which I share with you now as he has so generously shared it himself. It's a tale that has gone down in the annals of British theatre history – and, as I said before, there but for the grace of God go we all...

The Happiest Days of Your Life was John Dighton's fast-paced comedy revived by the Royal Shakespeare Company at the Barbican Theatre in 1984 (probably around the same time as I saw *The Comedy of Errors*). As a favourite television celebrity, Paul Greenwood was heading the cast. And it was the opening night. In what can only have felt like an unrelenting tragedy, Greenwood's memory failed him almost from the top of the show. The words just wouldn't stick. In fact, his memory loss was so devastating that he forgot almost every line. The house was packed with more than a thousand spectators, including most of the London press (and this was at a time when the London press still wielded considerable power). As Greenwood started to lose the lines, he began to ad-lib frenziedly. 'I suddenly heard my voice, saying "I'm sorry, we'll have to stop, because I'm talking nonsense up here." Then I heard myself saying to the prompter, "What do I say next?"'[98] Basically, he was 'choking'. Yet what was hell on earth for the actor was actually holding the audience in raptures.

Grabbing his script during the first interval, he later described to a fellow actor that he might as well have been reading Japanese: nothing made sense. By Act Three, Greenwood had departed so far from the script that he turned to the delighted audience once more. 'Shall I start again?' he asked. 'Yes!' they roared back. This was no blood-lusty bunch of bait-biting ball-breakers: this was an audience of wholehearted supporters. At the curtain call, he found himself with his colleagues bowing through the applause as if nothing untoward had happened. Sure, *The Times* hailed his performance as 'memory loss on a grand scale', and Milton Shulman in *The Evening Standard* understatedly described it as 'the actor's nightmare'. And it certainly was. Yet in the years that followed, Greenwood continued to have an extremely successful career in film, television and theatre. Public empathy prevailed. 'Nowadays the whole experience is like a bad dream,' he writes, 'all of it rooted in fear, domestic difficulties and a personal problem at the time of introspection.'[99] The public not only 'forgave' him (if forgiveness were ever necessary), but the industry has acknowledged his humanness by constantly employing him ever since. We should take faith in the fact that ultimately the audience's empathy and compassion can cancel out our stage fright. They won't eat us alive. They won't ruin our professional career. Because there but for the grace of God goes *everyone*...

Overview

In this chapter, we've explored the complex actor-audience relationship including the *proximity of producer and consumer*. We've noted how the *theatre architecture* itself can fuel our fears – not to mention the power of the *shared space* and the *live audience*, as well as the affect of the *professional (and amateur) critic*. Which led us finally to the communication that ignites across the footlights and the neuron-fired *empathy* that unites us all in storytelling. The final two tales are reminders that we needn't fear our audiences. They're not really our enemy: they're our advocate and ally. When Olympia Dukakis walked back out onto the stage after her terrible lapse in memory, 'the audience burst into applause. It so moved me... It was just so kind. I thought, "What am I so worried about out here? Look at these people. Look how much they're on my side."'[100] For all the hubris of the fourteen-year-old schoolgirl who gasped at the professional actor's temporary memory lapse, thank God we're all human – and we sometimes forget our lines. The earth doesn't stop turning. And we can keep telling the play's story.

That said, let's try to get to the bottom of the memory-loss issue. After all, it's so prevalent in stage fright that we should understand a little about how memory and learning operate. How does our brain retain information in the first place and why do we sometimes forget those lines when we *know* that we know them so well? As generals on the battlefield, it requires us to face the real enemy – it requires us to face ourselves.

3

How Do You Remember All Those Lines?

The Role of the Brain

'I was catatonic, gripped by sheer terror.
I had done the play about 376 times,
but my mind went completely blank…'[101]

Derek Jacobi

3. *How Do You Remember All Those Lines?*

'Will I remember the lines?'

How is it that something as mundane as remembering our lines can become the most terrifying aspect of our craft? What about conjuring up the fictional realm? What about interpreting and embodying the role? Does it really all boil down to remembering the lines? All too often the answer is: 'Yes.' Ask many actors what the main manifestation of stage fright is and they'll answer, 'I'm afraid I'll forget my lines.' Which – configured slightly differently is – 'I'm afraid I'll let myself down.' When it comes to memory, our Number-one Enemy is our self. And it can happen just as easily during a long run as it can on a first night. After years of performing the lead in *The Phantom of the Opera*, Michael Crawford started to doubt himself: 'I'd played the Phantom for three and a half years, I must know the words by now.'[102] Desperate to reassure ourselves, we repeat our lines over and over again. Just like the Oscar-winning actress Ruth Gordon, who would pace the wings 'like a caged lioness, waiting for showtime, muttering to herself... every night of the run in the same methodical restlessness'.[103] Not that she was actually reviewing her lines: it was 'a ritualistic attempt at self-comfort'.

What's going on here? How can Michael Gambon's fear of line-loss land him in hospital and put him on a drip? How can

Derek Jacobi's catatonic terror at forgetting 'To be or not to be' drive him off the stage for two years? How can great and experienced actors be so afflicted? Especially in an era when it wouldn't be difficult (in fact, it's quite common) for actors to have earpieces, into which their forgotten lines are whispered by an able ASM? Angela Lansbury flourished in *Blithe Spirit* on an earpiece – as allegedly have other actors including Matthew Broderick and Brian Dennehy. And we shouldn't forget that writer-performer Alecky Blythe has revolutionised verbatim drama by having actors on visible earpieces – in effect, being deliberately prompted. So why are we so hard on ourselves? Why can the root of so much performance anxiety be traced to mere memory?

In this chapter, we'll get to the very heart of it. We start by asking the basic question: *What is memory?* The meat of the chapter then breaks down into the three steps of the memory process: Step 1: How do we *learn* our lines? Step 2: How do we *store* lines in our head? And Step 3: How do we efficiently *remember* those lines when we need them? We then ask the key question: what's happening *when we forget our lines through stage fright*? And we finish by asking the remedial question of: How can we handle it better by changing our thoughts and *reconditioning* our brain?

We already know that much of the time we don't forget the lines because they've strangely faded away: we forget them because there's some other interference. And, perverse as it may sound, that interference can be our worry about the memory loss itself. It's back to the Fear Voice and those sabotaging imps that we encountered in Chapter 1. Robin Williams described it as the 'hardcore nervousness' of 'It won't work. It won't work. I'll forget the lines. Oh no!'[104] Derek Jacobi called it the 'worm' of self-doubt questioning, 'Can I do this in front of all these people?' The answer is: it *will* work and we *can* do it. We just have to diminish the demon's thrall. Which means finding out more about the mechanics of memory to that we can face those fears head-on. So at each stage in this chapter, we look at what the brain is doing *neurologically*. And then we address some *practical* ways that we can help it work efficiently. But let's start with the nitty-gritty: *What is memory?*

What is Memory?

'How much memory does it have?' We ask this all the time of our various technological devices. But what about the human device? How much memory do we have? Can we affect its size and efficiency? And what *is* it anyway? We've always been mystified by memory, considering it as much of a skill as any other, like speaking Spanish or juggling clubs. What's more it's a skill that can hugely impress our audiences. And therein lies the rub. 'At every post-show discussion,' notes actor Donald Carrier, 'the audience asks the question, "How do you learn all those lines?"'[105] So our ability to learn lines becomes almost synonymous with our talent as actors. 'And it's unfortunately taken on a kind of horrible pressure,' says Carrier. 'Actors who do have that skill – that *gift* – are very, very lucky. And other people just have to work very hard at it.'

There's no denying that learning lines can be darn hard, and in many ways it's getting harder. In everyday life, we're becoming more and more reliant on our technological devices to store information for us. Phone numbers. Things-to-do lists. Directions to destinations. But learning lines is something we can't depend upon our devices to do. *We* are our only resource. So to truly understand the process of memory, perhaps we need to return to a time before mobile devices existed. A time when human memory was considered 'the mother of the Muses' and an admirable gift of nature. Let's travel back in time to ancient Greece...

The Greek philosopher Plato was among the first people to articulate the mechanics of memory – specifically so that he could help orators remember their speeches. A memory system, postulated Plato, was like a wax tablet, a tablet that could do three things: *encode* information, *store* that information, and *retrieve* that information when it was needed. Although we now know that our brain is way more complex than a wax tablet, the basic premise of Plato's two-thousand-year-old postulation is still very relevant. As actors, we somehow need to *encode* the lines of our character; *store* those lines as long as the play runs or the film scene lasts; and *retrieve* them for every rehearsal, performance or take. Any difficulties we have in this three-stage process we call 'forgetting'. Simple as that.

Yet if only it were that simple. One of the major challenges of remembering anything is that, at any one time, there's a mass of information *available* to our brains, but only a small amount of that information is immediately *accessible*. ('I *know* I know that actor's name. Darn it – he was in that film called... you know.') Herein lies the issue: how do we access a particular piece of information – like a line or a monologue – when we need it? After all, it's not like retrieving data off our computers, where the storage system is static and we just click on whichever document we want, and the document is there and it's the same every time we click on it. Our brain isn't like that. The only way that our brain can access a memory is by creating it afresh every time. And that involves sending all sorts of signals to all the different neural regions and all at the same time. It's a very dynamic process – even with a simple memory. For example, a hammer. I want you to remember a hammer. Can you picture it? Clearly and distinctly? Its handle, its head, its colour and its weight? Would it surprise you to know that even in that simple memory of a simple object an enormous amount of brainwork is taking place inside your head? Antonio Damasio sums it all up:

> There is no single place of our brain where we will find an entry with the word *hammer* followed by a neat dictionary definition of what a hammer is. Instead, as current evidence suggests, there are a number of records in our brain that correspond to different aspects of our past interaction with hammers: their shape, the typical movement with which we use them, the hand shape and the hand motion required to manipulate the hammer, the result of the action, the word that designates it in whatever many languages we know. These records are... based on separate neural sites located in separate high-order cortices... Appreciating the shape of a hammer *visually* is different from appreciating its shape *by touch*; the pattern we use to *move* the hammer cannot be stored in the same cortex that stores the pattern of its movement as we *see* it; the [*sounds*] with which we make the word *hammer* cannot be stored in the same place, either.[106]

All that activity – just to remember a hammer? It's extraordinary that a simple hammer can ignite so many different patterns and networks in our brain. It's even more extraordinary that our brain can coordinate all these neuronal maps simultaneously so that they appear to us to be seamlessly integrated into what we picture as a hammer. So the answer to the question, 'How much memory do we have?' is: masses! In fact, the cognitive neuroscientist Michel Gazzaniga suggests that the only part of our lives that *isn't* memory is 'the thin edge of the present'[107] – that tiny moment of *Now* in which you and I exist. But how on earth does our brain do all this work? We need to study some basic neuroscience to deepen our understanding. Though we shouldn't be daunted. This is just another battle tactic, before we stride indomitably like generals through the battleground. After all, the more we know about the processes of stage fright – and particularly the mechanics of memory – the more directly we can Face the Fear.

What's the basic brain circuitry?

We'll probably never really know how the brain works, as our understanding of it evolves all the time. And it's not only our understanding that shifts. The brain *itself* is adapting as society and technology evolve. Even as I write – even as you read – there'll be some laboratory somewhere making some new mind-blowing discovery. Our brain is one of the greatest mysteries in the world. Yet what we *do* know is that it's one big energy powerhouse, generated by the tiny and miraculous nerve cells known as 'neurons'. We've touched on neurons already, so now let's probe a little deeper…

Neurons are probably the most valuable and extraordinary parts of our body. They're also the most communicative. They're constantly talking to each other by emitting and receiving electrochemical signals via the synapses (as we mentioned in Chapter 1). As we know, the gap between the end of a branch of one neuron and the branch of another neuron is called a 'synaptic cleft'. So what happens is that the electrochemical signals leap across these clefts creating patterned pathways, which enable everything we think, do, feel, and experience. As I sit here writing, there are about 100 billion neurons in my brain, each with about a thousand synapses; that means maybe one quadrillion synaptic connections are happening right now. That's an awful lot of activity over an awful lot of clefts. It's enough to make my brain hurt!

As you can imagine, all this activity means that our neurons are very sensitive to any change around them. And, therefore, they're very excitable. If they're not actively firing, they wither and die. If they are actively firing, then they're working unbelievably hard. Every second, they're responding to all the *outside-world* stimuli bombarding our senses – such as colours and shapes, touches and tastes. At the same time, they're responding to all the *inner-world* activities of our muscles, glands and organs. Here and now, I can hear the ticking of the clock at the same time as sensing that my heart is beating. In a simple moment of sedentary calm, there's a lot of neuronal activity. So just imagine the numerous navigations that are happening when we suffer a surge of stage fright! Our poor neurons are responding to the rumble of the audience as they fill the auditorium, the chill of the draft in the backstage wings, the butterflies in our tummy, and the muttering of our lines, the palpitations, the self-doubt, the imaginings of imminent disaster as we humiliate ourselves in front of the masses. That's a great deal of complicated communication between a great many complicated regions of our brain. However...

For our purpose of understanding stage fright even a tiny bit, we're going to keep it simple. We're not going to worry about all the complex regions of the brain. Here and now, we're just going to get to know two of them: the seahorse-shaped *hippocampus* and the almond-shaped *amygdala* (which we've already briefly encountered). Both of them are highly influential in our brain's evolution, and they're both at the epicentre of our memory and fear. That makes them major protagonists in the drama of our stage fright. So like the superheroes they are, I've called them the Memory Master and the Vigilante. And they're usually loyal warriors in our army. (Though – be warned – they're sometimes inadvertently coopted into the enemy's ranks. All the more reason to get to know them better.) As we look at how we learn lines – and what happens when we screw them up – these two characters will keep popping up in the drama.

First let's go back to Plato's wax tablet. We know this memory system comprises the three steps of *encoding, storing* and *retrieving*. So the first step in learning our lines is (obviously) *encoding* them.

Step 1: How Do We Encode a New Role?

Here's where our neuronal superhero – the hippocampus, or the Memory Master – springs into action. Located near the centre of our brain, the hippocampus is vital when we're *encoding* new information. And it's especially impactful when we're learning a new role. That's because the hippocampus helps us to create new memories in two particular (very actor-friendly) ways: *through our five senses* (sight, sound, touch, taste and smell) and *through our perception of space.*

Encoding through our senses

Once we understand that our hippocampus encodes *through our five senses*, we can start to consciously help it out. And there's one very immediate and easy way that we can help it...

What's the first thing we do when we're cast in a role? We look at the script, of course! Sure, we're reading to see what the piece is all about. But, if we're honest, we're also looking at how many lines we have. This is pragmatic, as much as egotistic. Our sensory perception of the script – the actual visuals of the lines on the page – will not only tell us how big (or important?) our role is, but also how much learning time we'll need to carve out in our schedule. In fact, one of the most immediate ways in which we begin to learn a part is by its actual *look* on the paper. I've even heard actors say in rehearsal, 'I can't quite remember the line, but I know it's at the bottom of the page.'

Whether or not they know their Memory Master hippocampus is at work here, many actors intuitively sense how important the look of the script is to their learning process. And they develop very personal feelings about it. Some don't want a single mark or highlight or annotation. Others (myself included) cover their scripts with notes and colours and scribbles and doodles. Tanya Moodie describes how:

> I separate the text with a pencil line into thought chunks, and sometimes even colour-code them with highlighters. I will circle first letters of words if there is a lot of alliteration, and mark out the antitheses. I try to make learning it a very active and muscular thing... so if I forget a word, I have a chance of remembering a colour or a feeling or an image or a rhythm. Sometimes if Shakespeare has used a complex antithetical image... I draw a picture of what I think that would look like next to the text.[108]

Moodie illustrates very clearly here that a strong sensory connection to the script can be very compelling in the learning process. And the sensory connection needn't just be the look: it might be the feel of the paper or the smell of the binding. Each of us has a different relationship to the actual script, and in every case, it's a sign that our hippocampus is helping us to encode the new material by appealing to our senses. So, we can do whatever we can to help it along the way.

Another way in which the hippocampus learns new information is by encoding through *space*. If we can learn more about what our brain is doing here, we can again understand how to assist in our own learning.

Encoding through space

I can remember almost every rehearsal room I've ever worked in. And I don't just picture it – I can feel where I'm standing or sitting or moving in it. In fact, whenever we start to put a play on its feet, our hippocampus's perception of *space* significantly leads our learning. This is a fact – a scientific fact that we know thanks to rats! By studying rodents, scientists have discovered that rats quickly learn the layout of a new maze as much by their orientation within the actual space as they do by any of their sensory perceptions (sight, smell, touch, etc.). In other words, it's innate in us as mammals to learn through our physical bodies in space.

While the scientific proof of this fact may be recent, our intuitive knowledge of the learning power of space is ancient. For over two thousand years, the arts of memory and public speaking have been linked to space and architecture. (Which is not surprising, considering that we haven't always had electronic devices to rely on.) In fact, it was the Greek poet Simonides, who first fathomed this around 500BC. He'd been giving a eulogy at a large banquet one day, when – shortly after he left – the roof of the hall collapsed, killing and mangling many of the diners. To help the authorities identify the bodies, Simonides pictured himself giving the eulogy in the banqueting hall and tried to remember exactly whom he saw sitting at each place around the table. He literally re-membered the dismembered bodies. As a result, he has been credited with what became known as the '*loci* method' of recall. This highly imaginative way of encoding new information builds on the Memory Master hippocampus's methods of learning through space and place.

Encoding through place: the 'loci *method'*

'*Loci*' means places, and the *loci* method was used in line-learning for centuries, long before we knew anything about the hippocampus. What's fascinating is that the *loci* method (intuitively) incorporates the way our hippocampus (biologically) helps us to encode new information through our awareness of what's around us. The basic premise was that, if you were trying to learn a long speech or oration, the first thing you did was to picture an architectural structure – say, a house – either real or imaginary. You then wandered in your imagination through the house, placing an image of each thing you needed to remember in particular rooms in a particular order. So you might put 'To be or not to be' (the concept of existence) in the porch; 'That is the question' (the existential dilemma) in the hallway; and 'Whether 'tis nobler in the mind' (the moral fortitude) in the sitting room, and so on. Then when it came to delivering your speech at a later date, you simply pictured yourself walking through your imaginary house and seeing each component of your speech in each room in the relevant order.

The *loci* method has had a massive impact across the centuries on how we learn – especially for actors. It was adopted and adapted by the Greek rhetorician Cicero (who suffered terrible stage fright, turning pale and quaking in his sandals whenever he had to give speech) and by the Latin orator Quintillius (who played a key role in developing early actor-training). Obviously the *loci* method was originally intended for orators, who would basically just be standing still and delivering a speech. So, taking an *imaginary* journey through a building *while* they were standing still could give them some specific pointers in their otherwise static state – and that helped them learn their lines.

We're not orators – we're actors. Most of our work naturally engages our whole body. And, indeed, the principle of linking memories to places is what rehearsing is all about. Be it stage or screen, our body and brain work together as we create a physical score within an actual space to encode the new material and help us learn the lines. We'll look at this later when we address muscle memory and physical scores. Suffice it to say for the moment, that these key functions of the hippocampus – our *senses* and our perception of *space*, as well as the details of *place* (whether it's real or imaginary) – are invaluable strategies for us when we're in the first stages of *encoding a new role*.

That's Step 1 of Plato's wax-tablet memory system. Yet how do we ensure that we don't just *encode* the lines, but that we *store* them efficiently? In other words, how do we transition effectively from Step 1 to Step 2? Again, we're going to unpack the basic neuroscience, so that we can then be more conscious in our learning strategies.

Transition: How Do We Ensure that Encoding a New Role Leads to Storing that New Role?

There are all sorts of terms regarding memory, and not only can they be confusing but they've also been constantly changing over the last few decades. Here, as ever, we're going to put it in simple layperson's terms and see that Step 2 actually involves three stages: *sensory memory*; *short-term memory*; and *long-term memory*. We've encountered two of these stages in Chapter 1 when we looked at 'choking'. The one stage we haven't yet encountered is sensory memory – and this is where the memory process begins.

The basic stages of encoding and storing new memories

At every waking moment, our senses are being bombarded with information: the sound of a passing car, the smell of hot tar, the taste of the coffee as we silently sip. For barely a second, our brain holds onto this information – this *sensory memory* – while it decides whether we need to do anything with it or if we can just let it go.[109] We simply don't have the head-space (or the time) to make every piece of sensory information relevant. If we attended to every noise, smell, or sip, we'd never get anything done! So most sensory memory stays on the peripheries of our consciousness. That cheeping bird... My husband's aftershave... The computer keyboard beneath my fingers... Drifting in... drifting out...

If, however, we *want* to remember something (such as the lines of our script), we have make sure that the information shifts from our fleeting sensory memory into something more conscious.[110] In other words, we can't just flip through a script and trust that the words will magically lodge in our heads. We have to invest some effort into bringing those words from the peripheries of our awareness to the centre. And that requires several stages of memory, starting with our *short-term memory*.

For *short-term memories* to be created, we actively have to register, recognise, or recall the particular information involved, be they 'numbers, words or statements, and they need to be recalled after a specific delay, usually five to ten minutes'.[111] In and of itself, our short-term memory can be pretty short. Indeed, it may last little more than a few minutes – maybe long enough to remember a phone number just before we dial it or a couple of last-minute script changes just before we shoot – and maybe up to a few hours.

Yet despite its comparative brevity, short-term memory is the first vital step in creating more durable, longer-term memories. In fact, it's short-term memory that we're using when we first need to recall the script, understand the blocking and the body movements, and remember all that information.[112] It would be almost impossible for us to create a *long-term memory* unless that information had passed through the conscious realm of our short-term memory first.

So how do we make sure that we set the whole storage process in motion? How do we convert a very fleeting *sense memory* into a slightly more enduring *short-term memory* into a rock-solid *long-term memory*? The answer is actually very simple: We give it some *attention*.

Pay attention!

Attention is crucial for us when it comes to encoding and storing our lines. (In acting terminology, we also know it as 'focus', 'concentration' and 'concentration of attention', and it's one of the four pillars on which Stanislavsky built his 'system' along with Relaxation, Observation and Imagination.) Attention is the fundamental tool we use to let our brain know that something is worth learning, and we do it through a series of split-second choices. Here's an example...

Let's imagine for a moment that we're in a rehearsal room and we're working on a new play. During the tea break, the playwright comes over to us and flashes a piece of paper at us. On it, there's a rewrite. First of all, our attention goes to the playwright and then pretty quickly turns to this vital, new piece of sensory information: the paper in his hand. Instantaneously, our brain sifts through all the other reference points coming to us at that moment in our fleeting sensory memory. (Maybe our stage manager is laughing in the corridor. A fellow actor is handing us a cup of hot coffee. Our phone is vibrating in our pocket as our agent calls us.) Immediately, our brain evaluates what we're up to in our present-tense activity and, from that instant evaluation, it determines what's most important for us to attend to consciously here and now. So at this moment in the rehearsal-room, the rewrite should probably get our full attention. (Our stage manager's joke, the cup of coffee, even our agent can wait.) If, however, we spill the scalding coffee – or the vibration of our phone becomes so insistent that it must be Hollywood calling – or our stage manager's hearty laugh turns into hysterical sobbing – then our full attention will switch from the rewrite to whatever else has now taken precedence. And thus a new short-term memory will be forged.

In many ways, we know the brain needs us to pay attention in the first stages of learning – because we know how hard it is to learn something if our attention *isn't* fully on it. Have you ever started learning your lines for a new role while you're driving the car, changing the baby's nappy, cooking the dinner? It's nigh on impossible. When we first try to encode our lines, it's much, much harder if we're multitasking. Once we've encoded them, then sure – we can knit, do yoga, jig, jog or juggle. But at the very first encounter, we need our full attention to pass from *encoding* new memories to *storing* those memories. We need to shift a stimulus from our peripheral (and largely unconscious) sensory memory to our more focused (and conscious) short-term memory. And the next stage in ensuring that we store something as important as our lines is to make sure that they then pass absolutely from our transient *short-term memory* to our durable *long-term memory*. Let's once more understand what's happening *neurologically* before putting *practical* strategies in place to help our brain with that process.

Step 2: How Do We Store Our Lines in Our Long-term Memory?

Lots of transitory, moment-by-moment activity goes on in our brain during sensory memory and short-term memory. However, when it comes to committing information to our *long-term memory*, our brain actually changes shape. If you were a London cabbie, you'd know this anyway – because you'd have taken the 'All-London Knowledge'. For the All-London Knowledge, 'Would-be taxi drivers have to learn 320 routes within a six-mile radius of Charing Cross, which covers a mind-boggling 25,000 streets and 20,000 landmarks and places of interest.'[113] A study by the University of London compared similar brain scans from taxi drivers and non-taxi drivers, and discovered that each person who had attempted the Knowledge had notably increased the size of their posterior hippocampus. Yes, indeed – they'd made their brains bigger through gaining long-term memories. That's quite a feat! I wonder what the results would be on actors such as Ralph Fiennes or Judi Dench – or all those actors with a canon of Shakespeare tucked inside their own posterior hippocampi? But how can creating long-term memories actually change our brains? Again, we'll keep it simple and laypersonable...

What happens when we interact with something in the outside world (e.g. an *object* such as our script, a *person* such as another actor, or a *place* such as a film location) is that our brain turns that outside stimulus into an inner representation. It's also known as a 'map' inside our heads. It does this by means of all that electrochemical communication that goes on between our neurons, and it uses proteins to actually change them. Some neurons become more active, some neurons become inactive. And the result of all this neuronal protein-chatting is that new connections are made in our brain to create the new inner map. And this new inner map is actually a new long-term memory. So you see, storing memories involves actively changing our brain. (Which is why stress can be so bad for us, as we touched on in Chapter 1. When we're under stress, we keep repeating negative thoughts; and those repetitions activate the changes that then lodge that negativity in our long-term memory.)

As we saw with Damasio's hammer, the process of remembering is incredibly complex. We know that our brain isn't like a computer where we can just press the iMovie icon. Nor do we have a screen located in one specific part of our brain onto which is projected the image of a hammer banging a nail into wood. Nor is the representation of the hammer in our heads one fixed map, like the map of the London Underground. As Damasio pointed out, how we *perceive* the hammer creates one particular map in one location. How we *feel* about the hammer creates another particular map in another location. And in a nanosecond all these diverse maps follow on one after another and relate to each other in astonishingly coherent ensembles.[114] These coherent ensembles are what we end up experiencing as the memory of a hammer. It's amazing!

It's even more amazing when it comes to building a fictional character. In making a long-term memory of a role, we're not just seeing the image of the text on the page (though, as we know, that does have some impact). Our actual experience of the black-and-white text includes maps of the research we've done, maps of our emotional lures into the role, maps of our rehearsed staging, maps of our fellow actors' faces and gestures, maps of the props we pick up, and maps of all the images provoked by the writer's language. All these multiple maps (created in multiple places in our brain) synchronise in a deeply mysterious way to give us our interpretation of Hamlet or Blanche Dubois or Superman or GI Jane.

The way in which our brain actually changes shape through these myriad maps – in order to lock in and store our long-term memories of a role – is literally mind-boggling! And it costs our brain quite some energy. That's why we really have to give the lines of the script some valuable attention. Otherwise, our brain doesn't know that it should bother with the effort of changing all those proteins in the first place. Long-term memory mapping only occurs for us when (in the words of biophysicist Stefan Klein) our brain is 'certain that the outcome warrants it. Only when the stimuli that are to be linked in the memory have appeared together often enough do new bridges grow in the brain – the reason that remembering takes *repetition* and *practice*.'[115]

What this all means – if we unpack it carefully – is that we actually have quite a bit of power here. As long as our brain is fit and healthy, we can consciously adopt strategies that make us more efficient, long-term learners.

So that's the neuroscience. What are the practical strategies?

Practical strategies for enhancing our long-term storage of memories

Learning lines is a vital part of our skill-set as actors. We can't avoid it. So it's great to realise how much control we have in strengthening that skill. In fact, there are three practical, manageable strategies that we can apply to help our brain convert our short-term memories into storable, durable, long-term memories. Those strategies are *repetition*, *meaning*, and (curiously) *downtime*.

Repetition

Be it television, film or the kind of Shakespeare summer festivals that proliferate in North America, we often have very short rehearsal periods and we may be preparing two or three projects at a time. So we have to do a lot of line-learning before filming takes place or rehearsals begin. Usually that line-learning can only be achieved through *repetition*. Unless we're a regular in a TV soap and we're in the habit of learning lines moments before shooting, most of us simply have to put in the 'grunt work'.[116] And how we go about that grunt work can vary hugely. Some of us drill the lines by going over and over them out loud or in our heads – maybe just before we go to sleep so that we can lull them into our subconscious. Some of us write them out a hundred times, like doing lines in school detention. Some of us move around the room, picturing where we might be on the set. Some of us repeat our lines while we're doing something deliberately unrelated: pruning the roses or washing the dishes. Some of us record our lines on our iPhones and listen to them again and again while driving or ironing or jogging. Some of us record the *other* characters' lines and speak out loud when it comes to our cues. Some of us hire a helpmate (or recruit a husband) to go through our scenes to the point of saturation (or divorce...).

The important thing to remember is that the line-learning is not rote-learning. Certainly one of the reasons for the constant repetitions is to store the lines in our long-term memory, but more importantly, the repetitions can be a direct route into the character's inner life. Actor Jay Whittaker describes:

> I'll sit on my sofa and I'll probably say a phrase twenty-five times in my head until it's stuck and then I'll move on to the next piece of the line. As the lines start to connect and actually make more sense, then they're not just repetition because images start to come. Then the ideas – the emotions behind the images – start to emerge. And I just keep repeating the

> phrases over and over. And as it starts to become emotional, the character starts to come out.[117]

And so it goes – from *repetition* to *sense* to *image* to *emotion* to *character*. When we're up against the clock of limited rehearsal, we have little choice but repeatedly to give our full attention to the actual physical script. It's the only way to convince our brains that the information is worth investing all that electrochemical and protein-changing effort. And nothing but that protein-changing effort will fix a map of those lines in our long-term memory. I repeat: we're not talking about mindless rote-learning here. As Whittaker points out, the repetition process allows the whole character to emerge. And that's partly because our imagination starts to give the lines *meaning*.

Meaning

It may sound obvious, but mindless rote-learning never works in the long run anyway. 'The mere repetition of information, with no additional thought about meaning or associations,' writes cognitive scientist Jonathan Foster, 'can help us to retain information for a few seconds, but it is generally a very poor method of learning for the longer term.'[118] I doubt many actors do the kind of cramming for a play that we did as teenagers swatting up on the English kings for our GCSE History. ('Willy, Willy, Harry, Ste, Harry, Dick, John, Harry Three…') That said, sometimes we simply have to. Sometimes we've only been given a few hours to get a TV audition onto tape – added to which, we've only been sent the sides for our part. So we have absolutely no idea what the lines might mean in the bigger context of the whole script and we have little choice but to fall back on line-bashing.

Trying to keep that information in our memory for a matter of hours is what neuroscientists Craik and Watkins call 'maintenance rehearsal'.[119] And I confess, I used to fall back on maintenance rehearsal all the time at drama school. I was so saturated by the constant stream of new material to be learned – monologues, dialogues, scenes, sonnets, soliloquies, dialects, songs – that sometimes I found myself doing last-minute cramming in a desperate attempt to maintain my memory for just a matter of hours. Sometimes it worked. Often it didn't – because, as Craik and Watkins also point out, if we want a deeper, more persistent memory, we need more 'elaborate rehearsal'.[120]

Elaborating on the text really just means giving it *meaning*. And it's one of the best ways of storing our lines for more than a few hours and ensuring that we're more likely to retrieve them when we need them. Added to which, it's something that we can consciously do. When we give a script meaning, we grant it some *personal value* for us as empathic human beings. We stimulate our imaginations with questions like: 'What do the character's words mean to me personally? Which aspects of my own temperament and history connect to these lines? What's the *context* of the material (i.e. what's the situation in which the characters find themselves)? What's the *function* of the material (i.e. what do they want out of this situation? And why did the writer script this scene in the first place?)' Suddenly there's a whole heap of images and ideas that help us to give the lines meaning and to elaborate on their context. And then of course they're easier to store. Here's another vivid description from Tanya Moodie, in which she illustrates how giving meaning to the lines can involve all kinds of imaginative hypotheses, as well as possible objectives and actions for the character:

> I associate the line-learning with understanding my character's objective. So firstly, after a readthrough of the script (or maybe two or three readings), I sit, pencil in hand, and begin to write down a few hypotheses of what might be driving the character, based on love or power, and try to encapsulate my ideas into one or two pithy sentences that describe their greatest desire (Overall Objective).

> Then, I start reading through from the beginning again, scene by scene... and I separate each unit with a pencil line. The units are when I change tack in my efforts to achieve my overall objective. I give each scene its own objective that feeds like a tributary into my character's overall objective, and I give each line an action that spurs forward my objective. I write all these things in and around the text of the script. I will also write down any snippets of inner monologue that I might be thinking while processing what another character has said to me. Then I will start speaking the text aloud while trying to express the action of each line in the manner in which I speak it. In this way, I am not only committing a text to memory, but I am also embodying a fundamental need to succeed in achieving my desires. The words and the character's rhythms come more naturally then. I do this unit by unit, so that all the chunks have clear psychological progression.[121]

We can sense the energy and impulse-to-action behind Moodie's descriptions. The work is elaborate, it's imaginative, and it's meaningful. (We'll look at the power of text analysis in greater detail in Chapter 5.)

While of course we need to give a text personal meaning, it's also very useful to research more broadly around the subject, and there are several avenues for this. First, there's the research we do by means of the third pillar of Stanislavsky's 'system': Observation. (The other three pillars are Relaxation, Attention, and Imagination, and they'll crop up again.) This kind of research involves the nitty-gritty of real life, and Antony Sher describes it as 'a wake-up call':

> Drama can be a kind of dream, a kind of sleep, where we imitate art rather than life, believe in fiction's received ideas, fall for Hollywood's view of the world. Look at the street brawl: it's messy, the blows mostly miss, those that land really hurt or stun; it's nothing like what some fight directors encourage actors to do, delivering and receiving blows with absurd grace – stylised, macho and pain-free – an insult to the victims of

> real violence. Look at real grief, too, or real drunkenness – it's not what you generally see on stage. We actors frequently copy previous interpretations of human behaviour rather than the real thing. Research takes you back to the truth.[122]

Linked to the research drawn from real-life observation, there's the research that comes from the fourth pillar of Stanislavsky's 'system': Imagination. This avenue of research is steeped in the facts surrounding the play – its historical, political, social or aesthetic context. Once we've collated the facts, then we can start to riff on them imaginatively. Through this kind of research, we give ourselves even more 'elaborate rehearsal' and that can really help us to lock in the lines. After all, there's 'a complex mutually reinforcing relationship between attention, interest, motivation, expertise and memory,' writes Foster, 'so that the more knowledgeable you become in a particular field, the more interest you will have in it – and your knowledge and interest will reinforce each other in *improving your memory for material*.'[123] So when Miles Anderson was learning the huge role of Salieri in *Amadeus* (as mentioned in the Preface), he started listening to and learning about the music described in the play. And before long, he had an emotional understanding of the musical references, as well as an 'interest' and 'expertise' in what the character was talking about. This elaborate, personal connection to the material gave it even greater meaning and helped Anderson consolidate his memory of the lines. It also consolidated the critical acclaim that he went on to receive in the role.

As if one large role wasn't enough, Anderson was also playing Prospero in *The Tempest* during the same season. Learning such a vast number of lines is a monumental task, and it really can exhaust the grey matter. Understandably, Anderson found that his brain couldn't keep on learning for hours on end: sometimes it just needed some *downtime*.

Downtime

We can actually strengthen our long-term memory by allowing ourselves some *downtime*: this is a scientifically proven fact – as well as being a great comfort. During the gaps between rehearsals, our brain is doing a huge amount of learning by itself. All too often when we have a mountain of lines ahead of us, we end up thinking that we have to line-bash intensively for hours at a time. (After all, knowing our lines is the least the director will expect of us, so we'd bloody well better learn them as quickly as we can.) Yet studies have shown that this kind of approach is misguided. Our brain works far more effectively if we take time off between our learning bouts. So we're allowed to have that cup of tea. We're allowed to have that game of online poker. In fact, we're not only allowed to, we *should* – because we're making our brains more effective. How wonderful!

It's what's Craik and Watkins call 'expanding rehearsal' or 'spaced retrieval'.[124] And we can be far more effective in learning our lines if we come back to them *after short breaks*. (So go and swim twenty lengths – or make a fish pie.) To be even more efficient, we should increase the length of the downtime every time we take a break. (So go and swim *fifty* lengths – or make a fish pie *and* a lemon tart.) And yet I know from my own experience that sometimes taking breaks can feel counter-intuitive. Especially if we don't have much time to learn a script. We whip ourselves into a frenzy of thinking, 'I've got to spend every waking moment *learning these lines*!' Yet it may surprise you to know that one of the best ways of strengthening our synaptic connections – and shifting those lines from our short-term memory to our long-term memory – is not only to take a break, but to leave the space between our retrievals to the point at which we've *almost forgotten them*!

This is remarkably reassuring. How often have we spent hours learning a script, then put it down till the next day only to find that, when we do come back to it, we can barely remember a word? There's no need to panic. This is actually a *good* thing. We should accept that we're using our brain very efficiently. We've spaced the retrieval of our lines to the point where we've almost forgotten them. So now we've given our neurons time between learning sessions to change those proteins, build those new synapses, and create a long-term, inner map of our role. Our brain can't do all that work if we don't give it time and keep bombarding it with line-bashing. If, instead, we allow some spaced retrieval, then the next time we come back to the script, our recall of the lines will be easier... and the next time easier... and easier... and so on. In fact, 'two spaced presentations of material to be learned are often twice as effective as two concentrated, unspaced presentations.'[125] (So head to the sea and swim the Channel – or cook a five-course dinner!)

It's important to understand this process of consolidated learning. And to understand that our time-out is improving our line-learning, not breaking our flow. Then we can adopt the right practices to make sure that our fragile memory of a new script grows stronger and stronger and stronger. At the same time, we can silence the panicky, self-sabotaging Fear Voice of, 'You're not working hard enough! You don't know the lines yet!' – Those interfering, totally unhelpful doubt-worms have *no* justification in trying to work us to a frazzle. When we allow a time of 'expanding rehearsal', we give our proteins time to synthesise. This in turn enables the new information that we've encoded to become stored as new long-term memories. And those long-term memories can last for weeks and months and even years. What kinder thing can we do to our brain, than take a break and have a cup of tea?

*

These are three manageable and practicable strategies that we easily implement to enhance our long-term storage: *repeating* the lines; giving them *meaning*; and taking some *downtime*. It's also worth reminding ourselves at this point of the power of our *body* in the learning process. After all, we know that we also retain memories through our perception of space and place. It's what's commonly known as *muscle memory* and it's another simple strategy that we can adopt to convert *encoded information* into *stored memories.*

Muscle memory

> 'Excuse me, please. Could you direct me to Oxford Street?'
> – 'Well, no actually, I can't: but I can take you there.'
>
> 'Excuse me, please. Could you tell me how to change a plug?'
> – 'No, I'm afraid I can't: but I can show you how.'

It's strange how our body seems to hold its own memory of space and instructions, even if our conscious mind doesn't know the exact words or logic. Biologically, of course, our muscles can't actually hold memory: it's our brain that does that. Yet certainly one of the most useful ways of remembering our lines is 'getting them into our body'. In many ways, we use muscle memory all the time: 'Now where did I put my keys? I came into the house. I dropped off the milk. I picked up the cat...' And we sometimes literally walk through the room trying to re-enact what we did, so that we can prompt ourselves into remembering where we actually put the keys. When it comes to acting, we know that part of the point of rehearsing is to build a physical score and imbue ourselves with some muscle memory. ('This is where I say the line about Moscow. Then, I go over to the chaise and ask Vershinin about his wife...') If we can associate lines with where we are in the space and what our body is doing on particular words, then it's much easier to recall them later – because the movement of our body and the actual space provide their own prompts. (It's worth pointing out that half the time we do this work intuitively. In which case, there's no need to think about it consciously. Don't forget, all these are strategies are really here to help us if we're suffering from stage fright.

If we're not, we can just get on with our usual process, whatever that might be.)

Personally, I do very little line-learning sitting down: I do most of it on my feet in a space, even if it's not the actual theatre or set. Obviously when we're working on detailed text analysis, we can't avoid a certain amount of sitting and imagining. Yet, throughout this book, we see that bedding in the lines for the long term can be so much easier when our *body* does as much work as our *brain*.

*

Let's recap: we've looked at the ways in which we *encode* a new role (through our *senses*, our *spatial perception*, and the details of *place*). We've negotiated the ways in which *encoding* a new role leads to *storing* a new role (through our fleeting *sensory memory*, our slightly more enduring *short-term memory* and our durable *long-term memory*). And we've looked at some practical ways of strengthening our ability to *store our lines in our long-term memory* (using *repetition*, *meaning*, *downtime* and *muscle memory*). We should now be in a strong position to tackle Step 3 in Plato's wax-tablet memory system – *retrieving* our lines when we need them. Here again, the Memory Master – the hippocampus – springs into action. Back to a bit of neuroscience, before we add the practical strategies...

Step 3: How Do We Retrieve Our Lines?

Have you ever noticed that when we first start to remember any new information, we're only too conscious of the fact that we're remembering it? It happens all the time in rehearsals when we first come 'off-book' – and there's almost always a bit of a set-back. We let go of the security blanket of the paper-and-glue script – and suddenly we're very aware that we're bashing our heads to remember our lines and we just can't get into the flow of the scene. That's because we're still in the short-term (working) stage of locking in the memories. So we're still very conscious that we're remembering to remember.

In the rehearsal room, this can be particularly frustrating, as we have to keep calling for 'Line!' It breaks our creative flow and it drags us out of the scene. And it feels like interference at every possible level. We've already seen that any glitches in our memory are usually due to some kind of interfering thought that pops into our head. At this stage in rehearsals, that interfering thought is 'I don't know these lines yet'. And that voice of uncertainty can be louder in our head than the actual lines of the script. Any experienced director will know that there's a time in rehearsals where he or she becomes a bit redundant. The actors are still in this phase of short-term memory – struggling through their half-learned lines as their brains forge the necessary, new, synaptic connections. And – yes – it *is* frustrating, but most of us know it's just a natural and transitory part of the learning process.

And, sure enough – once we've got over these the first Bambi-frail staggerings through the script – we begin to find that we don't have to consciously remember the lines any more. They're starting to lodge in our long-term memory. And this is when the true creative fun begins to happen and we really start to listen and play. That's because we're becoming 'habituated' to the scene. In fact, *habituation* (as it's known in psychology) is a great state to be in when it comes to remembering our lines.

Habituation

Habituation basically involves us becoming so used to a situation or an activity that it doesn't distract us.[126] This state is incredibly useful for us as actors – especially in the theatre. We want to become so habituated to our lines that we can almost forget we know them and just 'find' them in the moment of performance. In other words, we want to lodge them in our long-term memory (where we don't have to think about them any more) rather than in our short-term memory (where we're conscious that we're remembering them). When we're totally at ease with the habit of being on stage, there's no interference in our head any more. There's no 'What do I say next?' Instead, there's a kind of sublime alignment between our self as an actor and the 'life' of the character.

Part of my own process of facing and conquering stage fright involved understanding the creative joys of habituation. It was the Spring of 2015 and I was preparing a fact-based, one-person piece for the Hollywood Fringe Festival: *Nell Gwynne: A Dramatick Essaye on Acting and Prostitution*. Fairly early on in the process, I became aware that I was in danger of flirting with the imps of stage fright. It had been nearly ten months since I'd done any live acting (through circumstance rather than choice) and I knew that *Nell* would be my launch into the LA acting scene.

The whole process was fairly compacted. Between February and May, I researched and wrote the piece. Then I had just nine evenings of rehearsal over two weeks before the first preview. So it didn't take much for the worm of self-doubt to begin nibbling on my grey matter. I knew that the number-one solution to keep those doubts at bay was to do whatever I could to reach a state of habituation as quickly as I could. So, this is what I did *practically* to recruit my *neurological* processes: I simply went over and over and over the material as often as I could. In my head... in my body... at fast speed... at slow speed... on a mocked-up set... walking into work... wherever, whenever, however was possible. It was a discipline, a practice – just as people might practice their Buddhist chants. And I had one driving goal in mind: to habituate myself to the lines and the moves, to the point at which I could sustain one of two desired states in performance:

- *Performance State 1*: I would be totally confident in my autopilot knowledge of the play. Then, if the imps *did* start their sabotaging chatter mid-performance, I could easily deal with the situation by just allowing my body and mouth to go through the motions until I'd shut the imps up.
- *Performance State 2*: I would be totally at ease with the material: the moves, actions, desires, lines, objectives, emotional trajectory, direct address to the audience, all of it. That way, I could 'forget' I knew the words and simply play with them in the moment of delivery.

Obviously the second state was far more desirable than the first. The first would mean that I was not having a good time on stage and that I was battling with the interfering demon of stage fright and his minions, the imps. The second would mean that I was having such a great time on stage that I'd forgotten to let the imps in, let alone listen to them: and, thus, I'd defeated the demon!

These were the two 'ideal' Performance States. (The third – Total Public Meltdown – was unthinkable.) And I knew that these states would only be achievable if I could totally habituate myself to the play and its contents.

I cannot tell you how many times I went through those lines and moved through those stage pictures. I cannot tell you just how precisely I laid out the props and costumes at each rehearsal and performance. I knew exactly where I'd like them to be, so that they could literally and metaphorically guide me through the physical score if the imps started chattering. (That said, I wasn't so wholly fixated on it that, should a prop be moved or not even be there, I'd fall to bits. I was simply finding some *conscious* strategies to help the *unconscious* do its thing.) I was determined that nothing was going to stop me from successfully retrieving my lines – not monsters, nor demons, nor imps, nor worms!

Sure enough, by the end of the month-long festival – mission accomplished. Demon defeated! For this solo production, where I had no partner to bail me out, I knew that habituation was the best strategy for retrieving my lines and facing my stage fright. Sure, the props screwed me up sometimes and the costumes misbehaved. (There's no such thing as a 'solo' show – it's just that your partners are supposedly inanimate. The imps will find their way in somehow.) I even reached the point that, when I did forget the lines in performance (as I did several times, though I don't think anyone knew), I was so at ease, I could breathe into the moment in the knowledge that the stage felt like home and the audience was with me. Although we received various awards and nominations – including two for Best Female Performer – the highest accolade came from another actor with a one-person play. He came up to me after a performance and said, 'Oh, my God, you're so relaxed on stage. It's so sexy!' Mission definitely accomplished. Where habituation reigns, there's little space for stage fright.

Having said all that, it can be quite different for screen acting. Some actors find that there's a real benefit to *not* knowing the lines too well, and they enjoy the edginess of finding them on the brink of a breath. In fact, Marlon Brando was renowned for not learning his words. In a perverse 'anti-stage fright', he was apparently more afraid of *knowing* his lines than he was about *forgetting* them. If he knew them too well, his acting might be phoney; whereas if he didn't know them at all, he could really live in the moment. So he used to stick cue cards all over the set. He even stuck them on his fellow actors' bodies, as you can see in the famous photograph of Robert Duvall with a cue card held to his torso during the filming of *The Godfather*.[127] Allegedly, Brando's reasoning was, 'The audience doesn't know what I'm about to say, so why should I?' I doubt many of us could get away with that kind of genius or mischief or whatever you want to call it. (Indeed, as we'll see in Chapter 5, some screen actors have morphed Brando's chutzpah into a certain 'cool' of improvising their lines, regardless.) Nonetheless, there's still the safety net with filmed work that if we *do* forget our lines, we can record another take. Which is why so many actors who suffer fright on the stage find solace on the screen – as did Derek Jacobi and Michael Gambon and Ian Holm.

One of the great things about habituation is that it's a practical strategy we can achieve on our own through rehearsal and repetition. We've also got other practical strategies for retrieving our lines that don't rely so heavily on ourselves. One such example is to use the *theatre architecture* to give us points of reference.

Retrieving information through the theatre architecture

The basic premise of rehearsing (as we've already seen) is to map onto the stage set where the best moves would be to tell the story most compellingly. At the same time, we're giving ourselves some physical pointers – some muscle memories – to help us (consciously or unconsciously) to retrieve the lines each time. But we're not just restricted to the set. We can also use the entire *theatre architecture* as a prompt to our memory retrieval, if we think it's going to be useful. The specifics of how we map our moves may be really quite minimal. For example, with the many direct-address speeches that I had in *The Permanent* Way – where I was doing little more than sitting in a chair – I constructed a micro-score based on the theatre space itself to help me remember the text: 'On this line I look towards the emergency sign at the back of the circle. On that line I cross my right leg towards the left side of the stalls.' Little did I know that I was actually drawing upon a memory system that went right back to the early Renaissance. Since it's such a simple way of anchoring our memory (should we need to), let's do a little more time-travel to see where it all started...

It's 1530 and we're in the court of the French king. But more importantly we're in the company of one of the most famous men of his time: the Italian thinker Giulio Camillo. Camillo was actually the first person to make an explicit connection between memory and theatre architecture. He designed what he called his wooden 'Theatre of Memory', and his magic number was seven. In his memory theatre, there were seven steps divided by seven gangways representing the seven planets. On each of the seven gangways were seven gates decorated with cosmological and mythological imagery. And although Camillo's memory theatre wasn't intended for actual plays, the idea was that if you stood on the stage and looked out towards the auditorium, you could use the physical structure of the theatre to prompt you into remembering specific information.[128]

And this architectural practice didn't stop with Camillo. If you've ever seen the famous copy of Johannes de Witt's 1596 sketch of the Swan Theatre in London, then you'll have seen an allusion to the next evolution of Camillo's memory theatre. It was equally significant, and this time it was conjured up by the Elizabethan physician Robert Fludd.[129] Just like Camillo, Fludd created a direct relationship between the art of memory and the architecture of a theatre. He drew various theatre drawings (not dissimilar to de Witt's sketch), which depict his memory stages. This time the lucky number was five. In his memory stages, there were five entrances, five columns (two round, two square and one hexagonal), and five doors (white, red, green, blue and black).

This knowledge is all very intriguing, given all the discussion among theatre historians linking Fludd's memory stages to Shakespeare's Globe. What it basically suggests is that, at the very root of modern theatre architecture – including Shakespeare's theatre itself – lay a way of helping us as actors to remember our lines. You could say these architects were directly tackling stage fright! Whether they knew it or not, Camillo and Fludd were both tapping into our hippocampus's way of using the body in space and our physical context to help us retrieve our lines. Now that's pretty exciting – and we can still employ it today should we find that we're in need of a little aid to memory.

*

Thus we have two more practical strategies that we can use to strengthen our long-term memory: *habituation* (repetition to the point where we no longer have to explicitly think about what we're doing) and *using the theatre architecture* to prompt our memories (just as our Renaissance ancestors did – and possibly Shakespeare himself!).

We've now looked at the three-step memory process of successfully *encoding, storing* and *retrieving* our lines. And in so doing we've learnt from both our theatrical ancestors and our contemporary neuroscientists. But of course it's the *un*successful memory that can bring on our stage fright. So what's happening when we forget? And how can we forearm ourselves against such an eventuality?

What Happens When Our Memory Fails Us?

'How do you remember all those lines?' We know this is what audiences awe over. We also know it's the nub of our work as actors. Yet sometimes we *don't* remember them. Sometimes we suddenly forget them. And that unintended rupture in our fundamental craftsmanship can explode into an experience of stage fright. As we've already noted, the problem usually begins with a glitch in the retrieval part of our memory process. We've encoded the lines; we've stored the lines; but somehow our retrieval screws up. And the protagonist now in the drama of our stage fright is the other neurological superhero: the *amygdala*, the Vigilante. We encountered the amygdala in Chapter 1 when we looked at the evolutionary provokers of stage fright. So now let's look more closely at what it's up to when we forget our lines. We may not be able to stop the Vigilante, but at least we'll understand what it's doing.

When the amygdala – the Vigilante – becomes over-attentive

As we know, the *amygdala* is a tiny security system lodged in our heads as a kind of 'mind within a mind'. It's vigilant. It can be twitchy. It receives its data raw. So when we encounter a new situation (like a film location or an audition room – or worse, a sudden memory lapse when we're standing on the stage), the amygdala kicks into gear within milliseconds – far faster than our conscious mind. It scans our past experiences to see if it finds any matches with any previous life-threatening situations. And if it finds a close enough match with a past threat, it fires up our fear reaction of fight, flight or freeze.[130]

The amygdala's vigilance can be both a help and a hindrance. On the help side, it can save our lives if we're in real danger. On the hindrance side, it's not very precise and it sometimes gets things wrong. So, we forget our lines in the middle of a scene and – 'Attention! Scan the past! When were we last standing in the dark with a hot, blinding light shining in our eyes and faceless strangers waiting for us to say something?' (Sounds more like a Gestapo interrogation than a momentary glitch in a performance.) The trouble is that, even when it gets things wrong, the fear system is a very persistent memory system – because it wants to be sure it's doing its job. After all, if it misjudges a situation and it *doesn't* read the dangers, it could literally be a matter of life and death. And so the amygdala 'forms opinions' about what we should or shouldn't fear, and 'those opinions are very tough to change'.[131]

They're tough to change partly because, when we're experiencing moments of intense fear, the amygdala etches very detailed information into our brain. So much detail, in fact, that it can feel as if the event is happening in slow motion. That's certainly what I felt during my stage-fright experience in *The Permanent Way*. Everything went into slo-mo. I couldn't tell what speed the words were coming out of my mouth. I felt as if I was walking on the moon. And the detail and the robustness of the memory – as implanted by my amygdala – were very damaging. I couldn't shift the fear. For a long time afterwards, the stage space felt threatening and uncomfortable. Even though I knew it needn't be – after all, it was just a stage, it wasn't a Gestapo interrogation centre!

Yet once a fear memory is there, it's *there*! Once it's encoded, it takes a good deal of conscious effort to de-code it (not to mention a fortune on psychotherapist's fees). And this is why an experience of stage fright can be so impactful. It's like all fear memories, 'you can learn them instantly and they last a lifetime'.[132] There isn't anything else that you can learn that quickly. For all the amygdala's brilliance in saving our lives in a crisis, its combination of instantaneousness and imprecision isn't very useful for us on stage: 'With a single bad experience, we can become conditioned to fear things that are totally harmless... Fear is a sledgehammer, not a scalpel: it goes for power over precision.'[133]

But what's really so terrifying about forgetting our lines?

The answer to that question is: all the reasons we've looked at so far. 'How do you remember all those lines?' We know that's what many audience members applaud us for. Knowing our lines is the foundation of our craft – for the playwright, the director, our fellow actors, the people calling 'Action!' or the cues for light and sound. So of course if we forget our lines – if we 'dry' (as we say in the UK) or we 'go up on a line' (as they say in the US) – it can be absolutely mortifying. It's shameful and denigrating. And it can be just as mortifying, however established or nascent our careers might be. Can you imagine if a master electrician told you that he'd forgotten how to wire a plug? It's humiliating. And, for actors, that humiliation can be very public. That's why stage fright can kick in just as easily for seasoned professionals with numerous awards to their names. The stakes are higher. The audience's expectations are greater. They're willing to pay more for a seat to watch their favourite celebrity. Not to mention those Would-Be Hopefuls and Should-Be-Me Cynics, who have a particularly critical eye. Which is why Gambon and Dukakis and Cumberbatch and Jacobi are just as vulnerable as any recent RADA graduate. So, when we forget our lines, we punish ourselves with chidings of unprofessionalism and unreliability. We shudder with shame. We lose our artistic integrity, and our anxiety is overwhelming. Anxiety, as defined by the existential psychologist Rollo May, is 'a threat to some value that the individual holds essential to his existence as a personality'.[134] And, as actors, what could be more 'essential to our professional existence' than our ability to know our lines? So, if that ability is threatened *by our own brains*, we can suffer profound existential uncertainty.

Yet – stop for a moment! We've been through all this in the previous chapter. Half the time the audience is oblivious to the stumble or the hiatus, and – if they do note it – they're ultimately profoundly forgiving. These fears and anxieties are our amygdala working overtime; they're *not* the actuality of the situation. So the challenge is to 'know the enemy' – to suss out when the twitchy Vigilante momentarily switches to the enemy's side.

If we *know* that the amygdala 'forms opinions' about what we should or shouldn't fear...

If we *know* that 'those opinions are very tough to change' but they're sometimes wrong...

If we *know* that an unexpected moment of stage fright could kick-start unnecessary fear alerts for our amygdala in our *future* performances...

If we know all these things, we can take some control and apply some conscious willpower to break the unnecessary fear-hold. If we really are nothing but 'the thin line of the present' – and we really do exist only in the clefts between our synapses

– then we're very adaptable as human beings and we can make all kinds of conscious changes *right now*...

But we'll get to that shortly. For the moment, let's just see which lessons we can draw from the *glitches in our memory*. We still need to face a few demons...

What can we learn about our memory glitches?

Of course, not all the *glitches in our memory* are the same. There's a big difference between screwing up in early rehearsals (when the information is still new) and 'drying' on a well-known line (which can happen at any point in a run).

If it's *early* in the memorising process (like the first week of rehearsals or the first night of a show or the first day on a set), we're still in the short-term memory mode of consciously remembering our lines. Because we haven't had time yet to repeat the information very often, our brain hasn't made the neuronal changes that would shift it into our long-term memory. In many ways, this is the easiest to fix: we just need to rehearse or perform the piece more times.

If it's *later* in the process – like Michael Crawford being haunted by the *Phantom* or Derek Jacobi being bothered by 'To be or not to be' – then it's often because our long-term memory of the lines has gone horribly haywire. One of the glitches in the complex hard-wiring of our brain is that sometimes we can become so familiar with something – so habituated to it – that we start to *think* about it too much. As we saw in Chapter 1 with 'choking', we inadvertently yank it out of our *unconscious* memory (where we'd normally just get on with it automatically) back into our *conscious* memory (where we start to ask ourselves questions, like 'Oooh, how do I do that?'). And quickly consciousness leads to self-consciousness, which leads to self-sabotage. Which is why long runs of a show can be just as precarious as first nights. We start to think *explicitly* about information that we've already stored *implicitly*. Since this is one of the most perplexing issues about losing our lines, let's look at this phenomenon more closely.

Long-show-itis

We've seen how amazingly creative our brain is when it's making interior brain-maps. It does a lot of work, and it enjoys a lot of work. It likes stimulation. It likes the fun of learning new information. And so it needs new activities on which it can focus. But if it does the same thing for any length of time and at the same level of difficulty, our brain becomes bored – and we become anxious.

It was after five months in *The Permanent Way* that I suffered my own acute stage fright. It seemed absurd – this late in the game, out in the provinces, and after all the adrenalin-filled exposure of London. So haunted was I by the absurdity of my nerves that I began to speak to my fellow cast members about it. And as it turned out, I wasn't alone. Fellow actor Sam Graham was very open about the fact that he was experiencing stage fright – and about suffering it on two previous occasions. All of these occasions had happened during long runs and so he'd coined the term *long-show-itis*. The first time he'd suffered it, he was playing Phoebe in Declan Donnellan's production of *As You Like It*:

> Phoebe is a very strange character because she comes on stage about two-and-a-half hours into the play. You can already see people wondering if this new energy is of any value as they're already absorbed in the Rosalind story. As an actor, I felt a sort of antipathy from the audience, a kind of 'We don't need this.' And that of course fuels a kind of psychological angst, from which you can *subconsciously* create different symptoms – whether it be an undercurrent of 'I'm shit', or 'Actually I don't want to be here'. You then start questioning yourself *consciously*: 'Am I doing this wrong?'[135]

Graham was hounded by uncertainty as to whether or not his performance of Phoebe was relevant or any good. And what happened next was curious. He found that his long-show-itis became an almost unconscious way of recreating that buzzy kind of heightened arousal that we experience early on in a run, but which inevitably dissipates over time. His brain was seeking an adrenalin rush. It wanted a fix. 'It never happens in the early stages because you've got too much to think about. It creeps in when there's a possibility of "autopilot" – when you can become a bit complacent with the ease of performance – and that for me can trigger it.'[136]

Graham had studied Chemistry at university, so when the shakes and the trembles started, he turned to his Chemistry training:

> I thought, 'Right, so the brain is sending signals to your nerves, and this chemical is being sent out to your synapses. Why? Is this fear?' 'Yes.' So now fear is involved. 'So, what are you frightened of?' 'Well, I'm frightened that maybe all this work I'm doing might actually be meaningless.' And you ask yourself, 'So, why are you thinking that?' And you reply to yourself, 'Well, in practical terms, do you really think this is going to get me another job?' And you ask yourself, 'Why are you asking that now? You're supposed to be telling Shakespeare's story!' And all the time that you're dialoging with yourself like this, the character's speech is just coming out of your mouth.[137]

What's intriguing here is that there were several things going on for Graham. First of all, there were interferences between what he was thinking and the lines he was supposed to be retrieving. (As we know, that's not uncommon with stage fright.) Second, apart from experiencing all these self-judging inner monologues and doubts about his future, he found that the words themselves were beginning to sound like gibberish:

> I came up with the term 'long-show-itis' because I think my nerves were the result of my brain getting to the stage of knowing that the language (when spoken so often) starts to sound like nonsense – even though you're perfectly aware of the sense of what you're speaking. The thing about memory is that it's basically a series of connections in the synapses in your brain, and once you've learnt the lines, there's now a route map in there. It's almost as if, after a while, the route map somehow becomes a separate entity, and you start looking at it and going, 'What's that strange thing? What's that a map of?'[138]

And then you forget your lines.

Graham's chemical insights were very helpful. In the last few weeks of *The Permanent Way*, I too had found myself questioning the actual sense of my lines. The sound of particular words suddenly seemed really weird. And, in the split-second of performance, I'd find my brain asking, 'Did that sentence just make sense? Did those words actually mean anything?' Antony Sher describes a similar situation, playing in the long West-End run of *John, Paul, George, Ringo and Bert*:

> After the initial excitement of opening, a long run can become something of an endurance test. Round about the halfway mark, we all started forgetting the lines, despite knowing them inside out. That was the problem, actually – we no longer knew them in a way that made sense. We were on automatic pilot, thinking about the shopping, thinking about anything other than this endlessly looping story that had entrapped us like a recurring dream.'[139]

Matthew Dunster, a fellow actor in *The Permanent Way*, shared with me that he too was suffering performance nerves, even at this late stage in the run. Just like Graham, he had some pithy and instinctive responses that echo what we now know about the neurobiology of long-term memory:

> I think what has actually happened is that we've advanced beyond the task. Why should our minds be restricted by 200

> words on a page, four positions in a chair, one position to fetch a prop, one position to sit down with a prop? I know that when I'm saying my lines, I'm inhabiting them just as much as I ever did, and I'm inhabiting the moves just as much as I ever did... But my mind is four or five lines ahead, a speech ahead, the next project ahead – and there's nothing I can do about that. My mind is more athletic than the task that I'm currently applying it to. And I think that's why we're forgetting stuff: our minds have outgrown the focus.[140]

Again, Dunster was suffering brain interference, and it was in danger of jeopardising his retrieval of the lines. It's strange that when we stand outside ourselves as actors, we occasionally glimpse – in short, disembodied bursts – the mild madness of what we do for a profession. This madness finds all sorts of expression during long runs – because that's when the adrenalin kick inevitably wears off and we have the headspace to afford ourselves some out-of-body experiences. After three months of performing *Another Country* in the West End, Kenneth Branagh and his cast – all in their early twenties – were overwhelmed with bouts of laughter:

> The hysterical corpsing was partly induced by the unusual demands of a long run on inexperienced actors. After three months, I began to go a little stir crazy... my concentration wavered in performance until I dried desperately in the middle of one show and had to walk off while Rupert [Graves] saved the day with an ad lib – 'I think Judd must have a headache or something.' This produced terrible stage fright for the next two weeks.[141]

With *The Permanent Way*, it was deeply reassuring to face the fear with Sam Graham and Matthew Dunster. The ease with which they shared their articulate insights into what they were experiencing allowed me to feel that my own sensations were perfectly normal. Up until then, I'd felt horribly isolated and secretly alienated. In fact, the conversations with Graham and

Dunster were so poignant that they've stuck with me ever since. And in many ways, those conversations prompted me to write this book. Talking to them convinced me that the more we collectively look the demons in the eye and acknowledge their normal, biochemical reality, the less scary and persistent they can be.

Something that Sam Graham said struck a chord in me. Because our brain operates by making maps of our experiences, we have to be sure that we don't create new maps that lock in our stage fright *as the norm*. If that happens, we're in danger of developing what's known as *sensitisation*.

Sensitisation

Sensitisation is the opposite of habituation. Putting it simply, *habituation* involves us tuning out any unnecessary distractions that are *benign and unimportant*. (Such as the sounds of backfiring motorbikes and braking buses outside the theatre). On the other hand, *sensitisation* involves us learning the properties of a *harmful and threatening stimulus*, so that we can deliberately tune into it. Sensitisation is an important part of our survival tactics. As brain scientists Squire and Kandel describe it: 'By means of sensitization, people and animals learn to sharpen their defensive reflexes in preparation for withdrawal and escape.'[142] For example, soldiers become sensitised to loud noises: 'Was that a firework or a gunshot?' But most of us aren't soldiers in a war zone and, as we know, sometimes our amygdala's defensive reflexes are not always appropriate. Here's why...

When we learn a new memory, our brain locks it in by *decreasing* synaptic connections as much as by *increasing* them. In other words, it can only create a new brain map by killing off some of the old (now redundant) neuronal connections and basically freeing up more space. (It's a bit like our mobile devices really: 'I don't need those applications any more, so let's free up some bytes. Trash.') What happens when we become *habituated* to something is that our brain doesn't need that particular memory map any more. So it decreases the strength of those connections in order to use them for something else. And if there isn't anything else that immediately needs attention, our brain becomes bored. So it occupies itself with new activities. (Maybe it'll start looking for potential dangers or creating an adrenalin buzz.)

In fact, this could be the very root of our stage fright when we're performing in long runs. It could be that our brain becomes so habituated to our performance that it reckons it doesn't need that brain map any more. So, subtly, during the run, it decreases the synaptic connections that comprised the map in the first place – even though we still absolutely need that map in order to give our performance every night! Which could be why Sam Graham described his long-show-itis in terms of the route map becoming a separate entity. It's almost as if the map of our character's lines becomes detached from the intergalactic mother ship of the whole production. And, like a space-capsule with its oxygen line umbilically floating behind it, it spins out into the darkness of the abyss that leads us straight towards stage fright.

It's really important that we understand what's going on here. And we need to be on our guard. Because if our brain really is decreasing the synaptic connections to our character map (even though we still need it), this could be doubly problematic. Not only could our memory of the character's lines weaken, but now there's also space in our brain to make some new connections – connections that might have nothing to do with our performance. (Indeed, it could start actively looking for those potential dangers and creating that adrenalin buzz.) This is exactly where that twitchy Vigilante, the amygdala, springs into derring-do action...

With *habituation* (as we know), our brain alters because it's exposed to *repeated presentations of the same stimulus*. (That's how we learn our lines. We repeat them over and over and over, so that the brain can change its proteins and create a map of our lines.)

However, with *sensitisation*, we only have to experience a threatening stimulus *one single time*. And that one time alone is enough for us to respond way more vigorously to a whole heap of *other* stimuli that have nothing to do with the threat. In fact, they could be totally harmless.[143] So, if our ever-curious brain is looking for something to occupy it when it gets bored during a long run, then that backfiring bike outside the theatre or that braking bus suddenly sounds like a terrorist attack. Maybe that's a little extreme – but you get the point. When we're in a highly sensitised state, a totally harmless, unconnected distraction suddenly becomes weighted with imagined danger.

What I'm driving at here is that, when we suffer stage fright, two particular processes seem to kick into action, and they're linked to habituation and sensitisation. First of all, our bored mind is unhelpfully *habituated* to our onstage activity. ('Okay, I know these lines... I know these moves... Yawn, yawn.') So, it starts to scout for any new stimuli to keep it busy while we're doing whatever it is we're doing on the stage. Then if we suddenly forget our lines even for a milli-moment, that powerful kick of adrenalin could be just the very thing that our bored brain latches on to.

Then, that jolt out of habituation seems to trip the switch on our *sensitisation*. Our pounding heart prompts our brain to perceive that momentary memory lapse as disruptive and threatening. So now our brain is on the alert to see all kinds of other stimuli as disruptive and threatening – even when they're not. So my moment of distraction with *The Permanent Way* – 'Wow! The audience really are close, aren't they?' – gave my bored brain something to grapple with – a new buzz, a new fix. Once I got off stage, it didn't take long for me to become sensitised to a whole heap of other things that really weren't that scary:

'Oh my God! Max Stafford-Clark is out there!'

'Oh my God! This audience is terrifying!'

'Oh my God! I'll never work in British theatre again!'

My amygdala had done 'A-grade' work. It had vigorously responded to a mildly disquieting moment and had turned it into a five-act melodrama. From that moment on, my brain was sensitised to perceiving every other audience as threatening and scary, and for a long time I lost all the pleasure of live performance. And all because of one, tiny, momentary, interfering distraction.

When we don't know about sensitisation, we can start to create in our own synapses a fear-ridden connection between something that's benign (a regular audience who have happily paid to see a good show) and something that we imagine to be detrimental to our personal and professional survival (a critical mass of Gestapo-like interrogators determining our destiny). If we keep tuning into our stage fright, we then start to create an enduring, long-term memory map of that very fear. We start habituating ourselves to fear. And if we're not careful, we convince ourselves that we're going to forget the lines again. Like Robin Williams, our mantra becomes, 'It won't work. It won't work. I'll forget the lines. Oh no!' That dread then becomes our norm, instead of just getting on with the art we love.

Fortunately – as the pioneering behaviourist Ivan Pavlov discovered with his salivating dogs – our brain is highly adaptable. His drooling dogs only responded to the bell as long as the food was brought. As soon as the food no longer appeared, it didn't take long for the drooling to stop as the canine brains reconditioned themselves. It's true for us too. We can stop our brain from maxing-out at the mere mention of a matinee. In fact, we have the power *to recondition our brain* to respond to whatever we choose...

How Can We Create Strategies for Reconditioning Our Brain?

Our recovery from performance anxiety can actually be remarkably available to us. Our brain is very resilient and adaptable, and, since our brain is where our stage fright begins, it can be exactly where it ends. Indeed, nothing is more up for change than the human brain. We've already seen that whatever we think or feel or do is the result of changes in our neurons. And since *repetition* and *practice* are the means to secure those changes, then it stands to reason that the more we practise the anxiety of stage fright, the more we'll bed it in. Conversely, the more we practice the pleasure of being on stage, the more we'll bed *that* in. And for the purposes of overcoming stage fright, I'd suggest the latter is our favoured approach! So how can we go about that?

Repeat the thoughts we want to have

We know that it costs our brain cells quite a lot of energy to change for the long term. So, that change will only happen if our brain is absolutely certain that the effort warrants the change. This means that we have a huge amount of conscious power over whether we want to condition ourselves to stage *fright* or stage *pleasure*. We can either allow the actuality of standing in the wings or in front of the camera to persistently distress us. (And if that's what we want, then – like I say – we'll build the long-term memory of distress, and then distress will become be our newly formed map.) Or we can consciously and repeatedly connect to the excitement of the story or the magic of standing in the wings or the transformation of stepping out of the make-up trailer – or whatever the experience might be. Let's go back to Stefan Klein's quotation: 'Only when the stimuli that are to be linked in the memory have appeared together often enough do new bridges grow in the brain.'[144] So *don't* link together acting and anxiety! It's as conscious as that. Keep repeating pleasure and keep practising performance joy!

But only if that's what we want...

Ask ourselves what we really want

Let's remember: we *choose* to act. No one forces us to. This isn't the army; we're not in a military state.

Let's also remember that, because we have so much agency to change our brain, we can create whichever brain maps will serve us in the long run. If our stage fright is actually because we don't want to act any more and we're looking for a reason to give it up, then let that be our choice. If our stage fright is a temporary mis-linking of the pleasure and pain experiences of acting, then we can *change our thinking*. As Klein expresses it so pithily, 'Positive feelings tell us what we should do, negative feelings tell us what not to do.'[145] Horse-racing announcer Tom Durkin had a funny way of putting it, when he was dealing with his own performance anxiety:

> Let's say you're hitting your head with a hammer. The first thing you do is mask the pain, so you take an aspirin. It still hurts, so you put on a football helmet. But it's still hurting. And it's hurting so much your brains are rocking back and forth. At some point, you realize, 'What if I didn't hit myself with a hammer?'[146]

We'll know if we don't want to act any more, because it'll feel like we're hitting ourselves over the head with a hammer. Conversely, we'll know if we don't want to feel stage fright any more – because *that* will feel like we're hitting ourselves over the head with a hammer. As Klein says, 'Feelings of happiness aren't a coincidence but the consequence of right thoughts and actions.'[147] This isn't just positive thinking: it's biologically accurate. In fact, it's all about the chemicals...

We've already seen that what we *think* affects the chemicals in our brain: there's a very direct link between our *imagination* and our *brain's architecture*. So when we're depressed by our fears and doubts, the levels of the chemical neurotransmitter, serotonin (which is responsible for our mood, memory and learning), sink in our brain, and our neurons can die. Yet as soon as we're in a positive frame of mind, the levels of serotonin and dopamine (the neurotransmitter responsible for our well-being) rise. Rather than dying, our brain can then make new neurological connections. You really could say, our happiness starts in our head.

And I repeat – we don't *have* to be actors. If acting doesn't make us happy any more, then we'll find something else we can do instead. If we can't live without it, then we'll work to create new brain maps that signpost our pleasure not our fear. Little by little, through ongoing repetition and practice, we'll recondition our mind to disassociate acting from terror. For two long years, Derek Jacobi avoided the stage and lived in purgatory – 'and it really was purgatory, for I was being put through all those exposures of vulnerability, self-pity, speechlessness and self-doubt'.[148] And he knew that never again would he take his memory for granted. Yet, after two years of this purgatory, the Royal Shakespeare Company offered Jacobi a series of juicy roles – and he simply couldn't resist live theatre any longer:

> It took a long time before the panic wore off. Every day I still dreaded the thought of having to do it, of having to go on stage. I had this terrible disease, and the cure anyway, I was told, would be to actually *face it head on*. I had to get back on the stage and do a whole series of make-or-break parts. It was tough, and only by creating momentum did I have a chance of blasting my way out of difficulty.[149]

'Blasting his way out of difficulty' was basically Derek Jacobi's way of reconditioning his brain. And blasting, it certainly was!

Like a gymnast who has fallen off the beam and knows that they have to get back on it, Jacobi took on *Much Ado About Nothing*, *Cyrano de Bergerac*, *Peer Gynt* and *The Tempest* in quick succession. With that amount of lines to learn, he surely did blast his way out of his stage fright. We really can condition ourselves – thanks to the changing of our neurons – to overcome and to do pretty much anything we want.

Overview

In this chapter, we've looked at the role of our brain in memory and stage fright. We've addressed the *nature of memory* and its *basic brain circuitry*. We've examined the three steps of Plato's memory system – *encoding, storing* and *retrieving*. This took us on a mini-voyage into neuroscience and the way in which our brain creates maps. This enabled us to go deeper into the processes of encoding (through our *senses*, our perception of *space*, and imagining a *place* in the *loci* method); storing (through *attention, repetition, meaning, downtime* and *muscle memory*); and retrieving (through *habituation* and the *theatre architecture*). And that deeper *scientific knowledge* helped us note some *practical strategies*. Then, we faced what happens when retrieving our lines goes wrong and the Vigilante amygdala fires us up (through '*long-show-itis*' and *sensitisation*). And finally we contemplated the power that we have to *recondition* our brain (by understanding how to deal with the amygdala and create the experiences we want).

*

At the end of the day, learning lines is a very personal activity. Finding our own process is both important and challenging, especially in the rehearsal room. When I asked actor-director Donald Carrier, 'Do you think directors judge actors by the speed at which they learn their lines?' he replied:

> Yes, I do. I think an actor who has a problem learning their lines is somehow thought by a director to be inferior or lazy or someone who doesn't apply themselves. And there *are* actors who are lazy, who just don't learn the lines, who fudge around and then finally get down to learning the text. And other people just have to work very hard at it.[150]

In this chapter, we've certainly negotiated how we can work hard at learning our lines by understanding what's going on in the grey matter. So now let's turn our attention to what goes on in the black box, and see how our memory is shaped and sharpened by our all-important relationship with our directors in rehearsal.

4

What Goes On in the Rehearsal Room?

The Role of the Actor-Director Relationship

'You and your director are co-workers, not master and slave... it is ultimately the director's function to evaluate what *the actor does, and the actor's job is to find* how *best to do it.'*[151]

Robert Benedetti

4. What Goes On in the Rehearsal Room?

A 'magical, creative' place

A rehearsal room is a peculiar place. Its fluorescent lights and plastic chairs. Its angular floor-tapings in black and green that mark out on the lino (or brown nylon carpet) a sketch of the world we're about to create: the portals and staircases, bedrooms and pirate ships. Not to mention that strangely distinctive smell of 'blood, sweat and tears' – and the vague aroma of bleach. For all this hodgepodge of sensory stimulation, the rehearsal room is a place where (as Max Stafford-Clark says) 'magic and creation can happen.'[152] And it's pretty much the same with television and film, the main difference being that we're rehearsing in the actual performance location. Wherever we are, the birthing process that takes place in that magic space can last for several weeks with *Dr Faustus* or a matter of minutes with *Doctor Who*. And whatever happens during that invaluable rehearsal time can make or break our final performance.

Given all the variables of that birthing process, we should give some serious attention to the relationship between the actor and the director (the 'midwife', you could say). In this chapter, we focus predominantly on theatre, where the contact between the actor and the director is usually more extended; so it tends have more impact on our state of creative well-being.

First of all, we put the *actor-director relationship* under the microscope. Then – since our stage fright can ignite in performance as a result of what happened in rehearsal – we look at how to create a *good rehearsal environment*. This leads to the *principles of rehearsing*, and I offer some new approaches to 'experiencing' a role. And we finish with *two cautionary tales* about how we handle our rehearsal-incubated fear. (The first tale shows what happens when we feel disconnected from our partners, and the second takes a detailed look at working with new writing.) So let's start by looking at the complex dynamics of *the actor-director relationship*.

The Actor-Director Relationship

> It's a frightening and very daring thing that you're asking actors to do, so you need to treat them with care. As directors, we sit in our chairs and say, 'Go down there and do that for me. Go over there and be marvellous. Go up there and have some sex. Go over there and humiliate yourself. – And I'll just tell you whether or not it's working.' Actors go down the mines for us as directors. They go out into the jungle for us. And we sit here and don't have to mess ourselves up.[153]

With wry self-awareness, Mike Alfreds describes the curious working relationship between actor and director, a relationship that he also describes as being 'the most critical in the creation of a production'.[154] From the minute we enter the rehearsal room or film set, we all have a secret bond of faith in each other. After all, it's our job as actors and directors to work together to create the vision of the piece. And yet we may not even know each other. We may have met only fleetingly at the audition. Or – if we recorded our audition on tape – we may not have met the director at all. And – if it's television – the casting director may have had more input than the director. So immediately the spirit of collaboration between us requires mutual respect, generosity and humour. Yes, indeed – before we've even started working on the script, we're using all manner of human attributes to lay the best foundations for our collaboration.

So what sorts of qualities do we hope as actors that our directors will bring to the rehearsal room? Here are a handful of answers: Focus. Professionalism. Laughter. A quality of playfulness and ease so that we can take some risks and be inventive. A sense that the director believes in us and has faith that we'll be able to do whatever they're asking us to do. And a sense of forgiveness if we can't get what they want straight away. 'I want the director to have a method but not a restrictive one,' writes Antony Sher, 'and to possess an open, enquiring mind.'[155] In other words, a structure with elastic boundaries.

So, what kinds of strategies do directors adopt in the rehearsal room to help us keep our stage fright at bay? Here are a couple of invaluable insights from two leading directors:

'I try to work on simple principles,' says Rufus Norris:

> If the actor feels empowered, if the issues in the script that didn't support an actor's thought processes have been dealt with, if the actor can at any point come to the director and say, 'I have a problem' – then the issue of stage fright in a full-on way doesn't seem to arise. Or at least I have no memory of it happening on any show I've directed (which doesn't mean that it hasn't, of course).[156]

'Basically,' says Mike Alfreds:

> you try to create an atmosphere where people just want to come to rehearsals. I think it's actually about being a decent human being, and being as nice as you can in rehearsals. Giving actors the feeling that they're being supported. The feeling that you care about them... Giving them time. Not rushing them. Being warm with them. Making sure that if you're being critical, you're being honest but not unpleasant. The fact that you share your process with them. The fact that

you say, 'I don't know. I've got an idea and I'm giving you some boundaries and directions, but I'm not sure – so let's see together.'[157]

It's reassuring to hear a director with the impressive profile of Mike Alfreds saying so candidly that he doesn't have all the answers. After all, this is rehearsal. We should all be able to experiment and maybe even fail – and that includes the director. Yet it's a big deal – hoping that a director will be willingly vulnerable – especially given the unequal status that underpins our working relationship. We all know that, however collaborative and nurturing a director may be, at the end of the day they're the boss. The buck (usually) stops with them. So, in terms of the interpersonal dynamics, there's an unavoidable *power-play*.

The play of power

For most of us actors, we got the job because of the director: it's rarely the other way round. So inevitably there's a *power bias* in the relationship. (Mike Alfreds addresses many of these issues very insightfully in Chapter 5 of his book *Different Every Night*.)[158] Young actors can be particularly aware of this power bias. Antony Sher describes how he felt at the start of his career: 'Actors are taught to be passive, to be grateful for any work, to do as they're told, to not think for themselves, to leave everything to daddy director.'[159] And even as we grow in experience, there can be a certain undercurrent of 'they're important – we're dispensable'. So it's a relationship that can flicker with fear from the get-go, and the desire to impress our director in rehearsals can be very seductive. Especially if it's a famous director. Or a director we've not worked with before. Or a director whose work we particularly admire. Or a director who is known for being scary! The 'old school' directors (usually the male of the species) were renowned for being 'snide and arch and rude and they had whipping boys and they bullied actors into performance. No decent work can come of that,' says Alfreds. 'It may be very efficient, slick and "professional", but the performances will be dead at heart.'[160] Most directors nowadays are compassionate and creative and considerate. They want to collaborate and they certainly want us to succeed. Nonetheless, the mere identity of the director can surreptitiously stir our stage fright even before we've started. Not that a tinge of trepidation need be a bad thing. A little bit of awe can ramp up our game. If we're familiar with a director's body of work – if we know they've directed the great and the good – it can encourage us to give our best shots, at the same time as knowing we're undoubtedly going to learn something from them and thereby evolve our own craft.

At the end of the day, the power dynamic pivots on *trust*. We have to feel safe enough to make mistakes in front of these powerful people, as there's no way we can give our final performance at our first rehearsal. At the same time, the power isn't purely one-sided: they cast us because they trust us enough to come up with the goods. So, yes indeed – *trust* lies at the heart of our actor-director relationship.

Trusting the director

Basically as actors, we have to *trust our directors*. They're the outside eye, the direct mirror into our souls. They can appraise what we're doing. They can sense the bigger picture. They can see all kinds of things of which we're simply not aware. And that's because, when we're building a character, we're engaged in two complicated activities at the same time. On the one hand, we're *creating our character* (which requires us to be in a certain state of unconscious inspiration). On the other hand, we're *evaluating what we're creating* (which requires us to be in a certain state of conscious assessment and improvement).[161] The 'creative' component draws upon the right hemisphere of our brain, while the 'evaluating' aspect draws upon the left hemisphere of our brain (using the ideas of psychiatrist, Iain McGilchrist).[162] This is a very delicate operation that we're undertaking in rehearsal – striving to be playful and open while being constructive and critical. In fact, these two hemispheres are almost like two people in our heads seeing the world in two completely different ways. Our right hemisphere relates to other people and the environment in a spontaneous, fluid manner. Our left hemisphere, by contrast, likes control and stasis: it wants to fix our creative discoveries. So the challenge, particularly in rehearsal, is to have the two sides of our brain in a healthy relationship with each other. Too much right-brain creativity and we can't necessarily repeat what we did for the twentieth take or the thirtieth performance. Too much left-brain activity and we fix, control, and ossify our otherwise inspired performance.

This is why we need to trust our director. In the throes of rehearsal, we simply can't keep that balance without an outside eye. We can't accurately assess if what we're feeling inside is effectively coming across to our audience. We can't remember every detail of what we did each time and improve upon it every time we run a scene. So the director has to be our Best Audience of One. They have to laugh in the right places, applaud our good moments, critique our rocky moments, and reflect back to us why those moments aren't working. Our trust in this relationship is complex – and here are just three reasons why...

First of all, every actor has a different creative process. If there are fifteen of us in the rehearsal room, that means fifteen working methods. Not only does the director have to suss out our particular ways of working, but they then have to use that understanding to bring out the best in each of us.

Second, we have to trust that that really *is* what they're trying to do. As actors, we know we're being evaluated: that's almost the point of rehearsal, as Robert Benedetti indicates in the opening quotation of this chapter. The director has to evaluate whether a scene is working. And if it's not, how can we fix it? The director has to evaluate whether our choices are telling the story. And if they're not, how can we adapt them? Given all that evaluation, the power dynamics of the relationship can inadvertently trigger our sensitivity. If we're feeling at all unsure about what we're doing, the microscope of our own scrutiny can persuade us that we're being judged on something far more personal than the mechanics of the scene. And this is where some subtle seeds of stage fright can be planted. 'Do they think I'm any good? Are they regretting that they cast me? Will they forgive me if I'm not yet up to par?' And perhaps the edgiest question triggered by our twitchy, survivalist amygdala is: 'Will they ever employ me again...?'

Third, we're being evaluated within an environment where failure has to be an option. As actors, we have to be able to experiment in rehearsals. We can only be at our creative best if we feel we can try out various choices – and some of them simply might not work. Having the confidence to make a bold choice – to risk that choice being wrong and to trust that the director won't then question our fundamental talent (or lack thereof) – are vital conditions of the actor-director relationship. As Miles Anderson articulates it:

> Playing a character requires us to go from A to Z in our creative palette. If I'm frightened of falling down and looking stupid and making a fool of myself, I'll only ever go from A to G. If as actors we're afraid of pushing the boundaries and looking ridiculous, how will we ever know where Y and Z are? We'll never play those moments – because we'll always step back from them, always be afraid of them. Actors rarely use rehearsals for being able to stretch the boundaries and see how far they can go with something – because they don't want to be known as being 'bad'– even in rehearsal. Yet you have to be bad. You have to be allowed to be bad. You have to be able to risk something and go somewhere, rather than risk nothing and go nowhere.[163]

He's absolutely right. We need to be willingly vulnerable in rehearsals. And this kind of courage also requires us to have a certain objectivity about what we do. We need a healthy, creative *distance* – not only from our own work, but eventually from our director.

The necessary distancing

The actor-director relationship is just like any other relationship that involves a huge amount of interdependency. 'Will we bring out the best in each other? Will we make each other look good? If I'm willingly vulnerable in front of you, will you respect that vulnerability?' It's almost impossible to ignore that kind of intimacy. Whether we actually admit it or not, we're very aware of its tremors. The atmosphere changes – albeit subtly – whenever the director walks into the room: regardless of gender or sexuality, we *know* they're there. (How many actors and directors have crushes on each other – if not love affairs and marriages?) And as much as we're aware of the intimacy of the relationship, we're even more aware of the *distance*. During the rehearsal process, the logistics of intimacy and distance become very complex. And they can subtly affect our long-term fear or confidence. But what do I mean by 'logistically complex'? Let's take a closer look...

When we first start rehearsing a play, we want the atmosphere to be open and trusting so that we can take all those risks that Anderson just mentioned. During that time, there's usually lots of chat and camaraderie and nurturing dialogue with the director. And that's why theatre rehearsals can be so much fun. Yet, as we draw nearer to the opening night, the director's attention shifts. They're not just concerned with us any more. They need to evaluate the details of the overall production – the lights, costumes, sound, etc. And that involves a definite distancing from us – both physically and psychologically.

The *physical* distance is fairly straightforward. When we're in the rehearsal room, the director is literally very close to us – just a few feet or metres away. Some directors step right into the rehearsal space to direct. Some stick determinedly behind a table. Either way, they're still very close. And if the rehearsal room is small, the director is rarely out of our eyeline. When it comes to television, our brief rehearsal can be even more intimate. The director stands right next to us so that, amid all the hubbub of technical prep, they can hear how we're delivering our lines, and, likewise, we can hear their direction. As soon as the camera starts to roll or as soon as we get into the actual theatre space, that physical distance increases. And the director fades from our view – both literally and metaphorically.

The *psychological* distancing in our relationship is a little more complicated. At first, as actors, we can be quite reliant on our director. We want to give them whatever they envision. So we try to develop a dialogue with them that's intimate enough for us to check that we're doing okay, but cool enough for us not to take it personally if they're not yet happy with our choices. As we draw closer to tech rehearsals, their *psychological* intimacy with us fades at the same time as their *physical* proximity – because they have to shift their attention to the overall production. When the director stops being so connected to our rehearsal process, it can actually make us feel a bit uncertain. In psychology, there's a phenomenon known as 'separation anxiety'.[164] When a little creature first discovers its independence, it becomes very enthralled with itself and is totally self-absorbed. Then it suddenly notices its distance from its mother, and it stops being enthralled with itself and instead it becomes anxious about that separation. It's exactly the same for us as actors. There's often a point in rehearsal where the director has helped us to uncover all kinds of new and exciting interpretations and we're really enthralled with ourselves. Then we start doing runthroughs and tech rehearsals, and suddenly the director becomes more distant. In fact, they may only be communicating with us through note sessions. And even those note sessions become less and less frequent and more and more impersonal. At that point, we sometimes experience twinges of separation anxiety. Like a child being sent to school, we can feel a bit abandoned. Now we realise that we really are out there on our own – on that big, wide stage. And that can trigger mild – or even mounting – stage fright. That said, there are times when we totally welcome this distance, not least with the pressure of *previews*.

The peculiar nature of previews

Previews are strange experiences in their own right. They're *performances* in the sense that the public is there and they've paid for their tickets. But in a way, they're still *rehearsals*, as we know things may change from preview to preview – staging, sound cues, lines even, let alone our interpretations. Actor John Cariani sums up the proximity-distance ambivalence of previews very clearly:

> The figure of the director is right there at the beginning of rehearsals – and sometimes it can even be a bit suffocating. Then as my performance starts to grow more confident, I metaphorically push the director away – and that's thrilling. Once we go into tech, he's starting to get farther away. Sometimes, though, he metaphorically comes closer, and while I'm out there on the stage, I feel as if I can see him all the time in my peripheral vision. Not that I *can* actually see him, but there's a little 'thing' of him always around. And then in that first preview – if you make a mistake or you do something he asked you not to do – he metaphorically comes right into your face. And to keep him away, you silently say, 'I know, I know! I didn't do that on purpose! I'm going to fix it tomorrow night.' All that stuff is going through your head at the same time as the play. Which makes previews alive in a very different way from any other performance.[165]

Previews are becoming more and more peculiar with the omnipresence of mobile devices. And this is where it's important that *everyone* – audience and all – can understand what we go through as actors on the stage, so that we can preserve the unique and wonderful realm of live performance. Here's what I mean...

In August 2015 – a couple of weeks before the official opening of *Hamlet* at the Barbican Centre – Benedict Cumberbatch found that the previews of his performance were not only being reviewed by the national press, they were actually being filmed by the public on their mobile phones. One night during 'To be or not to be', Cumberbatch had to stop and restart the speech due to technical difficulties. This speech is one of the hardest places to begin any performance, advised Cumberbatch to his fans. (In fact, it's the speech that tripped the switch on Derek Jacobi's stage fright. Which is hardly surprising, since this is probably *the* most famous speech in the English-language canon, so everyone wants to see how each celebrity will deliver it.) Speaking to his fans at the stage door, Cumberbatch told them that during the performance he could see 'a little red light' of a mobile phone shining in the third row. 'It's mortifying,' he said. 'There's nothing less supportive or enjoyable as an actor, being on stage experiencing that.'[166]

This was, after all, a preview. The actors, the technical team, and all involved need these previews to coordinate the elements in front of a live audience. It's part of the excitement. (I was at the first preview of *Billy Elliot*, and we didn't leave the theatre till midnight because so many technicalities went awry. It didn't matter: we all knew that we were experiencing a unique event.) In support of Cumberbatch and the *Hamlet* production, the critic for *The Stage*, Mark Shenton, stressed that 'a lot will change between the first preview and first night. As critics, it is our job to respect the artistic process; and part of the process is an acknowledgement that they need previews to work on their show before we pass judgment.'[167] The professional press might honour Shenton's words, but fans are fans – and the public wants a piece of the newsfeed pie. Like I said in Chapter 2, every spectator is a reviewer now and every night is a press night.

These issues surrounding previews raise important questions about the nature of rehearsal. At the end of the day, it's us – the actors – who have to step out there, onto that stage or in front of that camera. And we know that that can be scary. One of the solutions to the tremors surrounding previews and performances goes back to the fundamental actor-director relationship. We have to know that we have the understanding and support of our directors till the birthing process is over. As a director, Mike Alfreds really gets it:

> Being an actor is all about being frightened. I think that goes with the territory and actors almost want to be frightened. I think that's the excitement – because it's so exposing being an actor. You're getting out onto the stage and you're saying to the audience, 'Look at me, look at my body, look at my voice, look at my taste, look at my judgement, look at my sense of humour, look at my emotional expressivity, look at my sexuality. Look at me!' Some actors do believe that they're hiding behind a character – but that's nonsense really because you can never hide. And it's a very frightening thing. I think all the problems I've ever had in rehearsals were very much about actors feeling very threatened.[168]

All the more reason for us to feel absolutely confident in whatever we've rehearsed, because – preview or press night – it's us out there.

Yet that doesn't always happen. Not all directors are like Alfreds or Norris or Stafford-Clark, to name but three. Sometimes our stage fright *in performance* can be directly traced back to moments *in rehearsal* when we didn't own the choices being made. In those situations, we find that we become literally – and metaphorically – *blocked*. Despite all the conditions that we all collectively strove to put in place in order to keep the rehearsal room creative, sometimes things go disquieteningly askew.

Unlocking the blocking

There are times when a director has a very specific vision for a production. And if we click with that vision – fantastic! We feel confident. We can flow in the rehearsal room. It's great. But if we can't find our way into that vision, it's incredibly hard for us to flow, and we silently dislocate both from our director and from our own performance.

In fact, Stanislavsky suffered his most acute stage fright when his relationship with the director broke down in exactly this way, and on more than one occasion. When he was playing Brutus in *Julius Caesar* for Nemirovich-Danchenko in 1903, he simply couldn't 'find' what he thought the director wanted. 'I see the tone and tempo of the second act, especially for Brutus, absolutely differently from you,' wrote Nemirovich-Danchenko. 'And I intend to follow my line without restraint.'[169] In the end, Stanislavsky's confidence was so destroyed that he had to pull out of the production. Fourteen years later, the situation was just as bad. At the dress rehearsal of *The Village of Stepanichikovo* in 1917, Stanislavsky was left weeping in the wings when, as 'a typical producer-dictator' (as he described it), Nemirovich-Danchenko ruthlessly suppressed the actor's deviation from his instructions for the role of Colonel Rostanev – and he pulled Stanislavsky from the show.[170] Stanislavsky was significantly immersed in his 'system' by that time, and he really wanted actors to create characters in the way that *they* perceived them – not as the director conceived them. Clearly, he and Nemirovich-Danchenko were not a winning team.

Although these situations are fairly extreme, it's reassuring to know that even Stanislavsky couldn't always incarnate his director's vision. Yet these stories raise a useful point. We have to find a delicate balance in rehearsals between *the actor's process* and *the director's result*. It can be very dangerous if we find ourselves trying to play the 'final result' in performance, simply because we weren't able to own the process in rehearsal. It can lead to interference in our heads, and, as we know, interference can lead to stage fright. If we try to play our director's superimposed form without any of our own imaginative connection, we can all too easily go hurtling into the abyss. We literally become *blocked by the blocking*. Here's an example...

Playing Don Pedro in *Much Ado About Nothing* at a prestigious Shakespeare festival in the States, Donald Carrier struggled for a five-month run to overcome his nerves in the opening scene. He and his fellow cast members couldn't fully understand the stage picture that the director had set in rehearsal. There hadn't been very much explanation behind the blocking, and so the actors were finding it challenging to retain the action because they didn't really own it. 'I still feel there might be other possibilities and other options that we've never gone to,' said Carrier. 'So a part of my brain feels a certain discomfort.'[171] That discomfort subtly stirred Carrier's performance anxiety. Even towards the end of the five-month season, he had to run over that scene a couple of times in his head before each show just to feel secure about it: 'I'm still not entirely happy with how it was eventually staged. The physical life and the psychological actions are just not quite matched – and that's when I get into trouble.'[172]

Let's rewind for a moment. Let's go back to the rehearsal room and see where the seed of that performance anxiety was planted. Early in rehearsal, Carrier had been encouraged to explore a certain sadness in Don Pedro about the potential loss of his friend, Benedick. Later in rehearsals, that choice was jettisoned without a wholly clear explanation and, instead, it was suggested to Carrier that Don Pedro is not sad, but rather he's happy. In fact, he's actually enthusiastic about Benedick's marriage to Beatrice. Of course, a director might change the blocking of a scene for all manner of reasons that make sense in the bigger picture of the production, though as actors we may not be able fully to perceive that perspective while we're enacting the moves. And if we don't fully own those staging choices, the seeds of doubt can be planted in us. As Carrier discovered:

> When it came to performance, my brain kept asking, 'Where did that intention come from?' The physical life of the scene [which was still informed by the old choice of being sad] was not supporting the action that I was now trying to play (which was to be encouraging and enthusiastic towards my friend). As a result, my performance in that section is kind of 'stand and deliver' (for lack of a better phrase). It's what I call '*reportage* acting'. My character is saying, 'I'll do this and this', but there's nothing *dynamically* happening between us as actors to support those words... It gives me great anxiety before I play that moment, and it's a scene in which I'm constantly afraid of losing the lines.[173]

Carrier's stage fright *in performance* was the consequence of an issue *in rehearsal*. He was self-aware and generous enough to pinpoint exactly what the issue had been. Because Don Pedro is essentially a supporting role rather than a leading role, he didn't feel able – in a short rehearsal period – to insist that the scene wasn't working. Although he tried to address it several times, he was placated with, 'No, this is fine. It's good. There's nothing wrong with this scene.' 'It's always difficult,' he noted, 'when you're not one of the main characters, as you don't want to take up valuable rehearsal time or be perceived as the "squeaky wheel". So you just try and make it work.'[174]

Finding the courage to really be heard when the 'blocking' is doing just that – *blocking* us – is incredibly hard. Of course we want to do everything we can to nurture and sustain the rehearsal-room relationship with the director. After all, it's their overall vision that we're incarnating. And a serious breakdown in communication can really spur our stage fright. To some extent, the problem lies in the word 'blocking' itself. Whenever I'm directing, I try not to use the word – because 'blocking' does just that. It blocks us as actors when we need to be able to flow. Besides, actors aren't 'blocks' – they're living, breathing, interpreting, intuiting, imaginative, human beings. If (as Rufus Norris states) a director enables the actors to come to them at any point and say, 'I've got a problem' and it can all be discussed – then there *is* no problem. If, on the other hand, the director isn't able to accommodate the problem for whatever reason, then there *is* a problem. To an extent, it all boils down to director-training. The kind of dynamics we're talking about here – the balance between the actor's process and the director's vision – is something young directors can't learn in the classroom. This sort of intricate knowledge only really comes about through hard graft and experience.

So you can see how provocative and exciting the actor-director relationship can be. It's packed with power. It teeters on trust. Sometimes we find ourselves on a roller coaster of intimacy and distance. Sometimes we find ourselves in the hands of a master midwife. And sometimes we find ourselves locked within the blocking. So how can we ensure that the relationship is at its most creative? And what does the *rehearsal environment* need for it to be a hotbed of magic in which there's minimal room for stage fright?

Creating a Good Rehearsal Environment

The prop store on the top floor of the Lyric Hammersmith Theatre, London. The leaky, freezing cavern of the basement theatre, Moscow. The back room of a pub just off the Fulham Palace Road. These are all rehearsal rooms that I have known and loved. For all the joys of a clean and tidy studio, we can create pretty much anywhere – as long as we experience the right atmosphere among the collaborative team. As Max Stafford-Clark said, a rehearsal room is a place where magic and creation can happen. And I'd suggest that magic and creation require two important factors – *play* and *feedback*.

The power of play

The best acting teachers are children. Just watch them at play. It doesn't take long to see the freedom and wonder that infects their natural state. And that state is innate in all of us as adults – if we're able to give it voice. For decades, theatre gurus – including Michael Chekhov, Jacques Lecoq and Peter Brook, to name but three – have all insisted that we need to access our inner child when we're in the creative process. In fact, one of the quickest ways to banish our stage fright is for the director to allow us (and for us to allow ourselves) to *play*.

All too often in rehearsals the 'evaluation' mode (that I mentioned earlier) morphs into the 'judgemental' mode. In other words, a healthy degree of 'evaluating' whether or not we're telling the story mutates into an unhealthy degree of 'judging' whether or not we're any good. ('Is this what the director wants? Will I have it under my belt by Thursday?') Yet, as my Russian mentor Vladimir Ananyev would regularly remind us during my own actor-training in Moscow, it's impossible to play and judge at the same time. They're two mutually exclusive actions – like simultaneously trying to open and close the door. We can't be playfully open and fearfully closed at the same time. So in the rehearsal room we have to find some means of diverting our energy away from trying to 'get it right' all the time (whatever 'right' may be). And, instead, we should look for constructive opportunities to play.

To some extent, we're dependent on the director's process. If they're able to share a portion of the rehearsal time with us thrashing about in the murky unknown of the script, it's wonderful. That's when we make real and unexpected discoveries. That's when we become so absorbed imaginatively that we forget to censor ourselves. Stafford-Clark is particularly good at this. He allows chunks of rehearsal time for true, creative play. For example, one afternoon when we were working on Goldsmith's *She Stoops to Conquer*, he suggested that the whole of the rehearsal building, as well as the cul-de-sac outside, was the Hardcastles' estate. During an extended improvisation (which must have lasted for well over an hour), he gave each of us a secret objective to fulfill. By the end of the afternoon, the collected ensemble had tripled its sense of play, its dynamic interaction, and its understanding of the relationships: it was time well spent. Obviously the power of play always has to be harnessed towards the production, as it was with Stafford-Clark. Yet it doesn't have to be quite so organised: we can aim to bring playful inventiveness all the time to our work. It just has to be relevant. And that's where the director's *feedback* comes in.

The need for feedback

The power of play switches to the play of power in our actor-director relationship when notes are given. We need notes. We need *feedback*. It's how we elaborate and improve our work. Yet the specifics of *how*, *when* and *how often* those notes are given can have a profound affect on our confidence. Some actors like a lot of notes. Some actors like very few notes. If we don't get any notes at all, it can be either hugely relieving or mildly disconcerting. And directors have different modes of feedback: some directors give us no notes if we're doing well and some directors give us no notes if we're doing terribly. Short of them telling us on day one which type of director they are, we have to figure it out for ourselves and build our own sense of faith in our performances accordingly.

How we respond to those notes is a whole other psychological task. Some actors like to be pushed. Some actors like to be coddled. No actor wants to be humiliated in the rehearsal room (as that rarely achieves anything other than adding to our performance nerves). Yet we do want to grow as artists. In fact, many of us find that wholesome feedback builds our creative strength. As actors we like to be told the truth. We like to be told when we're doing a good job and it's important for us to know when we're doing a bad job. (Better to hear it in the rehearsal room while there's still the time and intention to change it, than wait till we're reading it in the reviews section of the *Guardian* or the *Los Angeles Times.*) Some actors want feedback to be given very directly. 'I actually respond rather well when people tell me I'm not up to the job,' writes Antony Sher. 'I get quite determined.'[175] Similarly, John Cariani says, 'I don't like to be treated carefully. I love directors who push and don't coddle. I feel most safe in a rehearsal room when the feedback is direct – because then I know that the director cares enough not to leave me to mess up.'[176]

Whether we prefer to be coddled or we prefer to be cajoled, there are some note-realities that we simply can't avoid. If we're cast in a big role, for example, we're going to get a lot of notes. If we're playing a complicated part, we're going to get a lot of notes. If we're struggling with the role, we're going to get a lot of notes. The trick is to be sure that, when we're receiving all those notes, we're really *hearing* what the director is saying to us, rather than raising our defences. That means listening to those notes openly, rather than letting them suffocate us. In fact, the only time Stafford-Clark remembers an actor suffering stage fright in rehearsals was when he was giving him notes:

> I don't have much direct experience of actors with stage fright, but I did work with a very good actor a year ago who subsequently revealed he had not been on stage for fourteen years. He had trouble with lines and had begun to repeat the same mistakes in each runthrough. I picked him up on it each time and he began to resent it and asked me not to sit so close to the stage taking notes as it put him off. I declined and said I was simply doing my job. By about week two of the production run the lines had sunk in and there was no larger problem. In retrospect if I had recognised his problem earlier I would and should have been more sensitive.[177]

Stafford-Clark works a lot with new writing and he's gloriously fastidious about the specifics of a playwright's text. And yet we don't have to make ourselves overly dependent on a director, whatever their status or experience.

Finding our rehearsal-room independence

Indeed, we shouldn't be totally dependent on the director. While all these conditions for what makes a good rehearsal environment are great, we don't have to be too needy. It's back to the 'necessary distancing' – and it goes both ways. As Tanya Moodie describes:

> I've trained myself not to *need* anything from a rehearsal environment and have the buck stop with me. As long as I get a mid-morning break and a mid-afternoon break, I'm good. I've had too many rehearsal situations become toxic, or unstable, or unreliable. I've had cruel directors and crazed scene partners. I've worked with injury and illness (mine), bereavement and drunkenness (not mine). I've had six-week rehearsal periods and three-day rehearsal periods… I've learned that feeling creatively free and supported starts and remains with me.[178]

Moodie hits the nail on the head. The rehearsal environment can be unpredictable. The relationships between actors and directors – or actors and other actors – can be nuanced and complicated. But whatever might happen, we have to own our process.

In fact, there are all kinds of *principles of rehearsing* available to us. These are principles that we can adopt on our own to keep our fear at bay, while still being open and collaborative and generous in the rehearsal room. Here are just a few of them. But – be warned. They actually require us to recalibrate the nature of acting itself...

The Principles of Rehearsing

Basically, there are two main reasons why we rehearse a piece. *Collectively* we want to work out how to tell the story. *Individually* we want to build our particular characters. 'Building A Character.' That's no small task. And the demon of stage fright frequently raises its head when, for some reason, we feel dislocated from the character that we're building. Instead of just acting the role, we suddenly become *aware* that we're acting the role. Or rather, *we're* here and the *character* is there – and we're falling into the gap between the two. To some extent, this dislocation can happen all the time (and inevitably) when we're rehearsing, as we don't even know what the character is yet.

But let's just pause for a moment. What do we actually mean by 'character'? And how can we stop ourselves feeling disconnected from it? Could there be a way of creating a character in rehearsals that *never* actually dislocates us from it? Perhaps it's time to reconsider what exactly we're doing when we're acting.

Feeling is listening

So often, as actors, we believe we have to *become* the part and *feel* what the character feels. First of all, that's very difficult in the fragmented process of rehearsing. We start. We stop. We discuss. We share a joke. We restage. We take a tea break. We start again. All as if we're little Duracell rabbits that can bang the drum of our feelings at the simple flick of a switch. So we shouldn't beat ourselves up too much if we have dislocations from the character during rehearsals, as our creative flow is inevitably and constantly being interrupted.

Second, perhaps we need to change our whole philosophy. 'Becoming the character' is actually a misguided definition of what we do as actors. Let's take David Mamet's approach for a moment. We can't 'become' the character, because the character doesn't exist. It's just lines on a page. So unless the paper-and-glue script can cry when we rip it or laugh when we scrunch it, the character doesn't feel anything. It's us, the *actors* – living, breathing, sensate human beings – who imagine and interpret and embody. We're the ones who *feel* something.

Yet the truth is that we rarely *let* ourselves feel. In trying to feel what we think the character should feel, we bypass the *Most Important Step*. We Stop Listening. We stop listening to ourselves. To our own words. To our bodies. To our partner's bodies. To our partner's words. To the space in between us. To the director. And this lack of listening is no small surprise really. We're so busy in rehearsals multitasking on a major scale – trying to remember our lines, trying to remember the staging, trying to be intimate with people we've barely met – it's hard to really listen to *anything*.

And if we widen the picture...

...if we take that consideration beyond the walls of the rehearsal room...

...we actually rarely allow ourselves to listen *in everyday life*. Really listening to what's going on in the world can make us incredibly vulnerable to the vast, emotional content of all the massive, global narratives. Climate change. Superbug epidemics. The 'so-called Islamic State'. Immigration crises. The collapse of Europe. Disappearing jumbo jets. It's all too much. Our contemporary life is such that we almost *have* to stop listening, for fear of imploding under the emotional weight of humanity's current state.

So this sets up a conundrum. As actors we *want* to feel. Our profession gives us *permission* to feel. In fact, we're professionally *obliged* to feel. It's the main tool of our trade. Yet because we've got out of the habit of really listening in everyday life, we've blocked our channels of feeling at all levels of our existence. It's no surprise that stage fright can sneak up on us, even in rehearsals. We feel dislocated from the character – because half the time we're dislocated from *ourselves*.

So what can we do, as actors, to make sure we *re*connect? How can we press the restart button on our own sensory existence? We can start by truly listening to ourselves in the rehearsal room. We can start by looking at what it means to play a character. We can start by asking ourselves *what it really means to 'experience' a role* – because somehow, somewhere the definition became confused.

'Experiencing' the role

Let's turn back the clocks to the birth of contemporary acting and the cross-pollination between Stanislavsky and Strasberg. Somewhere in the early twentieth century, it seems as though maybe the wires got crossed when Stanislavsky's 'system' migrated to New York. Between the 1920s and the 1950s, a few myths began to emerge and their grip across Western acting has been very persuasive. At its most simple, it's the 'I have to feel what the character feels' epithet. And there's no doubt that some of Stanislavsky's own ideas about 'becoming' the character are very compelling. Here he is, writing about what he calls 'the state of "I am"':

> *I am* in our language refers to the fact that I have placed myself in the centre of imaginary conditions, that I feel myself situated among them, that I exist in the very depth of imaginary life, in the world of imaginary things, and that I begin to act from myself, with my fear and conscience.[179]

'Existing in the very depth of imaginary life.' That's sounds exciting!

But – stop!

Let's look more closely.

Those last few words – 'with my fear and conscience'. They hold a very significant clue. We know Stanislavsky was afraid as an actor. We know Stanislavsky suffered self-consciousness as an actor. What I believe he's saying here is that when we allow ourselves to 'become' the character – to say, 'I am the character' – we're really just integrating our two realities. We're taking the fictional life of the character and our actual life as actors – which means our nervousness and self-consciousness as much as our creative brilliance – and we're allowing those two lives to fuse. In other words, we're not *ignoring* our fear or trying to push it away like a whining child tugging on our sleeve. Instead, we're embracing it. We're validating it. We're channelling it directly into the character and alchemically turning it into something useful and not disruptive.

Let's unpack this idea a little further...

Some people have interpreted Stanislavsky's 'state of "I am"' as the point at which we're so fused with a character that we lose our self. And sure – 'getting lost' in the character can seem sexy and beguiling. 'Hey, man – I really *became* Hamlet or Hedda or the King of Siam or the Duchess of Malfi.' It's like a state of altered consciousness and that's kind of cool... And we feel we let ourselves down – or we're not proper actors – if we don't experience that altered state. We've failed in our actor's craft... And then we get stage fright!

Yet Stanislavsky explicitly stresses the opposite. We don't *lose* our self. We *fuse* or *merge* our self – along with all our complicated feelings – with feelings that are appropriate to the character's given circumstances. It may sound semantic and pedantic, but there's a subtle and important difference between 'becoming' the character (or 'losing ourselves') and 'merging' (or 'fusing ourselves') with the character. In fact, there's another tool from Stanislavsky's toolkit that can really help us to understand the difference and (more importantly for us here) to overcome our stage fright. This term has only come to the fore in recent years. It's what he called *perezhivanie.*

Perezhivanie literally translates as 'living through' a role. *Zhivanie* means 'living' and *pere* means 'through', and it was the term Stanislavsky adopted for 'experiencing' a role. And this is where our own *actual* experiences really can merge with the *imagined* experiences of the character. Let's be clear. Living through a role doesn't mean 'suffering'. Living through a role doesn't mean 'enduring' what the character might be enduring. Living through a role actually refers to our natural dual consciousness on stage (as we explored in Chapter 1). And what that means is that we inhabit the fictional world of the script at the same time as we're experiencing the reality of being on stage (or in front of a camera). In other words, 'living through' or 'experiencing' a role allows all the conditions of acting to be as much a part of our here-today-now actuality as any of the fictional given circumstances.

That includes our awareness of the boom mic above our heads.

That includes our knowledge that this is a mid-shot.

That includes the passion that we're experiencing playing Cleopatra.

That includes the fact that we're a bit nervous about this scene.

That includes the fact that our husband is in the audience and he's taking us out for dinner afterwards.

That includes the tears streaming down our face as we speak our character's farewell speech.

From this perspective, there *is* no divide between our self and the character. The character can *only* feel what *we're* feeling. Whatever is going on for us in this very moment can't help but be part of our performance experience. And that's because our brain cannot differentiate between the two worlds. (I mentioned this in Chapter 3, when we looked at the brain's inability to differentiate between imagination and reality.) Our brain has only one experience of the present nanosecond. So we can call it 'self' or we can call it 'character' – but our brain just knows it as 'Now'.

This is incredibly liberating. It releases us from the hangman's halter of 'I'm not feeling what the character feels. So I must be a bad actor!' Or 'Darn it – I just broke out of character!' I'd actually go so far as to say that the genuine process of facing the fear and embracing our stage fright involves us recalibrating what it fundamentally means to act. We don't have to fake anything in the rehearsal room. We just have to listen to what's really going on. The character isn't out there somewhere and we have to imagine our way into their existence. The character is Here-Now-Us – with *all* our feelings. It's that autobiographical self that we met in Chapter 3. And it includes the adrenalin-kick of our nerves, as much as anything else. Those are very real emotions that we can't ignore. They're what we're experiencing here-today-now *as human beings*, so let's embrace them as a legitimate part of whatever we're experiencing here-today-now *in the role*. By allowing all our complicated, contradictory sensations to be part of one unified experience, we can unite our sense of actor and character. We can truly *merge* with the role. And then we find we've bridged the abyss that can manifest as stage fright – because there's no longer a gap between what we *should* feel and what we *do* feel. It's all one experience!

So what does all this mean in practice?

It means we start by actually listening to ourselves in rehearsal. We acknowledge what we're really feeling as our autobiographical self. If those feelings seem to contradict the character's given circumstances, we then gently and imaginatively justify to ourselves why the *character* could be feeling what *we're* feeling. So instead of saying, 'I feel terrified, but my character is really confident – so I'm totally dislocated from that character,' we look for reasons why the *character* could feel terrified. And if we work playfully, it doesn't matter how tangential or off-the-cuff or bizarre those justifications may seem at first. Ultimately – and very cunningly – we *diffuse* our nerves by making them a legitimate part of what we're allowed to feel. We con the conman. We disconcert the demon – by embracing him, not running away from him. And by doing so – he disappears – like a genie in a puff of green smoke. Enough analogies: here's a concrete example...

I was rehearsing *Richard III* with the wonderful director Tina Packer at the Colorado Shakespeare Festival. It was Act I, Scene iii, where Queen Margaret is cursing the royals and I was thrilled to be discovering a great sense of flow in the scene. Mare Trevathan as Elizabeth was giving me wonderful attitude. Nigel Gore as Richard was visceral and raw. It felt really good. Then one day in rehearsals, a particular staging was set up to accommodate certain sightlines. And suddenly I felt trapped. All my flow vanished and I began to experience a disconnect. I knew myself well enough to know that if I wasn't careful, that disconnect could open up like the San Andreas Fault and gradually gape into an abyss of stage fright. Not wanting to bother a director whom I respect so much with my banal insecurities, I quietly turned to the voice coach, Margaret Jansen.

'I feel like a bull stuck in a stall,' I explained. 'It was all going so well, but now I just feel blocked. I don't even feel I can move my feet.' Jansen's immediate response was, 'Fantastic! Use it! Let that be exactly how Queen Margaret feels! She's unable to walk around her old castle freely. She has to plant her feet where other people want them to be. And all the while she has this pent-up passion of a bull inside her.'

Instantly, I understood the 'state of "I am"'. All the insecurities that I'd been feeling as the actor in the rehearsal room disappeared. Instead, they were miraculously transformed into amazing fodder for the given circumstances of the character. To prevent any gap opening up between myself and Margaret – to halt that potential San Andreas Fault opening up – we'd synchronised *my* experiences with *the character's* experiences. No longer was Queen Margaret at one remove, with me as the actor trying to feel whatever she might be feeling. Now I really *was* experiencing what the character might feel. I really *was* 'living through' her given circumstances. In the next rehearsal, everything felt different. I was curiously excited by the staging. We'd unlocked the blocking and it all made perfect sense. In fact, I'd subtly *merged with the character.*

Merging with the character

When we weave the fabric of our character together with the fabric of our own sensations *in rehearsals*, we lay the grounds for us to feel as if we've merged with the character *in performance.* It may sound like a paradox, but the closer the weave between ourselves and the character, the greater the potential for us to truly transform. This certainly happened for me playing Margaret in *Richard III.* There were times during performances when I'd come off stage and I had no idea what I'd done out there. Like an empty flute, I'd temporarily vacated myself, and let the breath and the language and the actions play upon me. It was exhilarating and exciting: I'd merged with Margaret. Don't get me wrong – it wasn't a question of 'feeling' Margaret's grief for the loss of her murdered son, lover and husband. How could I? Mercifully, I've never had anything so dreadful happen to me as having a son, lover or husband murdered. It simply meant that there was no gap between the words of the character and my existence on the stage. I was so driven by everything that we'd prepared in rehearsal, there was no space left in performance into which self-consciousness could creep.

If we can use rehearsals to synchonise our actual moment-by-moment sensations with those of the character, we give ourselves the potential for great flights in performance. We allow every stumble to be part of the dance.

Two Cautionary Tales

I end this chapter with two cautionary tales. Each tale tells a different story of how unaddressed issues in rehearsal eventually led to out-and-out terror in performance. The first is a wonderfully honest account of how isolated we can feel when – for whatever reasons – we can't connect to our onstage partners. The second is an autobiographical tale of the wonders of working with new writing. I share these two tales as part of our ongoing talking cure as we face and embrace our fear.

Falling into the Pitt

Jay Whittaker was playing the Prime Minister, Mr Pitt, in Alan Bennett's *The Madness of George III* at the Old Globe, San Diego, directed by Adrian Noble. It was a role in which he was really rather brilliant. Yet despite the critical acclaim, he spent the entire four-month run suffering chronic stage fright. When I quizzed him about it a year later, he identified the primary cause of his fear as a sense of isolation in performance:

> Real stage fright is where you're worried you're gonna fuck something up – and you're scared! I had that feeling in almost every performance of *George*. What caused [the stage

> fright] was that I wasn't sharing a journey with any other character. The writer hasn't given William Pitt a particular arc; he's given him a kind of straight through-line. And there was so much time offstage between scenes that I never really got into a flow. I would do a scene. I'd walk off stage. I'd have time to let all my energy down. And then I'd have to start it all up again. So the entire role ended up being a series of technical manoeuvres. It wasn't heart; it was completely head. And because it was completely head, I was terrified before every entrance. In every show, I thought I was going to lose my lines. All the way through to the last performance of the four-month run, I would sit or stand backstage before every entrance – going over the lines that I had to say – terrified that I was going to drop them. It was an excruciating show for me, because I had such stage fright.[180]

If you'd have seen his performance, you'd find this tale hard to believe. And I suspect none of his fellow actors knew. Yet Whittaker's stage fright was intensified by the poor predicament of a fellow actor:

> One of the other actors had a lot of problems with stage fright of his own, and he would drop lines on a nightly basis and just make the words up. He was terrified. And because we made every entrance of the whole play together, *his* terror – *his* stage fright – would infect *me*. I'd be standing there in the wings and he'd be shaking and mumbling his lines before going on. And that would totally go into me and then *I'd* feel that way, too. I tried with all my might to just get into my own space and not be affected by it. At the same time, I *wanted* to be connected to this person, because onstage we *needed* to be connected. So I was trying to find a fine line between shutting him out when we were offstage and then trying to connect to him when we were onstage. Ultimately what I had to do was just shut him out *period*. I had to act in my own world and make that a character choice. Mr Pitt was so into his own thing that he didn't really give a shit about what anybody else thought or said. And *I* did that, too, out of pure self-preservation.[181]

Like I said, Whittaker was brilliant as Mr Pitt, and so his choices (albeit out of self-preservation) were absolutely appropriate. But let's rewind. Let's go back to the rehearsal room and see what could have been done to prevent this state of anxiety, had the director known anything about it.

One of the surest ways for us to kill the potential for stage fright *in performance* is to ensure *in rehearsals* that our partners remain our main point of contact. After all, we are who we are in relation to our environment, and other people are the biggest influence on how our environment changes. And actually that's exactly what Whittaker wanted to do: to connect to his partner. Yet his fellow actor was a very experienced performer with endless Broadway and international credits. So I've no doubt that it would've been way too difficult for him to reveal to anyone (director or fellow actors) that he was suffering stage fright. When Derek Jacobi was working with Sir Laurence Olivier in *The Merchant of Venice*, he describes how: 'It was during the run that for the first time I became aware of Sir's stage fright. It filtered through after the play had opened, for naturally he never spoke about it during rehearsals or run-throughs, or on the first night.'[182] Of course 'Sir' didn't! It's a mighty thing to do – to 'fess up to our stage fright. Yet if we don't, we can feel terribly isolated. And yet if we can focus on our partners – both as empathic people engaged in the same profession and as fictional characters dialoguing in a scene – then we can start to address the situation and alleviate our feelings.

In fact, neuroscientists have examined how we need human contact, especially when we're in extreme danger (which is absolutely what stage fright can feel like). Combat historian, S.L.A. Marshall, explains that, when soldiers lose visual contact with their buddies under fire, a 'moral disintegration' of the line is produced.[183] Taylor Clark goes on to say that 'in an emergency, we invariably seek out the company of others to reduce our stress and fear. Immersion in a group makes us feel safer... and the better we know our companions, the greater the comfort we derive... Fear proves no match for the social bonds between us.'[184]

This can be so useful for us when it comes to stage fright. If we can build a strong ensemble in rehearsals and if we can truly create our characters *in relation to each other*, we reduce the potential sense of isolation once we're in performance. By then, we know that there'll be others out there on the stage with us, who really will help us out if there's a crisis.

The more we talk about it – which this book constantly advocates – the stronger the bond between us as performers. Then we can acknowledge that our stage fright is a normal part of being an actor and it's nothing to be ashamed of. In fact, it's a boon! As chronic stage-fright sufferer Sara Solovitch reminds us, without that anxiety, 'there is no excitement, no passion, no peak performance'.[185]

*

I want to finish this chapter with a tale of working on new writing and the intricacies of rehearsing it with directors and playwrights. There's no doubt that the flexibility required of us when a script can change right up to the last moment is very exciting. It can also be absolutely bloody terrifying. Again, in this tale, we found that talking about it as a company – once we realised that we were each experiencing it – dispelled some of that terror. So, on with the talking cure...

Teetering through Topless Mum

Working with new writing is exciting. It's also very challenging in ways that are quite unlike working on scripts that have stood the test of time. Of course every television or film script is a piece of new writing. And it's not uncommon for lines to be changed between takes or even for whole scenes to be improvised – and that can really keep us on our creative toes at the time of filming. Of course, at a later date the editor and director will craft the finished product and use our best version. But theatre is different. When it comes to new writing in the theatre, the rehearsal room, rather than the editing suite, becomes the laboratory of intense scrutiny. Will the play work? Does it have longevity? Is the story clear? Are the characters compelling? Is that speech right? Is that line right? Is that word right? Is that comma right? Under this degree of scrutiny, it doesn't take much for the seeds of our stage fright to sprout, flourish and rampage.

This is the tale of Ron Hutchinson's *Topless Mum*, which premiered at the Tobacco Factory in Bristol, 2008. The story focuses on British soldiers faking photographs of Afghan detainees being 'abused', 'humiliated' and 'tortured'. While the play hinted at the real-life events of the *News of the World* newspaper publishing faked Iraqi photos, Hutchinson had added his own personal twist. He proposed that a fictionalised 'mock-up' might be potentially more 'truthful' than a documentary record. This premise in itself was intriguing.

Both writer and director were extremely charming to work with, so I choose this production simply because it's an example of extremes. We had an extremely short rehearsal period for a new work. The director and writer were very keen for a London transfer. The writer was abroad for much of the rehearsal period. And the material itself was particularly meaty and challenging. The nature of all these extremes really charged our collective anxiety. And this is how the process unfurled…

The play

Whenever we're rehearsing a new script, we desperately want it to work – primarily for the playwright. Judi Dench describes how much easier it is to relax with a Shakespeare play because you *know* it works and you know *why* it works: 'In a new play you're so anxious about telling the author's story and making it come across.'[186] With *Topless Mum*, the entire creative team really wanted this play to succeed. After all, the script had something meaningful to say in exciting and thought-provoking ways. Added to which, Hutchinson is a sharply intelligent writer with a clear passion for language. He writes very articulate characters, who express themselves fluently. Yet that articulacy was deceptive. While the language of *Topless Mum* seemed to be very realistic, the speed at which the characters took some big decisions was *not* psychologically real. And so as actors we had to be mentally very agile. We quickly realised that the play wasn't as straightforward as it first appeared.

The rehearsals

One of the criteria of a good rehearsal room (as we've seen) is that we have to be able to take risks and potentially get things wrong. Yet with a new play, there's an added complexity to that risk-taking. All the time in rehearsals, the writer and director are trying to hear whether the lines are working and whether they're telling the story. (Hence, Max Stafford-Clark's fastidiousness with new scripts.) Meanwhile, as actors, we're trying to piece together our interpretation of the character. Sometimes, our experimentation can be mistaken by the writer for a case of the lines being clunky, and then they think the words need changing. But half the time they *don't* need changing: it's just that we're still trying to fathom the appropriate way to interpret them. With *Topless Mum*, I was nervous about taking risks in case the writer took it as a sign that the play wasn't working and then rewrote the lines. Added to which, we had such a short rehearsal time for this new and textured play that we found ourselves making decisions about our characters as quickly as we possibly could. This was partly to reassure the writer and director that the play as it stood was strong. And partly so that the lines would be finalised and we could start to get inside the characters' complex thought processes.

There's another tricksy little rehearsal challenge with new works. As actors, we have to remain creatively very nimble. Every time a line is rewritten, our character's thought processes change and their rhythms alter. What might seem like a minor adjustment from the writer's perspective can feel (from the inside) like a major shift for us. Sometimes a writer will take a line or even a speech from one scene and weave it into another: this can be challenging if we've been tracking our character's through-line. Sometimes lines are taken from one character and given to someone else: this can be tricky if we've been justifying our character's motivations. Sometimes whole speeches or scenes are cut: and this makes us worry that we weren't doing them properly and the writer and director didn't like our choices.

You can see how delicate the relationships can be in a rehearsal room when you're working with new writing. If a character is in constant development, it can be hard for us to trust that the way in which we're forming our interpretation is logical or right or appropriate. Like I said, we have to remain creatively very nimble – and more than a little thick-skinned.

My nimbleness was certainly put to the test with *Topless Mum*. At one rehearsal, I mentioned to the writer that he'd given my character an ambiguous final moment. Did he want me to play that ambiguity, or did he want me to bring her journey to a specific conclusion? He thought about it for a moment and then turned to the director. 'Let's take a tea break,' he said. (From the focused look on his face, I guessed he'd gone off to draft a few final lines to round off the character's story.) Fifteen minutes later, he came back with a complete, new scene. This in itself was very exciting. Nonetheless, it totally changed the trajectory of the character in the overall arc of the play.

With only a matter of days to go before opening night, I was beginning to feel more than a bit shaky. The production was a challenge for me, anyway, as I was still in the aftermath of my stage fright in *The Permanent Way*. So I had many conflicting feelings about performing in live theatre. Added to which, the rehearsal room at the Tobacco Factory was very, very narrow, so the director was always in our eyeline. And a mild claustrophobia gently cranked up my anxiety about the lines.

Then there was another little challenge. As is usually the case with new works, the writer took time out during the rehearsals, so that the actors and director could get on with it. A few days before opening night – again as is usually the case – the writer returned. And it quickly became clear that we'd been rehearsing the production in a direction that was far more realistic and documentary than he'd anticipated. He imagined (as I understood it) something more epic and Brechtian in its style. Suddenly there was a panic in my stomach. Was I barking up completely the wrong tree? If so, and with the first night looming dangerously close, I hadn't got time to fix it – and I'd just have to keep on barking!

The performances

The first preview was pretty stressful for the creative team – on both sides of the footlights. One of the actors completely lost his lines during a very long speech and improvised his way meanderingly through the main points. (He simply hadn't had enough time to bed-in the rewrites.) Added to which, in the traverse performance space, the audience seemed claustrophically close. They were just centimetres away from us on both sides of the stage. So every time I turned my head, I was eyeballing a spectator. (It reminded me horribly of *The Permanent Way*, when I'd found myself looking an audience member directly in the eye, and my whole epic stage-fright journey had begun.) Added to which, the stakes were high: we all desperately wanted the play to be a success as the writer and the director were so hoping for a London run. Those stakes surreptitiously rattled us, and, in the dressing rooms during the interval, we began to mutter our concerns. One actress sensed that she'd been terribly miscast and was feeling overwhelmingly uncertain about what she was doing out there on the stage. Several other actors were suddenly very vocal about how nervous they were feeling. Given my own history of stage fright – and the fact that I felt unavoidably underprepared for the first preview – I had to work very hard that night to keep a firm focus.

The second preview was no better. Another of the leading actors completely lost *his* lines and struggled rather painfully to find his way through the scene. Speaking to him afterwards, he shared how ghastly he'd felt. He didn't yet know the *thoughts* of the character, as the rehearsal process had been too intensive to get much further than line-bashing the evolving script into his short-term memory. For a brief (misguided) moment in that second preview, he'd allowed himself to flow with his character and, during that brief moment, he'd had a split-second interference of thinking, 'Oooh, this is going well!' And – bingo! Self-enthrallment nabbed him! The lines completely eluded him and any possible link in the thought processes vanished into the ether. Struggling to get back on track, he improvised for what seemed like an eternity. But – boy, oh boy – he was out there on his own! Nobody could help him, because nobody else on stage was any more familiar with the play than *he* was at this early point in the run. The result was that, in the interval, the stage manager came into the dressing rooms and slapped our collective wrists. There was an overwhelming sense that we hadn't done our homework well enough and we were being badly behaved. This ratcheted up our adrenalin even more and it made me realise that no one but an actor really understands the nature of stage fright. We undergo massive mental multitasking in performance under *normal* circumstances, let alone with all the complexities of *this* particular production.

Throughout the month-long run, I put myself under immense scrutiny and the whole experience was decidedly discomforting. For a start, it hadn't yet dawned on me that I could convert this feeling of insecurity into something appropriate to the character. I hadn't yet fully understood the nature of 'experiencing' and 'the state of "I am"'. So instead of allowing my real feelings to weave into the fabric of the role, I found myself dislocated from both the play and the character. ('How can I feel all this nervousness when I'm supposed to be a tough, military lawyer?')

To make matters worse, the audience still seemed claustrophobically close because of the smallness of the venue as well as the traverse nature of the stage. Often the director was in the house, and halfway through a scene I'd suddenly catch her in my eyeline: her own anxiety for the production was palpable and present. In the end, I wondered whether the talking cure could be useful all round. So I suggested we had a chat. She seemed as grateful as I was to break the amnesty on 'It's all right... *Isn't* it?' In fact, during that mid-run interview, she candidly and generously illuminated her own complex process, and sharing our feelings was an immense relief. She confessed that she'd been so engrossed with the minutiae of the language in the rehearsal period, it was only in the performances that she really started to see the whole piece. Because of the traverse stage, she became super-aware of the production's strengths and weaknesses as she could now watch the *audience* as much watching as the play.

The audience

With a new play, we have an inevitably heightened awareness of the *audience*, as we have no idea how the play will be received. It has no performance history yet. No heritage. We're relying on this very first audience to start creating that history. And the uncertainty is scary. And it's very difficult. And yet, as Stephen Wangh writes, 'your task as an actor is to allow yourself to come face to face with whatever *is* difficult for you, and thereby to transform it.'[187] What was difficult for me in this circumstance *was* the audience! Not to mention my head's interfering imp – that Fear Voice – which goaded me every night into believing that I was going to forget my lines and humiliate myself in front of all these people! I Had Stage Fright. Simple as that. And in almost every performance of *Topless Mum*, I felt as if I was tiptoeing on a high wire in an ill-fitting pair of stilettos. And the situation worsened. When we heard that the stage manager had been instructed to give us line notes after each show, the discomfort was magnified. I knew for sure that I was being watched and scrutinised – by the audience, by the director, and by the stage manager. I was doing my best to follow Wangh's advice: I was certainly 'coming face to face' (literally and metaphorically) with what was difficult for me. But how on earth was I going to 'transform it'?

Being watched is the crux of it all – as we acknowledged at the start of this journey way back in Chapter 1. Wangh even suggests: 'What we are used to calling stage fright is the energy of feeling watched. In other words, it is the essential energy of performance itself. And it is the same substance whether you call it stage fright or just energy.'[188] It was around the time of *Topless Mum* that I began to get the inkling that I might write this book. I really wanted to find a way to transform 'the powerful energy of fear, an energy we usually oppose as an energy, into a creative source.'[189] And then I realised the *power of eyes*. I'd given away so much agency to the power of the audience's eyes (those hungry wolves out there in the darkness, those Gestapo interrogators scrutinising me in silence), that I'd forgotten the power of my fellow actors. As film director Mike Nichols once said, 'If you ever felt you were getting lost, drown in each other's eyes.'[190] And veteran actor Oliver Ford Davies backs him up, 'Performance should be a time, with so much rehearsed and decided, that you really can lose yourself in your fellow actors.'[191] Part of the problem was that, with our all-too-brief rehearsal process for *Topless Mum*, so much *hadn't* been rehearsed, so much *hadn't* been decided, and I'd simply forgotten to lose myself in my partner's eyes.

The actors

I started talking to my *fellow actors* about our collective energy. One of the leading actresses revealed how vulnerable she was feeling – on the traverse stage, with the large textual arias that could sometimes sound more like the author than the character. Like Nina in *The Seagull*, she didn't know what to do with her hands. She wobbled on her high heels. Her legs felt too long. Her hands felt too big: she was (in effect) a 'helpless witness to her own malfunctioning'.[192]

Hearing that she was experiencing so much discomfort was – strange as it may sound – wonderful! We both realised that, as a result of sharing our personal vulnerabilities, we could now work onstage as a real team. We could really drown in each other's eyes. We could provide strong listening. We could connect and support each other – because now we knew what each other was going through. We could do the very thing that Jay Whittaker (as Mr Pitt) couldn't do with his fellow actor. As Wangh stresses, 'the surprising thing about fear is that if we acknowledge it and put it into the work, it disappears, or rather it seems to convert itself directly into excitement.'[193] (Like that genie in a puff of green smoke.) However, as Wangh also points out, 'it will not serve to *try* to make the fear disappear. It disappears in the process of naming it, of letting yourself know, "Okay, this is fear." It takes real courage to say, "I am afraid," so in the act of naming it you are already converting the fear into usable energy.' That's what we were doing: we were naming it out loud, and in so doing we were converting it into usable energy. Just as had happened with *The Permanent Way*, sharing the experience of *Topless Mum* enabled us actors to consolidate our fears and reconfigure our processes. From that moment on, we actually started to enjoy ourselves and the words began to flow. We even felt comfortable on stage. There was a twinkle in each other's eyes. And suddenly we were no longer the ones feeling naked in

Topless Mum. Our vulnerability was willing and no longer out of our control. Furthermore, the writer and director secured the London run. It was a happy ending all round!

Overview

In this chapter, we've put under the microscope the all-important actor-director relationship. We've looked at what we need from a director and from a healthy *rehearsal environment* (including *trust* and *playfulness*), whilst also acknowledging the *power-play* and the necessary *distancing*. We've examined the unique nature of *previews*. We've looked at what can happen *in performance* as the result of glitches incubated *in the rehearsal room*. We've touched upon the *principles of rehearsing*, including developing strong listening and recalibrating what it means to act and 'become' the character (using Stanislavsky's tools of *perezhivanie* and 'the state of "I am"'). We've reminded ourselves of the power of our partners, especially when handling our collective fears and especially when working on new writing.

*

In response to her own stage fright – which (as we've seen) crippled her during the one-woman show, *Rose*, at the National Theatre in 2000 and sent her scurrying mid-sentence off to her dressing room – Olympia Dukakis picked herself back up and walked back out onto the stage to tumultuous applause. Fear is 'just all part of the work,' she said. 'We're confronted constantly with new experiences, new experiences that shake us up: If you deny that, it's going to catch up with you.'[194] As we know, this whole book is about *not* denying our fear so that it *doesn't* catch up with us. Through the course of the last three chapters, we've acknowledged the roles of the *audience*, the *brain* and the *director*. Now let's turn our attention to what we ourselves can individually do as actors. How can we till the most fertile grounds for the fruits of our artistic pleasure to grow? How can we be kind enough on ourselves to face the fear, to welcome it, and to diffuse its pernicious hold? Once more unto the breach, dear friends…

5

How Do We Develop Good Practices?

The Role of Our Self as the Actor

'I don't fight it any more. I let it happen. If that's who I am, that's who I am.'[195]

Olympia Dukakis

5. How Do We Develop Good Practices?

What can we control?

We started Chapter 1 with the image of the generals going into battle. We know our ultimate goal is to face and embrace our Fear Foe, rather than fight it. That said, one of the main strategies of war is to take control – of supplies, routes, landmasses, not to mention the hearts and minds of those to be conquered. If we know that we can control a situation, we feel a certain ease.

When it comes to the acting industry, however, there are so many aspects that are *out* of our control, it's not surprising that our fears ratchet up. Our whole life is built on uncertainty. Never quite knowing if our agent will call. And if they do, will we get the audition? And if they don't, can we pay the bills? And if we can't, will we lose our homes? And if we lose, will we survive? And on and on the fears conspire. Yet we needn't be adrift on the sea of our tempestuous industry. As Beth Klein, Senior Vice President of Talent and Casting at Universal Television, advises, we should forget about what we *can't* control and focus instead on what we *can*. So what can we control? Our 'preparation' and 'good choices' are two sound and simple places to start, suggests Klein.[196] So in this chapter, we'll look at how we can control those two very things.

We begin with our basic acting instrument, and how to be *physically* and *psychophysically* prepared. (These instructions are fairly obvious, but it's still worth including them here.) Then we turn to the craft of acting itself, and look at it from four perspectives. First of all, how we can prepare ourselves *in general* for our creative work. Second, how we can guard against stage fright *at the rehearsal level*. Third, how we can tackle stage fright *in performance*. And fourth, how we can maintain our creativity *in the long term*. Then we consider what it really means to *face* the fear rather than *fight* it. And we finish off with best practices for dealing with *auditions* and *post-performance practices*. By the end, we should've equipped ourselves with some fairly comprehensive strategies for dealing with those stage-fright demons, whenever they choose to appear. After all, in the art of war: 'Invincibility depends on one's self.'[197]

So let's start our tactics for invincibility by preparing the instrument we use for our creative work: *our body*.

Tending to the Physical Needs of Our Instrument

There are certain obvious things that our body *needs* if we're to maintain our well-being in everyday life, let alone when we're dealing with the stresses of an actor's lifestyle. Obviously we need enough sleep, we need sufficient exercise, and we need good nutrition.[198] Fortunately it's more or less in our control to make sure those three things can happen.

At the same time, there are several, equally obvious, things that we should *avoid*, including caffeine, alcohol, nicotine, and recreational drugs. It's even more in our control to deal with these avoidances, especially if we're suffering stage fright: to put it bluntly, it's up to us whether or not we put them into our mouth. And it's important to understand the impact on our system if we do choose to consume them. The affect of caffeine is very much like the affect of adrenalin, so if we're already excitable, the last thing we want is more adrenalin. The same goes for alcohol, nicotine, and recreational drugs. They all affect the chemical balance of our brain. When our brain works right – we work right. And when our brain is troubled – it's hard to be our best self.[199]

In fact, when we're suffering ongoing stage fright, we can find ourselves in something of a chicken-and-egg scenario. Which came first – the stage fright or the stressed brain? So whatever we can do consciously to be kind to our brain – be it more sleep and exercise, less alcohol and coffee, more nuts and leafy greens, less high-fat meat and sugar – the more we can exponentially reduce our stage fright. These are good practices that we can easily adopt to prepare our physical instrument and control our stress. And it's pretty much up to us whether or not we do them. Yet we know that stage fright isn't just physical – it's psychophysical. So we should also look at our *psychophysical needs.*

Tending to the Psychophysical Needs of Our Instrument

Every musician know that the less tension in the player, the more freedom in the playing. And the same is true for us as actors: it's much easier to be creative if we're feeling physically relaxed. Similarly, every potter knows that the clay must be on the centre of the wheel if the pot is to be easily shaped. And again the same is true for us as actors: it's much easier to be creative if we're feeling centred (i.e. focused or concentrated). In fact, Antony Sher refers to the concentration-relaxation balance as the 'ideal state' for actors.[200] So, when we're preparing our creative instrument, the balance between the two – feeling relaxed and feeling focused – is our main *psychophysical need.* We've already seen that Relaxation and Attention (or Focus or

Concentration) are the first two of the four pillars on which Stanislavsky built his 'system' (along with Observation and Imagination). And since our Relaxation helps with our Attention, we'll start with that pillar first.

Relaxation operates on two levels: there's our Small-picture Relaxation (i.e. the particular state we achieve as actors before a rehearsal, shoot or show) and there's our Big-picture Relaxation (i.e. the ongoing state we achieve as human beings that affects our whole lives). Let's start with the Big Picture. In fact, let's start at the very beginning – with *breath*.

Breathing

When I was a kid doing school productions, my mum would tell me to stand in the wings, breathe deeply in and out three times, and say to myself, 'Keep calm… Keep calm… Keep calm…' And it worked! I just thought it was a family ritual; little did I realise it was a biological strategy. Well, of course – my mother was a biology teacher. Not only did she know that it was a good strategy for immediately distracting my thoughts from my nerves and giving me something very concrete to focus on, she also understood that developing a good connection to our *breath* is vital for us when it comes to reducing our fear. This is a fact that even combat trainers put into practice. They encourage their students to use what they call 'tactical breathing' – and it's just as useful for us actors as it is for soldiers. Tactical breathing is simple: 'breathe slowly and deeply into your abdomen (not your chest) for four counts, hold for four counts, exhale for four counts, and repeat. Our breath… is like a bridge to the parasympathetic nervous system, which [as we saw in Chapter 1] is in charge of calming the body down. By slowing the breath, we send a subtle message to the unconscious mind that everything is going to be okay.'[201] (This is exactly what my mother was teaching me in my nascent performing years.)

Part of the reason that tactical breathing is so vital is that, often when we're anxious, we inadvertently start to breathe shallowly and quickly. This increases our susceptibility to fear, as our inadvertent gasping sends the stress-message to our body that something is wrong. Because there's such a direct connection between our breath and our parasympathetic nervous system, the research on anxiety suggests that 'if you keep your breathing under control, it will be impossible for you to experience the strong physiological symptoms of performance anxiety.'[202] This is extremely useful for us to know. Our breathing is something we can actively and consciously control (in the wings, in our trailer, wherever). In other words, we have the direct and simple means to actively and consciously begin to control our anxiety. (If only I'd remembered what my mother had taught me as a child, when I was suffering my own adult stage fright.)

Linked to our breathing, we have some other Big-picture Relaxation Practices that can help us train our control. They're useful both for life and for acting – and they include *meditation* and *yoga*.

Meditation

At the heart of our stage fright (as we've seen throughout this book) is often our perversely self-sabotaging, inner Fear Voice insisting, 'I can't do this! I'm going to screw it up!' When this voice starts chattering, it's really just our imagination at perverse play – and our imagination can be a very powerful force. And yet it's a force that's remarkably at our beck and call, so we can choose to use it just as easily for therapeutic ends as we can for destructive ones. This is where *meditation* comes in.

The basic principle of meditation is that we take direct responsibility for our inner monologues. We reprogramme how we talk to ourselves. So instead of envisioning the future as full of anxiety ('Oh, no! I'm going to screw up!'), we choose to see it as full of optimism ('Oh, yes! This is going to be fun!'). Again, science has proven that people who practise meditation are able to calm their brains more quickly than those who don't. Of course it takes discipline and practice. And it links back to the second of Stanislavsky's pillars: Attention (or Focus or Concentration). So now let's turn to that pillar.

We all have minds that swing quickly from one thought to another like a monkey through the jungle. (From the scene that we're performing – to our tax bill – to our audition next week – to the line we just stumbled over – to the doom of our acting destiny. All in a matter of seconds.) If we practise meditation regularly – by concentrating our thoughts – we can train ourselves to focus our monkey-mind and stabilise our attention, so that we can have a little more control over where it swings to next. Obviously it's nigh on impossible to discard our interfering thoughts entirely. In fact, many meditation (or 'mindfulness') practitioners say that the interfering thoughts are the equivalent of the weights in a gym: we need them there in order to strengthen our ability to work against them. Or, to put it another way, they *are* the grit that makes the pearl in the oyster. The trick (in simple terms) is to acknowledge that those negative thoughts are there, but not to give them any value or precedence. Instead, we just observe them. And the rewards are twofold. On the one hand, meditation trains us to let go of our distracting (self-sabotaging) thoughts much faster than we would otherwise. And on the other hand, it quickens our ability to refocus on the fun of performing. So there's a double-whammy diffusion of our stage fright.

The handy thing is that our mind doesn't have to do all this focus work on its own. Since our body is way more biddable than our mind alone, we can increase our level of self-control by harnessing our *body's* energy to our *mind's* meditative practice. Small wonder that so many actors practise some form of *yoga*.

Yoga

The word 'yoga' means 'yoking' – and *yoga* directly yokes our physical body to our mindful awareness. As we saw with tactical breathing, when we consciously use our breath in particular patterns, we can relax our muscles. And when our muscles are relaxed, we can be much more mentally present to what's happening here and now. What that means when we're acting is that we're far more available to our intuitive responses and our in-the-moment impulses. And then, as we know, our acting feels much more alive. We're making new discoveries here and now, rather than fixing a 'perfect' performance. Besides, yoga is great for our overall physical suppleness and mental agility.

Because yoga integrates our body, mind and breath, it's a wonderful means of handling and overcoming stage fright. This is no new practice in the theatre. In fact, yoga has been a significant part of Western actor-training for over a hundred years and for many, many centuries in the East. Stanislavsky actually used it in the Moscow Art Theatre (although he had to keep it well under the radar of the materialist Soviet government, as it was way too esoteric for them). When you consider that he was creating his 'system' while he was suffering a crisis in his own acting – as well as dealing with chronic stage fright – it makes perfect sense for yoga to be one of the tools in his kit. Now more and more practitioners and actor-trainers across the globe are using yoga as part of their Big-picture Relaxation Practices. So it's not merely a fad of the last twenty years.

*

Those are a few examples of how we can prepare and maintain our instruments physically and psychophysically on an ongoing basis. They can also help us with some of the external factors of our industry that we saw in Chapter 1 (such as *loss of control over our careers* and *the vagaries of casting*). In other words, balancing our body and mind can be a great (inner) antidote to the madness of the (outside) world.

Now let's turn our attention to some Small-picture Relaxation Practices that we can use when we're preparing for our creative work as actors.

Preparing Ourselves for Our Creative Work

Before offering some specific practices for *working on a role*, I'm going to propose some basic guiding principles for our acting *in general*. As ever, these guiding principles are as much about mindset as anything else – and they can help us remain relaxed enough to handle our performance anxiety in both *rehearsal* and *performance*. These three guiding principles are: (1) keep it simple; (2) get out of our own way; and (3) know what we need to warm ourselves up. Let's look at what each of these means.

Guiding principle 1: keep it simple

Keep it simple means just that! Sometimes we're so desperate to transform ourselves into a character, we try to be too clever. We overcomplicate our choices in rehearsal – coming up with all sorts of smart ideas and clever constructs. And then in performance we want to be sure that the audience 'gets' all those ideas and acknowledges how smart we've been. Our clever construct then becomes like a suit of armour. Not only is it metaphorically hard to move in, but it also grows metaphorically rusty. As we stagger about in our rusty armour, there's a risk – in the words of director Ingemar Lindh – 'of not giving space to what exists'.[203] What actually exists is our *live connection*: with our partner, with the space, with the given circumstances of the script, and with the audience. It's the life of that in-the-moment core self that we talked about in Chapter 1. If we can dare to *not* have everything worked out in advance, we can genuinely follow new impulses as they arise. In fact, there's actually less to worry about... because there's actually less to remember. We're simply allowing ourselves to listen to the here and now. And that's way more pleasurable than stomping around in our rusty armour.

It's one of the curious paradoxes of acting: the less we feel we have to give a fixed and perfect performance, the less nervous we are. When we're less nervous, we can be more playful. When we're more playful, we can dynamically listen to each other. When we dynamically listen, we can respond to each moment as it unfurls. Which takes us to guiding principle 2...

Guiding principle 2: get out of our own way

The degree of dynamic listening that we're talking about here is really all about *getting out of our own way*. The image I usually use to describe the ideal state for an actor in performance is that of a flute. A flute is well constructed and well maintained – but it's empty. If we've done our preparation on a role and we're feeling physically relaxed and mentally focused, we can almost vacate ourselves in performance like a flute. (It's what I described in Chapter 4 with Queen Margaret in *Richard III*.) We don't have to think about all our preparation; instead we can trust that we've assimilated it. And then we can simply let the music of the playwright's script sound through us as we speak it, playing its notes on our body, on our imagination, our emotions and our soul. And then the notion of stage fright doesn't even dawn on us.

*

Ultimately these two guiding principles help us to be in (what Stanislavsky calls) a 'constant state of inner improvisation'. If we really want to exist in this wonderfully liberating and exciting state – this fine balance between preparing ourselves thoroughly and daring to let it all go – we need our third guiding principle. We need to *warm ourselves up* effectively.

Guiding principle 3: warm ourselves up

Every actor has a different way of *warming up* – and part of our good-practice preparation is to understand what we each personally need. After all, a tailor-made warm-up can help us enormously in dealing with our stage fright. It may be vocal. It may be physical. It may be quiet like a meditation – or vigorous like a child at play. The main thing is that a warm-up shouldn't feel like a chore. Rather, it's 'a *gift* you're giving to yourself and to your co-workers,' describes Stephen Wangh. 'It is a gift you choose to help you grow as actors. It can provide both safety and excitement.'[204] *Safety* – in the same way that scales and arpeggios provide a musician with a structure that can be rehearsed and refined. *Excitement* – in the same way that those scales and arpeggios prepare the player for flights of musical majesty. In other words, we don't just warm up for the sake of warming up. We're getting ready to propel ourselves into vast and imaginative realms.

It's also a conscious means of transforming the state that we're in when we arrive at the theatre or the film location. A warm-up, as Wangh puts it, 'is a bridge between the conditions of mind, body and voice you have been using in everyday life and the conditions of mind, body and voice you need to act.' Whether it involves the whole company or it's a solitary activity, a warm-up helps us transit from the distracting detritus of our daily life to the seductive anticipation of the performance space.

That said, some actors don't do any warm-up at all – perhaps because their whole existence is one big creative warm-up so they're always in tune. Others begin the whole process hours before the performance time. Some actors adapt their warm-ups according to the character they're playing, as different roles require us to get into different rhythms and headspaces. And sometimes we need to change our warm-up, because we ourselves have changed. After my stage-fright experience in *The Permanent Way*, fellow actor Matthew Dunster pointed out that my warm-up (a highly structured combination of physical and vocal exercises) might actually be *adding* to my stage fright, rather than diffusing it:

> The warm-up you currently do is very detailed and it's basically about repetition. It's very routine – which is what our performances have become at the moment. So when our routine is *broken* in performance – like when we forget our lines – we're not equipped to deal with it; we have nothing to save us. What you need to do is scare yourself witless. If I was working with you as a director, I'd make you do a warm-up that was different every night – because, when that repetition deserts you in performance, you're fucked if you haven't got the facility for playing about.[205]

What Dunster is saying is crucial in terms of understanding that a warm-up should be adaptable. Like a cyclist training at high altitude or a gymnast training during a Russian winter, a warm-up needs to be fit for purpose, and – if it's not – we need to change it. At the end of the day, we're trying to prepare our inner creative state so that we can achieve the ideal balance between relaxation and focus.

*

So far, we've looked at the Big Picture of our whole lives and the Small Picture of our general acting work. Let's make the circle of attention smaller. Let's look at how to prepare ourselves for working on *a particular role*. First, we'll look at some good *rehearsal* practices, and then turn our attention to some good *performance* practices.

Developing Good Rehearsal Practices

Whatever happens during rehearsals (as we saw in Chapter 4) can sow the seeds of our confidence or (conversely) our fright. Yet we also know that we're not entirely at our director's mercy. We have plenty of strategies that we can adopt on our own to keep the fears at bay. Going back to Beth Klein's idea of the things we can control – i.e. 'preparation' and 'good choices' – the rehearsal practices I offer here are intended for that very purpose. They're designed to help us feel more *prepared* – practically and philosophically – so that we can make *good choices* when we're working on a role. And the starting point for our rehearsal preparation is pretty much always the *text*.

Rehearsal practice 1: mining the text

Before we can begin to make any creative choices, we have to know the territory that we're entering: i.e. we have to analyse the script. The term 'text analysis' can sound academic and boring; but when we embark on proper text analysis, that couldn't be further from the truth. Some directors, including Adrian Noble, call it *mining the text*, so that we can excavate the real gems. The whole process of fathoming everything out is an intricate and fascinating forensic science. (Why does a character use certain words? Why are there certain silences? Why did the writer choose particular punctuation? Why are certain activities specified or certain points of view adopted?) The forensic investigation is filled with possibility. In fact, putting together a skeleton from the tiny shards of paper-and-ink bone – and cladding that skeleton in our own flesh and muscles – is one of the greatest thrills of acting. And just like any other aspect of our craft, real and thorough text analysis is *physical* and *psychological*.

Physical text analysis

On the *physical* side, the clues are often not hard to find, as the writer may be explicit about the character's physicality. We know Richard III has a hump; we know Epikhodov in *The Cherry Orchard* has squeaky shoes; we know Walter White in *Breaking Bad* has cancer; we know Susy Hendrix in *Wait Until Dark* is blind. And once we've gleaned the hard facts, we can start to use our imagination to embellish the other physical details. A really good provocation for our physical text analysis is: what's the character's occupation? If we're playing Joan of Arc, we know that she's a soldier; Walter White is a chemistry teacher; Friar Lawrence is a Friar – and the Nurse is a nurse! If we can pinpoint a character's occupation, we can come up with all sorts of imaginings about how they might walk, how they might use their hands (do they cut down trees or do they mend intricate clockwork?), how flexible or otherwise their body is, how musical or otherwise their voice is. And, to some extent, these physical details aren't too hard to fathom.

But our forensic research can take us deeper. There are less obvious and more intricate physical clues embedded in the text. For example: what are the character's rhythmic patterns? Are their sentences long? Are the rhythms staccato? Do they talk in iambic pentameter? And it's important to uncover these rhythms, as they'll actively affect our breathing. Then there are other equally physical and yet even subtler clues, such as: what's the shape of the vowels in our mouth? What's the bounce of our tongue and teeth around the consonants? And how does it actually feel when we say the words? These tiny physical sensations can vividly fuel our imagination. Take Shakespeare's line from *King Lear*: 'Blow, winds, and crack your cheeks! Rage! Blow!' There's a range of vowel sounds here and a vastness in the images. And then take Mamet's line from *American Buffalo*: 'Fuckin' Ruthie, fuckin' Ruthie, fuckin' Ruthie, fuckin' Ruthie.' There's a joy in the rhythmic consonants, and there's a pleasure in the expressiveness of the character's inarticulate repetitions. Verbal and oral clues like these – and the feel of them around the resonators of our face – can provide our imagination with just as many stimuli as the images themselves. So the physical choices available to us when we really dig into the text analysis are both obvious and embedded – visual and sensory. And the discoveries can be very rewarding.

Psychological text analysis

On the *psychological* side, we're looking in our text analysis for the intentions beneath the words. Language is one of the main ways as human beings that we let the world know the nuances of all our feelings, our needs, our beliefs and desires. If we didn't convert our inner experiences into language, no one would have much of a clue about our perspective on the world. It's exactly the same with scripted characters. Their external words are clues to their internal lives. Yet (whether we're talking about real people or fictional characters), those feelings, needs, beliefs and desires can be very hard for us to pin down to concrete expressions. Because what we actually *say* and what we actually *mean* can't be always be laid on top of each other as exact carbon copies. After all, sometimes we simply don't know how to express ourselves. Our words might be just the tip of an 'iceberg' of emotions that lies hidden beneath the surface of our external expression. A brushed off 'Sure, I'm fine,' after my grandmother just died doesn't really mean that I'm fine. 'Sure, I'm fine' could really mean, 'Please don't talk to me right now – or I'll fall to pieces…' So our real craft as actors is to hold the human soul up to the light like a quartz crystal, to twist it and to reveal the subtle nuances of the character's (and the writer's) myriad intentions. And in this way the forensic process of text analysis becomes very exciting – and very playful.

Psychophysical text analysis

And it doesn't stop there. Beyond the physical and the psychological, text analysis also has a *psychophysical* side. Many actors find that breaking down a script into its 'bits of action' (or units) is an extremely useful way of getting inside the text. (Tanya Moodie illustrated this in Chapter 3, with her vivid description of pencil lines and coloured highlighters. And, personally, I don't know how to go about learning a script unless I've done this kind of analysis.) What we do when we break a script into its bits of action is to subtly combine the *physical structure* of a scene with the *psychological intentions* of the characters. If we can see how a piece is structured (how long a scene is, how many characters exit and enter, the number of monologues or soliloquies or overlaps, etc.), we can unpack two lines of enquiry at the same time. We can trace the various changes that happen *in each character's thoughts* (i.e. the specifics of the scene) and at the same time, we can chart the *overall dramatic tension of a scene* (i.e. its general shape). Lots of books detail how to do this prep (not least my own *The Complete Stanislavsky Toolkit*),[206] so I'm not going to go into that here. Instead, I want to highlight why this kind of text analysis can directly allay our stage fright.

When we break down a text into its bits of action, what we're basically doing is 'bundling' sections of text together. Bundling information, stresses psychologist Sian Beilock, can be very beneficial when we're performing under pressure: 'Combining what you need to remember into meaningful wholes helps to ensure that some pieces don't get lost when it counts the most.'[207] This is exactly what breaking down a text into its bits of action does: it unlocks the scene's structure, it reveals its emotional and narrative arc, and it bundles information together into meaningful wholes. Rather than having a whole heap of individual items strung together on a string of our short-term memory – or one big blob of text that we're trying to line-cram – we now have globules of connected ideas that we can pattern and link. Dividing our lines into 'bundles' (so to speak) makes them much easier to remember. And if this kind of 'bits of action' text analysis isn't a process that our director brings overtly into the rehearsal room, it's something we can do on our own.

So text analysis is physical, psychological, psychophysical, and we can do it on our own. In other words, it's a great rehearsal practice that gives us some control over our creative *preparation* and enables us to make some *good choices*. Thus it's one way to allay our fears. It also helps us to become more precise in our learning of a text. After all, *being dead-letter-perfect* is another very powerful way for us to take control of our preparation and overcome our stage fright. Which takes us to rehearsal practice 2...

Rehearsal practice 2: being dead-letter-perfect

Words are more important than we can possibly imagine. Very subtle information is carried in the nuances of language. And that subtle information can cue certain responses within us. It's the premise on which most advertising and newscasting and political campaigning is based. Look at the public outcry in Summer 2015 when Prime Minister David Cameron referred to a 'swarm' of people migrating from France to the UK. And as I currently sit here writing, Donald Trump is running for Republican candidacy in the USA. Every day, words are being bandied about and subsequently justified.

When we really tune into the subtleties of language – and the surreptitious way that information cues our responses – we realise just how important it is to know our lines reliably. Not only because of how our words affect other people, but also how they affect us – not least in terms of staving off our stage fright. So it pays to be *dead-letter-perfect*. Here's what I mean...

Take the word *piano*. An experiment was conducted, in which one group of people was given the sentence, 'The man *tuned* the piano,' and another group was given the sentence, 'The man *lifted* the piano.' Later, both groups were asked to name objects associated with the phrases, 'Something heavy' and 'Something melodious'. The group who'd been given the 'tuning' image offered 'piano' in response to 'something melodious'. The other, 'lifting' group, offered 'piano' in response to 'something heavy'.[208] This was because each group had encoded the same object – a piano – with a specific image: one involving pleasant music, the other involving physical exertion. When we encode information – be it a piano or a poem – the whole process is as *emotional* as it is *literal*. In other words, we associate *feelings* to what we're learning as much as we associate literal *meaning*. So the idea of listening to a melodious piano concerto conjures up inside us a completely different emotional resonance from the idea of trying to haul a heavy piano up a set of stairs – like the chimps in the old PG Tips commercial! So it's important that we learn a script dead-letter-perfect right from the beginning – rather than learning our own paraphrased version of it. Otherwise we start to forge different imaginative and emotional associations from those that will ultimately help us to remember the script-as-writ. When this happens, our interpretation of the role is always a little bit 'off' – a bit too generalised. And that can add low-level anxiety, because we know we're slightly off-key.

Which leads to another reason for us to develop the rehearsal practice of being dead-letter-perfect. When we're not 'DLP', there's always a little distracted part of our brain occupied with thinking, 'That's kinda-sorta what the text is... Not quite that word, but nearly...' And that little distraction can act like a niggling worm of doubt. It nibbles away as a mild interference. What's more, we end up asking too much of our brain. Instead of just getting on with connecting to the actual script, we're trying to improvise a new script on the spot, creating our slightly 'off' version of what the playwright gave us. And that's a completely different task in its own right. After all, we're trained actors, not professional writers. Besides, just imagine what would happen if everyone in the cast did that: you'd end up with a script which was nothing like the writer's original. At the end of the day, it's simply much easier to know the lines exactly, rather than a 'kinda-sorta' paraphrase. And not just for our own sake – but also for our partners – so that we can help them with (what's known as) their *cued recall*. Which takes us to rehearsal practice 3...

Rehearsal practice 3: understanding the processes of cued recall

This is another compelling reason why we should learn a script dead-letter-perfect. It goes back to how our brain works and the network of neuronal patterns that fire when we remember something. We've seen several times throughout this book that, neurologically, there's a very clear match between what we've *encoded* in our brain (i.e. learnt) and what we're trying to *retrieve* (i.e. remember). So when our brain can't make that match, we're in trouble. Here's an example...

Have you ever forgotten a line on stage and the other actors just look at you completely blankly? It's like *everybody* has suddenly forgotten the whole script. That's because there's a lack of what's known as *cued recall*. The other actors haven't detected a match between the cue that they were expecting you to give them (i.e. the cue in the script that would trigger their memory) and the words (or silence) that you've just uttered. Here – as ever – art is imitating everyday life. Here's how...

In everyday life, certain cues trigger certain recollections for us. For example, if I ask you: 'What did you do on Friday night?' it'll trigger different responses in you from if I ask, 'Where did you go on Friday night after you left the movies?' The first cue is fairly open. The second cue provides us 'with more information in an effort to extract some specific material.'[209] (Police and prosecuting lawyers use this strategy all the time: 'So what did you do after you left the casino and went to the victim's apartment?'

– I was never at the victim's apartment, but now you're making me think that I might have been...) In other words, we can manipulate someone else's recall by using particular cues. If we're performing a script and the match between the words and the cues doesn't happen, it can lead to all sorts of inner mayhem. And not just in theatre.

There's an increasing tendency in film and television today for actors to deliberately adjust the lines – as if that little frisson of improvisation will make their performances seem more 'truthful'. I recently heard about a very successful actor who was filming a TV series. He was frustrated at how many of the other actors didn't bother learning the scriptwriter's lines. They didn't want to rehearse, and they weren't giving him the cue lines, and it was really screwing the performance which, as the series lead, he'd carefully and conscientiously crafted. During a shoot, he'd be expecting to hear a particular line, and, if some other cue were thrown his way instead, there'd be a split-second adjustment in his head as he tried to figure whether or not his own scripted line would still fit the dialogue. In the end, he went to the producers and asked for a gentle riot act to be read. How could they collectively serve the script or the narrative of the drama if several actors were giving their own rendition, rather than the one agreed upon?

When there's a constant lack of cued recall, we're not being given the necessary triggers to retrieve our lines effectively. And more often than not, our memory will fail us if what's being cued is different from what we've encoded. Or to put it another way: we're less likely to remember the right line if our partner doesn't give us the right cue. And *vice versa*. Acting is collaborative, after all; so we need to help our partners out, too.

However, there's another rehearsal practice that we can adopt to be sure we've prepared ourselves as thoroughly as we can – regardless of the cues that our partners end up giving us. And that's to *personalise the images*.

Rehearsal practice 4: personalising the images

One of the ways in which we can help ourselves to effectively encode new information (i.e. learn the lines) so that we can reliably retrieve the stored information (i.e. remember the lines) is to *personalise the images* in the script. (This is a valuable rehearsal practice that stops us getting anxious if our partners don't give us the right cues.) Let's go back to the word *piano*. When we see that word in the script, we can personalise the image by giving it as much detail as possible. What kind of piano are we picturing? Is it our brother's polished Steinway grand? Or our nephew's dusty Casio keyboard? Or the out-of-tune piano in the village hall where we once learnt Beginner's Ballet? The more refined we make our images – i.e. the more we personalise them – the more specific will be the feelings we attach to those words, and, therefore, the more consolidated our memory of those words will be.

Now let's go back to the *hammer* that we talked about in Chapter 3. As we imagine picking up the hammer, we've probably got enough history with hammers to know how to assess its weight and we'll probably know how to bang something with it. We might recall the little wooden mallet we had as a kid for bonking round pegs into round holes as our tiny self discovered its amazing powers of coordination. Let's now suppose we're playing the farm manager Shamrayev in *The Seagull*: suddenly that hammer will have a heap of other connotations for a man who works on a farm, who mends fences and shoes horses. What kind of hammer do we picture now?

Let's now put an imaginary *axe* on the table. How is the axe different from the hammer? And are we the woodcutter in *Little Red Riding Hood*, killing the wolf and saving the granny? Or are we the student Raskolnikov in *Crime and Punishment*, bashing out the brains of a little old lady? At that moment of imagination, our brain is remembering the weight, the length, the metal and wood of some axe from our past when perhaps we went on a camping trip and chopped up firewood. At the same time, we're creating an imaginative understanding of what exactly our body would have to do to chop down a tree or kill a wolf or bash out a little old lady's brains. With each of those images comes a particular emotional stirring – and our association with the *axe* will be different from our association with the *hammer*. So you can see that personalising the images (which goes hand in hand with the precision of being dead-letter-perfect) is key to consolidating our lines so that we can retrieve them easily. And when we can retrieve our lines easily, we don't get so nervous. It's an invaluable rehearsal practice. Again it's something we can do on our own, and again it's playful and exciting.

*

So there's quite a lot of practical text analysis we can do during rehearsals to prepare ourselves independently and take control of our choices. We can find the *physical feel* of the text, the *psychological undercurrents*, and the *psychophysical bits of action*. We can make sure we're *dead-letter-perfect* so that we can help our partners with their *cued recall*, and we can help ourselves to be dead-letter-perfect by *personalising the images*.

That said – however thoroughly we prepare ourselves on our own – there's always that moment in rehearsals when we share this work for the first time and still the jitters can hit us. A very good rehearsal strategy for dealing with our nerves is to actually celebrate the opportunity to *practise under stress*.

Rehearsal practice 5: practising under stress

The first time we go public with something that we've been preparing behind closed doors can be more than a little stressful. How often have we said (or heard fellow actors say), 'I don't know why I'm screwing this up – I did it brilliantly in my room last night'? It's actually perfectly normal. The room in which we prepped the material last night was probably quite different from the space in which we're sharing our prep today. All this new information bombarding our senses (a new space, new people, different props, cameras, etc.) can inevitably screw us up temporarily. And the reason for this – as scientific studies have shown – is that our memory is more reliable if we're in a similar physical environment and emotional state at the time we *remember* something, as we were at the time we *first learnt* it. It's what psychologist Endel Tulving calls the *encoding specificity principle.*[210] He suggests that what we remember depends on the similarity – i.e. the 'match' – between the two environments (the *learning* environment and the *retrieving* environment). So the more alike they are, the better.

And the match is twofold. On the one hand, the *physical contexts* need to be the same – and we all know how much easier it is to perform something in a space in which we've already learned and rehearsed it. On the other hand, the *psychological state* needs to be the same – so that we're remembering our lines in the same kind of state we were in when we were rehearsing them.

It's not always easy to find a match, though. In terms of *physical context*, we've no idea necessarily what the film set will look like until we're there – or what our costume will be. Even with something as simple as a first readthrough of a script, we can feel vulnerable – all these people we've never met before, in a room that's new to us – and we're trying to show them why we were chosen for the role over any other actor.

As for the *psychological state* – it's often even harder to find a match. All the comfort of rehearsing our audition speech in our bedroom flies out of the window when our heart is pounding and the adrenalin is pumping in front of a panel of judges.

However... all these *mis*-matches can also be accepted as useful fodder here-today-now, and turned on their head to our creative advantage. If we allow even the mild stress of a readthrough to be a constructive part of our experience, we can ultimately reduce our chances of suffering stage fright when we find ourselves under greater pressure at a later time. How so?

Because *practising under stress* can actually change the hardwiring of our brain so that it can learn to stay cool under any condition. People in physically dangerous jobs do it all the time. Soldiers and firemen regularly practise their drill: they know that rehearsing under stress is as important for them as any kind of rehearsing is for actors. So whenever we find ourselves feeling anxious in a rehearsal ('Will the director like this idea? Am I working well with my scene partner? Will I hit my mark?'), we should actually embrace and enjoy these feelings. After all, they're helping us to train our brain to deal with the higher octane situations of previews and press nights and final takes.

*

So those are five easily implemented rehearsal practices. They are very much in our control and we can use them to prepare ourselves so that we can make some bold choices. So let's now fast-forward to performance. What good practices can we put in place there to deal with the monster if it suddenly rears its head?

Developing Good Performance Practices

As Laurence Olivier said, the monster of stage fright can come at any time and in any form. Yet that doesn't render us powerless. In fact, what I offer here are six strategies for handling stage fright if it does strike us in performance. As ever, these strategies mix practical actions (that we can take) with psychological mindsets (that we can adopt), so that – as ever – our body and brain can work together. And they're also strategies that allow us to take some personal control.

The first performance practice returns us to one of the key tools we used for learning our lines in the first place – attention – and more specifically for us in performance, *refocusing our attention on our partners and our actions.*

Performance practice 1: refocusing our attention on our partners and our actions

Stage fright is basically a misdirection of our attention. We've seen throughout this book that if we choose to attend to and prioritise our fear, then that becomes our reality. If, on the other hand, we choose to attend to and prioritise the joys of acting, then *that* becomes our reality. Where we put our focus is very much within our control. So if we suddenly convince ourselves that the audience is out to get us, then it's a sign that we're holding *that* particular thought in our attention. As Peter Coyote describes: 'Stage fright is imagining somebody else, out in the audience, thinking about you in a disparaging way. That means, your attention has gone out into the audience and you're not concentrating on stage. To me, stage fright's a dead giveaway that your concentration is off.'[211] Taylor Clark adds to this perspective. He suggests that 'the culprit in cases of meltdown under pressure isn't *fear*, but misdirected focus'.[212] So performance practice 1 is to take our attention *away* from our churning feelings, and to focus it instead *towards* our partner and the acting environment. And that act of refocusing can be as simple as if we were shining a torch beam. If we can take this simple, practical action, then what we perceive to be the critical eye of the audience becomes less important to us than what we're actually doing on stage or in front of the camera. This is exactly the strategy adopted by actor David Annen in Kenneth Branagh's 2013 production of *Macbeth*. So to unpack this practice further, we're going to use a little more of the talking cure...

David Annen had always prided himself on being one of those performers upon whom actors and directors could rely – 'dependable, solid and useful.'[213] When stage fright struck him after more than twenty years in the business and just three nights away from the end of a highly successful run, he was totally shocked and somewhat devastated. His agonies were exacerbated by the fact that he was playing the comparatively small role of Seyward – a role that should have been easy. By the time Seyward appears for his major scenes, the play is well into its course but – just like Sam Graham playing Phoebe in *As You Like It* – the late arrival of Seyward on the scene only made Annen's anxiety worse. In fact, by the end of those three final performances, he was almost crippled with fear. Rehearsing his lines 'like an addict' – backstage, in the street, and even in the moments when he was standing on stage just before his speech – Annen knew that he had to find a remedy otherwise he was screwed.

The production was set to go to New York's Park Avenue Armory in collaboration with the Manchester International Festival. It was a big gig that really excited him, and he didn't want the experience to be sabotaged by his mind-created panic. So sure enough – he faced his fear during the New York run. And he actually found his remedy in two strategies directly involving his focus of attention:

> The first strategy was obvious really and was just about relationships and intentions. As Seyward, I was commanding the army and there were about twelve people on stage, one of whom I actually talked to (the young prince) and one of whom I referred to (Macduff). So to overcome my fear, I made sure I knew who all the other lords were and what my relationship with each of them was. I created imaginative connections for them. So when I looked each one in the eyes – and this strategy *encouraged* me to look them in the eyes – I knew why I was saying those particular lines to that particular lord. 'You're the hot-headed one, so I want to cool you

> down a bit.' 'You're the scared one, so I want to gee you up a bit.' It was only a few lines of script but I knew that if I looked them in the eye, I would know why I was speaking to them.
>
> The second strategy was even more effective and involved just finding a really simple physical score to go with the words – particularly the speech that I was hung up on. As I said the words, 'The time approaches, / That will with due decision make us know / What we shall say we have and what we owe', I found that if I clenched my right fist on the world 'will' and my left fist on the word 'know' – which were both concrete, positive, powerful words – that would get me through those two lines. So that's what I did – every night for three weeks. And I got the lines right every night for three weeks. And the panic lessened and at the end of those three weeks in New York, I was really pleased. I thought, 'I'm a recovering stage-fright addict – and it's all right.'[214]

By refocusing his attention on his partners and on some simple physical actions, Annen overcame his stage fright. He successfully lured his focus away from his fear and back to the basic storytelling. Like Mike Nichols said, when we get lost, we just need to drown in each other's eyes.

That's all well and good if we have an onstage partner. What about, for example, the situation that faced Benedict Cumberbatch and the blinking red eyes of the mobile phones during his Hamlet soliloquies at the Barbican in 2015? I suppose that if I were he – knowing that we can't really police our audiences – I'd try to welcome in those red eyes. I'd twist the crystal on the situation, and rather than being frustrated by the phones, I'd use them to my advantage and turn them into partners. I'd see them as the eyes of God, questioning my existence. Or the eyes of my father, watching me from purgatory. Or the eyes of hundreds of souls, shining a light on what I'm doing. Which is exactly what they are... People in the darkness, recording for all time the quality of my performance as a living being. I'd invite those red eyes. Welcome them in. I might even suggest having a performance where everyone *has* to have a mobile phone, so that all I could see would be a sea of red-eyed monsters drawing me into 'To be or not to be' and 'what dreams may come'... Since what we resist persists – and since we have to befriend our audience, rather than seeing them as the enemy – I'd relinquish my frustration, and if I can't beat 'em, join 'em! The truth is, we're in a technological millennium. The devices aren't going away. It may be that live theatre is the last bastion of real, true in-the-moment, unmediated experience. But it's going to be hard to enforce it, so we must do whatever we can to prevent the technology wrecking our focus or scuppering our love of acting.

At the end of the day, we all have these monkey-minds that leap from thought to thought. And if we can try to consciously refocus our attention in the moment of performance, we can go a long way towards taming them. While we can't control our minds entirely, we can adjust our mindset so that we accept that monkey-spirit and live with it with humour. ('Oh... there's those mobile phones again!... Welcome... Welcome... Welcome...') In order to be that playful, we can start by getting some *perspective on perception*. Which takes us to performance practice 2...

Performance practice 2: getting some perspective on perception

'It is not what happens to you in life that determines how you feel; it is how your brain *perceives reality* that makes it so.'[215] This sound insight from psychiatrist Daniel Amen means that it's not just what we *attend* to that creates our experience: it's how we *perceive* what we attend to. As we saw in Chapter 3, our brain isn't like a camera that simply takes an objective picture of the world. We derive all sorts of *meanings* from what we see in a situation – meanings that are influenced by our beliefs, our past history, and our expectations. And how we evaluate those meanings is what we call *perception*.

When it comes to stage fright in performance, perception can be pretty darn powerful, as (in the words of Amen) 'The view that your brain takes of a situation has more reality in it than the actual situation itself.'[216] Our perception is incredibly creative. It manipulates reality. And therefore, it's very unreliable. It's so unreliable that, during moments of acute stage fright in performance, we can experience a complete collapse of our professional, social and artistic identity – and yet the audience wouldn't have a clue! For all our catastrophic inner collapse, they may detect nothing more than a tiny blip in the rhythm of the play – perhaps a stutter, a stumble, a momentary glimpse of an actor on the edge of a breath. But that's all. They have no idea about what we're actually going through. So performance practice 2 is to *get some perspective on what we perceive.*

David Annen had just such an opportunity, as he had the unique experience of watching his own stage fright. The last night of *Macbeth* in Manchester was simultaneously streamed by National Theatre Live – across the world to literally millions of viewers. It was three nights into his awful, high-level performance anxiety, and in 'preparation overdrive', Annen's panic couldn't have been higher. 'I just didn't know how to cope, I didn't know if I should tell anyone. I *had* to do the live broadcast, so I was thinking, "If it all goes wrong, I can give up acting, there's probably something else I can do." It was completely embarrassing and unforgiveable.'[217]

The live broadcast began. And the fateful time approached for his fateful 'time approaches' speech – and sure enough he fluffed it. But was it 'completely embarrassing'? Was it 'unforgivable'? Absolutely not at all! Annen has subsequently had the chance to watch a recording of the broadcast and 'It's an extraordinary experience to watch what looks like a fairly calm and confident actor on stage, when *I* know that in my head is this paroxysm of fear. We get to the line and, sure enough, I mangle it again – but not so as you'd really notice. I say sort of the right lines in sort of the right order. It doesn't quite scan, but you sort of get the sense of it.' The audience really wouldn't have noticed. After all, as Annen points out,

> I think what happens anyway with audiences – especially with Shakespeare – is that they're getting the gist of what's being said, and if there's something they don't quite get, they're on to the next thing straight away. So when people said to me afterwards, 'It didn't matter,' I really think that either they hadn't noticed or they thought it was fine. – Or they were just glad it wasn't them! And actually I wasn't the only person to make a mistake that night. Or any other night, for that matter. There's always someone who fluffs a line or forgets something. So when I saw myself on the broadcast, I thought, 'It's really not the end of the world – but I've got to handle this better next time'.[218]

We can learn so much from Annen's tale, as few of us actually get to see those fear-fuelled performances when we think we've utterly screwed up. What he illustrates is that it really is all about perception – and we have to remember that the audience often doesn't notice, and they rarely really mind. The worst thing they're going to perceive is an actor stopping completely, exiting to the wings, finding the lost line and coming back on stage – which is what Paul Greenwood and Olympia Dukakis both did. And the sky won't fall our heads. And the earth will continue to turn. And the show *will* go on. And our career won't judder to a terrifying halt. It's vitally important – when we experience stage fright in performance – to check our perception of the situation. We need to review the 'reality' that our brain has momentarily constructed – and to let ourselves off the hook.

The provocative question here is: 'Why did someone as experienced and reliable as David Annen suffer stage fright on this occasion?' Answer: he was trying to *deal with a small role.*

Performance practice 3: dealing with a small role

It's not uncommon for us to suffer stage fright just as badly in small roles as we might in leads – especially if we're used to playing large roles. With a large role, we have the chance to experience a sense of flow – the arc of the character, the trajectory of the emotional changes, the development of relationships. We can get on a roll. It's much, much harder to experience that in a small role – partly because we're on stage so little (or so sporadically), and partly because every word and every move suddenly becomes so darn important to us. We've got so few lines to focus on, that – if we screw them up – it feels monumental. Whereas screw up a phrase or two in a big role and we've got plenty of chances to redeem ourselves.

In order for us to really assess what's going on with small roles – so that (once again) we can be forewarned and forearmed – we're going to turn to creativity expert and writer on flow, Mihaly Csikszentmihalyi (pronounced 'cheek-sent-me-high').

First of all, what is this thing called 'flow' that eludes us with small roles?

Flow (as Csikszentmihalyi describes) is 'an optimal experience'.[219] We become so involved in an activity, that nothing else seems to matter: the activity becomes all-consuming in and of itself. And for us to experience this optimal state, we need various conditions to be in place.

First of all, we have to know that we can *achieve something* with a particular activity.

Second, the activity has to *line up with our goals.*

Third, there has to be *enough challenge* involved in the activity to keep the task exciting for us.

And fourth, we have to be able to enjoy the actual task *for its own sake* with no other agenda or expectation about it.

Looking at these four conditions, you can see what the problem is if we've only got a small role. How can we flow when we've only got thirty lines? It's difficult! And when it's difficult to flow, it's easy to feel stage fright.

So let's look a little closer. Let's take the first condition of flow – *achievement* – and go back to Sam Graham playing Phoebe, as well as David Annen playing Seyward. In each of these smallish roles – which both occur well into the narrative of each play – the two actors began to feel a sense of inadequacy. Were they *achieving* anything with these roles? For us to experience flow, there has to be a healthy balance between *something that we have the skillset to achieve* and *something that pushes us to achieve it.* It's just like working out on a resistance machine. Too much weight and we can't lift it. Too little weight and we don't achieve anything. Both Graham and Annen are very adroit actors, who are used to taking leading roles: they're used to lifting bigger weights. So the inner voices of self-doubt began asking whether they were achieving anything in the plays' narratives with these smaller, more peripheral roles.

As for flow condition 2 – *lining up with long-term goals* – Graham found himself asking himself if the role would get him any future work. We can't help it as actors: in the throes of one job, we find ourselves questioning where that job fits into our longer term career trajectory. After all, our ongoing concern about how to sustain our professional profile significantly contributes to our low-level anxiety.

As for flow condition 3 – *the degree of challenge* – it's rare for a small role to bear any real responsibility for a play's narrative. Unless of course it's the Messenger in a Greek tragedy. Added to which, David Annen felt that he'd 'cracked' the role of Seyward fairly early in rehearsals and Kenneth Branagh as director was happy with what he was doing, so there was nothing for his curious brain to grapple with. And by the end of the run, his brain had gone stir crazy and was cookin' up mayhem. Herein lies another paradox of acting: the *harder* the role, the more it consumes our attention, so that the task of acting becomes *easier* – and then we can flow.

And flow is a good feeling. Flow is addictive. Flow can give us a real high. It's that feeling on stage or in front of the camera when we merge with a role – just as Stanislavsky described. (And, indeed, as I experienced with Margaret in *Richard III*.) We're not making conscious choices in advance of a moment in order to elicit a particular response from the audience. It's all just happening. It's effortless. It flows. And when we're in flow, any thought of stage fright doesn't even come onto our radar. For actor Jonno Roberts: 'It feels like being at the crest of a wave or skiing in front of an avalanche. It's that kind of focus, where discoveries are tumbling along behind you.'[220] For Jay Whittaker: 'Flow is when I'm fully connected to the emotion of what's happening and there's no thought about the words or the blocking or the character... When I'm flowing, my mind is completely silent and there's nothing going on beyond the play.'[221] When actors are just *talking* about flow – they flow!

Yet there's a fourth condition for flow: *enjoying the task for its own sake*. We need the first three conditions to be in place for the fourth to kick in. However...

This fourth condition could actually provide a chance for us to take some conscious control. In our heart of hearts, we know that not every role is going to satisfy our creative needs. Not every role will give us flow. That's just a fact of the business. Yet for Graham and Annen, the gigs were big. (One was with Declan Donnellan, and one was with Kenneth Branagh.) That fact in itself made career-sense. So when the role doesn't challenge – but the gig excites – we should take solace in the fact that, although we're not getting the full injection of creative flow in the role, we can at least just enjoy it for the simplicity of what it is. And, even if it's not a big gig, sometimes it's nice for the pressure to be off. Sometimes it's nice for a job to be just a job.

That's a philosophical mindset which can sustain us in the long term. But let's come back to something more immediate. Which performance practices can we adopt if we're actually in mid-scene when the stage fright gets us? Well, here's a curiously intuition-based strategy that can really help us out – one that keeps our body in flow until our mind has had a chance to catch up...

Performance practice 4: switching our brain-channels from talking to moving

Remember Tim Orr's story right back in the Introduction? The moment he forget his lines, he started doing physical activities – moving around the stage and picking up books. On the one hand, this gave him a concrete sense of being anchored to physical objects. (At least he had the security blanket of a prop to hold.) On the other hand, he was doing something very instinctive and very clever: he was *switching channels in his brain*. Basically (as we saw in Chapter 1 when we looked at worry), we can't sustain two conversations at the same time – which means we can't talk to ourselves in the Fear Voice whilst also trying to speak the lines of the play. Both of these activities are language-based, and so they're using the same networks in our brain. The result is a bit like two trains trying to get along the same platform at the same time. If we can't switch one of them to another track, there's going to be a crash.

'Doing two things at once that rely on similar brain regions,' stresses Beilock, 'is generally harder than doing two things that call on separate pools of brain power, because in the first case there are just fewer neural resources to go around.'[222] So when Orr started moving around the stage, he was intuitively switching tracks. He was changing from his *language*-based synaptic networks to his *spatially* based synaptic networks. And as soon as his body was occupied with moving through space, his inner computer was no longer overloaded with too much activity in the language neural networks. The joy was that, within seconds, the words that he'd been wracking his brain so hard to remember came flooding straight back to him. The 'language' platform was now vacant, so his 'lines' train could pull into his 'performance' station!

Although he was able to deal intuitively with the immediate situation, Orr still had to haul himself on stage every night to get through the rest of the run. In other words, the knock-on effects of the momentary lapse were more long term. And it's true – big role or small – it haunts us when we screw up. However, if we do find ourselves replaying over and over what we think happened – how we dealt with it, how we think the audience might have perceived it, whether news of our glitch got back to the director – we need to stop! Instead of entertaining that Fear Voice, we need to use our imagination to a far healthier end. Which takes us to performance practice 5...

Performance practice 5: imaginatively rehearsing the success

We know that our imagination is active – how can it not be? We're actors, for goodness' sake! Our imagination is our most useful tool. Yet sometimes it's not just active, it's *over*active. If we've had a performance screw-up, the stress-fuelled Fear Voice can endlessly replay that dreadful moment until we're mortified to incapacitation. But we know that what we rehearse (even in our imagination) is what we bed-in – and we don't want to bed-in dread. So let's not! Let's rehearse something different.

In fact, *imaginary rehearsal* – or 'mental rehearsal' – is used all the time by sports psychologists with athletes. They encourage them to picture the course, picture the race, picture the winning, picture the response of the crowds, picturing raising high the trophy – and this imaginary rehearsal can seriously improve their actual performance and reduce their chances of 'choking' (as we saw in Chapter 1). Science hasn't yet proven the exact reason why our mental rehearsal can be so effective in dealing with performance anxiety. But that hardly matters. The important discovery is that, when we *imagine ourselves* performing a particular action, our muscular activity actually increases in those very muscle groups that would normally perform this activity if we were doing it *in real life*. In other words, our body and brain can't tell the difference. As far as they're concerned, *imagining* is *doing*. This just endorses all the extraordinary discoveries that we've learnt so far. Our brain – along with all its messages to our muscles – can't tell the difference between reality and imagination. It really is extraordinary – because it means we have a huge amount of conscious control. It's back to what we talked about in Chapter 3. If we've had an experience of stage fright in a performance – and it's haunting us during the day so that we end up dreading the next performance – then we can stop in our tracks! Right here! Right now! We can change the inner channel – just like we'd change from BBC 1 to Channel 4, or from CNN to HBO. Instead of *hard-wiring the panic*, we can imaginatively *rehearse the success*. So, right now: imagine standing backstage in complete composure. Imagine sailing through the glitchy moment with complete aplomb. Imagine taking a bow with a well-won flourish. It's not only simple; it's pleasurable. I've said it before – and I'll say it again: stage fright begins in our head, and that's the very place it can end. We can recondition our brain to experience whatever we want to feel. We can imaginatively rehearse the performance that we want, and erase the performance that we fear.

But – yes, of course – we're human. And the cynic inside may insist that this sounds like a miracle cure. So let's suppose that, despite our strongest efforts, the willful monster still raises its ugly head (or, at least, we allow it to) when we're actually in performance. We have a sixth practice that we can do for instant, short-term calm and confidence.

Performance practice 6: three anti-stress manoeuvres

Okay – we're mid-performance – and the monster has arrived. (Don't forget: 'Know the enemy and know yourself.' And we're certainly getting to know our self here.) First things first – we finish the scene if at all possible. Then as soon as we come off stage, we follow three very tangible, physical, anti-stress manoeuvres. Those manoeuvres are:

- Sit down as soon as possible.
- Pause for a moment.
- And have a drink of water.

These three steps are adopted by soldiers in combat. So if it works for them, it should work for us. Indeed, science has proven that the very act of slowing down... then pausing... then drinking water gives our brain a chance to realign, refocus and calm down. Now, what could be simpler than that? If we can employ these battle tactics, General Sun Tzu would be proud.

*

So, we've looked at some practices to stave off the fear at *the rehearsal stage* and we've looked at some practices for tackling it if it comes up *in performance*. Let's look at some strategies for facing and embracing the fear *in the long term*, so that we can aim for all-round health and professional longevity.

Long-term Strategies for Facing and Embracing the Fear

We've seen throughout this book that the one of the biggest mistakes that we make when we're dealing with our fear is to *avoid* the situations that we're scared of. 'Avoidance ensures that the fear lives on,' writes Taylor Clark.[223] And that's because, when we avoid something that makes us anxious, we don't give ourselves a chance to see that whatever we're scared of isn't really so significant. (This is what Derek Jacobi tried to do for two years.) Nor do we give ourselves the opportunity to discover that we're actually much better at dealing with the situation than we ever thought we would be. (This is what Derek Jacobi achieved after two years.) So rather than avoiding our fear, we need to coexist with it. We probably can't annihilate it, but if we can coexist with it (as Clark points out), we learn *how* to be afraid. So here I offer some long-term strategies for *facing* and *embracing* our fear. If we can use them all in some way, shape or form, it may well be that, not only can we *coexist* with our fear, but we can actually *overcome* it. After all, when we sincerely and open-heartedly embrace an enemy, it's impossible for them to feel like an enemy any more.

Long-term strategy 1: acknowledging our stage fright exists

All along we've seen that our mindset is half the battle. Successfully Facing the Fear really means *acknowledging that our stage fright exists.* And that may include sharing it with other actors. This was certainly a pacifier for David Annen when he finally voiced his fear to some of his colleagues in *Macbeth*. And it was an absolute clincher for me in *The Permanent Way*, when my conversations with Sam Graham and Matthew Dunster saved my acting life. As a result of which – little by little – I began to change my whole attitude towards stage fright. Rather than seeing it as a shameful, 'dirty secret', I took it as a chance for personal growth and an opportunity for courage. After all, 'Bravery isn't being *fearless*. Bravery… is being scared and doing the right thing anyway.'[224] It was also the chief motivator in eventually writing this book. It took some time to truly face my fear, but once I did, it really did diminish. I'm now as close as I *can* be to having embraced it and finally overcome it. (Fingers crossed and a following wind, of course – but that's all part of the game.) The purpose of this book is to speed up the whole process for you, so that it might only take days or weeks, rather than months and years. And that process can begin by welcoming the Fear in…

Long-term strategy 2: understanding risk sharpens our creativity

What's the benefit of welcoming the Fear in? Well, the truth is that our stage fright actually *sharpens our creativity*. In other words, it's not really a foe: it's a friend. Let's have a look at what that means…

According to Csikszentmihalyi, we have two contradictory sets of instructions within us as human beings. They're instructions with which we're born, so we simply can't escape them. The first is our conservative tendency for *self-preservation* (i.e. we need to go carefully so that we don't hurt or even kill ourselves). The second is our risk-taking tendency for *exploration* (i.e. we need to throw caution to the wind so that we learn all about the world around us).[225]

Although we need both of these tendencies to survive, it's actually our risk-taking tendency for exploration that enables us to be truly creative. And yet that's the tendency that's hardest to follow: we're far more likely to protect ourselves than take a risk and see what happens. So if we want to be truly creative, we have to consciously nurture our curiosity and actively take some risks. Otherwise our creativity will wilt. Facing our stage fright is one of those risks; in fact, facing our fear is a direct way of becoming truly creative. So all the more reason to do it. And being more creative might mean that we have to *care less*...

Long-term strategy 3: caring less

Perfectionism is no good. We saw that in Chapter 1. Those of us who are perfectionists and want to get everything absolutely right before we step on stage are actually *less* likely to be creative than those of us who are naturally more extrovert and enjoy a certain danger. So basically we don't *want* to be perfectionists. If we seriously want to face our stage fright and become more creative, we actually have to *care less*! Obviously that doesn't mean that we don't care about our craft and our work. It simply means that we're not overly *full* of cares. We need to allow the risk of *not* getting things perfect to be a legitimate – nay, a necessary – part of our creative process. After all, we already know that there is no such thing as a perfect performance. Therefore, it's incumbent upon us to quieten the perfectionist streak that can thwart us. This imperative is urgent because our perfectionism doesn't just fixate on perfecting a role: it also fixates on perfecting our career. And that's just totally out of the question. A 'perfect career' is impossible in our highly competitive and wholly unpredictable profession. No one's career is without the dark times...

Long-term strategy 4: dealing with the difficult times

As we've seen already in this book, everything in nature happens with equal and opposite force. I may be full of self-confidence when I'm *Singin' in the Rain* – and filled with self-doubt when I'm waiting at tables. In other words, any creative impulse within us inherently has a destructive force in equal and opposite measure. So for us to develop any long-term strategies for our acting careers, we have to *deal with the difficult times* when we're not being particularly creative.

One of the hardest facts of life for us to handle as actors is how inadequate we feel when we're not working. We enter this tantalising profession with open eyes, knowing that huge chunks of our life involve giving away control of our destiny. We know that, much of the time, we're at the mercy of other people to determine how, when, where, and whether we're going to express our creative energy. So, for our professional longevity, we have to know how to handle the pendulum-swing of despair (when we're out of work) – because, almost without fail, it follows the pendulum-swing of euphoria (when we're in work). And there are a couple of practical realities that we need to face.

First of all, it's a biological fact that, when we're out of work, we're not getting the adrenalin fix that usually comes with performance. There's no dopamine pumping every night and day, making us feel good as the audience applauds or we watch the dailies. Which means there's an actual, physiological change in our chemical make-up. We're neurologically different when we're performing from when we're not performing. That's a fact of life we can't avoid. So we might as well reconcile ourselves to it and adjust our mindset accordingly.

Second, it's worth accepting that, not only is a certain despair unavoidable, but – as Stephen Nachmanovitch proposes – it could actually be a vital part of our creative process: 'Creative despair feels rotten when it overtakes us, but it is necessary – it is a symptom that we are throwing our whole being into the problem.'[226] In fact, Nachmanovitch goes on to suggest that, 'Unbeknownst to [the actor], the momentum of all his practice carries through, unconsciously, during the dark night of the soul.'[227] In other words, our creativity doesn't die when we're out of work. It incubates. It waits. It silently revitalises. Our creativity needs the dark night of the soul, just as much as the fertile earth needs the dead of winter. So we shouldn't try to avoid the despair simply because we prefer the euphoria: we need both. If we can adopt this perspective, it can be remarkably empowering. We're no longer scared by the pendulum-swing between creative euphoria and dark despair: we understand that it's an intrinsic and vital aspect of our long-term creative flow. And then it's much easier to face it.

So those are four strategies for *facing* the fear: let's see if we're ready to *embrace* it.

Long-term strategy 5: talking back to the Fear Voice

One of the first things we can do in embracing our fear is to treat it like a friend. We'd embrace a friend – so let's embrace the Fear. That means we can *talk back* to our self-sabotaging Fear Voice, even if it starts up in performance. Rather than buying into our toxic introjects, sports psychologist Don Green suggests that we answer the Fear Voice with 'a very conscious, logical, knowing response'.[228] 'Look, buddy, I'll listen to you later once this performance is over, but for the moment I've got a job to do.' That way, we're not ignoring the monkey-mind's desire to indulge the imps of mischief – we're just saying, 'Not now. Later.' – Just as we might to an insistent child, who's tugging at our sleeve because they want some chocolate.

Long-term strategy 6: reframing the situation – and having a laugh!

Our final strategy for embracing our fear in the long term is to *reframe the situation*. Time and again in this book, we've raised this as an option. And it really is invaluable. One way to reframe the situation is simply to use different vocabulary. So rather than seeing stage fright as *a problem that can beat us*, we see it as *a challenge that can be met*.[229] The simple mental repackaging of 'problem' as 'challenge' can be surprisingly effective. And then maybe we can change 'challenge' to 'game'. And 'game' to 'fun'. After all, we know that fun and fear can't coexist, so why not let the fun diffuse the fear?

Which takes us to another means of reframing the situation, and that's to use humour. 'Your humour is a definite ally,' says Green. 'When your humour kicks in, it's really wonderful.'[230] By relocating our fear in the *funny* zone, we can't help but yank it out of the *fear* zone – because we start to see it from a new angle. And this is because humour 'is about playing with ideas and concepts,' explains clinical psychologist Rod Martin. 'So whenever we see something as funny, we're looking at it from a different perspective.'[231] It's true that, when stage fright kicks in, we can become locked in a rigid, almost claustrophobic mindset of '*I can't do this. This is terrifying! I'm useless! I've got to get out of here.*' Yet (as Martin suggests), 'if you can take a humorous perspective, then by definition you're looking at it differently – you're breaking out of that rigid mind-set.'[232]

When you think about it, we're lucky as actors, in that our craft is all about play, pleasure, games and entertainment. Where's the humour in being a tax collector? Or a sewage farmer? Or a shelf-stacker? *We've* got it for free. As my publisher Nick Hern recounted: 'Long ago, a friend told me about one of her tutors who was playing King Lear in a university production. At the dress rehearsal before a small audience of friends, this guy was working himself into a real state as he tore the part to pieces, when, from the audience, came a voice, "For God's sake, Harry, it's only a *play*!"'[233] It *is* only a play, so we *should* play. The very nature of what we do – putting on costumes and pretending to be other people – can be a liberating way of hooking us back into the childlike joy of our work. So next time we find ourselves wavering in the wings or fluttering on the film set, we should stop for a moment and look at what we're doing. These strange clothes. Someone else's words. The mass of people bashing their palms together to thank us for our work.

So the next time you think the monster of stage-fright is tracking you down – just picture Herman Munster.

Morph the mind-gripping demon into Taz the Tasmanian devil.

Morph the self-sabotaging imp into Rumpelstiltskin in *Shrek*.

Morph the worm of self-doubt into the Inch Worm in *Sesame Street*.

Our imagination is capable of playing this game, and it's hard to take any of the stage-fright monsters seriously when they look so silly or childlike.

*

So we've had some strategies for *life at large*; some specific strategies for acting (*in general*, in *rehearsal* and in *performance*); and some *long-term strategies* for facing and embracing our fear. The last two sections of this chapter look at how we might face our fear at the two bookends of our professional activity: *auditions* (before we've even hooked the role) and *post-performance processes* (which can be just as useful as anything else when it comes to conquering our stage fright).

Best Practice for Auditions

Auditions are immoral. In what can be as little as two minutes, we have to show to a panel of career-carving judges the arsenal of our artistic ingenuity. In fact, their very format undermines our real creativity, in the sense that it sets the right hemisphere of our brain (the creative part) against the left hemisphere of our brain (the organising part). The right brain needs freedom and flow, and for us to be really present to a situation, that situation has to be free of judgement or agenda. But we know that that's exactly what auditions are all about – judgements and agendas. That's their point – to assess whether or not we're right for the role and to get the piece cast. Added to which, auditions and showcases are full of all sorts of 'left-brain' organising rules: 'Don't let your piece be longer than ninety seconds. Don't look your auditioners in the eye. Your headshot must be this dimension. Your CV must be in this format. Don't ask questions unless asked for them', etc. All those left-brain regulations are totally at odds with our right-brain flow. And whenever a situation pulls us from right brain to left brain, our body can change significantly: we feel tense, our heart pounds, our anxieties are aroused. And with all those psychophysical changes, it's incredibly hard to be really present and inspired. So auditions are (by design) inclined to off-balance our creative natures.

Yet – as ever – forewarned is forearmed. We know auditions are unavoidable: they're the gateway between us and the industry. So we may as well learn to love them, and one of the ways to do that is to acknowledge how they implicitly challenge our creative ease by inadvertently pulling us from right brain to left brain. Once we acknowledge that – forewarned, therefore forearmed – we have the choice to harness some of that left-brain organising potential to our own advantage. Here's how...

Do you remember right at the beginning of this chapter, Beth Klein of Universal Television suggested we should forget about what we can't control and focus on what we can? Since there so many things that we can't control in an audition set-up, we simply have to focus on whatever we can fix. So what can we use our left-brain organising potential to control? We can do our preparation on the role. We can do our research on the director or the writer, the play or the television series, the theatre or the film company. (That way, we can know the full context of what we're going into.) We can find out logistically where we've got to be – which area, which street, which building, which room. We can arrive there in plenty of time. And then we can focus on our *mindset*. We can use our left brain to help us consciously with the frame of mind we choose to adopt. You could say that nowhere is mindset more important than in auditions. So here are just a few prompts to help us with that mindset.

Mindset prompt 1: 'They need us as much as we need them!'

First of all, we can remind ourselves that auditions have very little to do with our talent. They don't test us as artists; they simply assess whether or not we're right/useful/appropriate/castable (delete as appropriate) for a particular role. Part of the mindset is reminding ourselves how nerve-wracking it can be for the auditioners, too! At the end of the day, they've got to find the best possible cast for this particular production or film or TV pilot. They need to ascertain whether the person who walks into the room can do the job with talent, personality, charm, charisma and commercial certainty. After all, a lot of time, money and kudos depend on whether or not their production is a success. So don't forget: *they need us as much as we need them*! We're all here to help each other to make the best possible piece of work.

Mindset prompt 2: 'Enjoy it for its own sake!'

Second, auditions have a lot to do with our behaviour. Given how nerve-wracking it is for the casting team, the more we can demonstrate that we actually *like* being there, the better. In his seminal book, *Audition*, veteran casting director Michael Shurtleff advises: 'You're not at an audition to do the scene right, but to show the auditors who you are. Give yourself a chance. Worry less about the material and more about what you would do and feel if you were in that situation. The play gives you a situation; your job is to put yourself in it.'[234] By shifting from 'Will I get this part?' to 'What would I do if I were in this situation?' we adapt the context of the audition from 'being judged as an actor' to 'telling a mini-story'. If we think of the audition as something that's pleasurable in and of itself, we can change our whole perspective and radically reduce our nerves. Then we're not overwhelmingly obsessed by whether or not we get the part: we're just doing our job here and now – and *we're going to enjoy it for its own sake*!

Mindset prompt 3: 'There's no one like us in the whole world!'

You could say that these shifts in mindset and behaviour are just semantic. Yet – hold! Throughout this book, we've seen just how vividly our brain responds to the thoughts and words we give it. So we might as well give it the right thoughts and words. We might as well give it the prompts of, 'Hey, this is fun – I can strut my stuff!' rather than the prompts of, 'Oh my God – I'm being judged!' As Shurtleff reminds us, what the auditioners want to see at an audition is 'the real you reacting to a remarkable situation in a remarkable and unique way. There's only one person like you in the entire world. Trust yourself to use *that* with truth and imagination.'[235] Don't forget that, as actors, we already have all the materials we need inside us. We've got the emotions, the imagination and the technique. Now we just have to 'get out of our own way' in the audition, so that we can reveal and share those invaluable materials. *There's no one like us in the whole world!* Now, isn't that fantastic?

*

If we can change our perspective like this – helped by these mindset prompts – we can start to relinquish the nerves of auditions and embrace the absolute pleasure of the challenge instead.

Now from one bookend of our profession to the opposite other...

Best Post-performance Practice

The mindset that we develop *after* a performance can be just as powerful for allaying or whipping up our stage fright as anything we do before or during. Of course we all want praise. Isn't the applause part of the reason we went into acting in the first place? Yet culturally, applause is expressed differently the world over. In North America, audiences love standing ovations. In England, they can be gently muted and very polite. In Russia, they might slow handclap. In Germany, they famously boo. We tend to have various expectations of audience responses in the theatre – and at the same time we know that the audience's chance to respond is actually scripted into the end of a show! So it's all a bit of a ritual.

With television and film it can be different, as we're usually less aware of how our work has been received at the time we actually do it. We may receive a few words on set from the director at the end of a day's shoot – and obviously much more at the final wrap of the film. But everyone is so up-against-the-clock that there isn't much time for backslapping and handclapping. So why do we care so much about our post-performance reflections? Why do we mull over our work so doggedly once it's done? And how do we stop it? Well, actually it's back to *having a sense of perspective.*

Post-performance practice 1: have a sense of perspective

When we feel that we've given a bad performance, we often want to scurry off in a sorry state of self-judgement and self-punishment. Yet the director can think it was our best show to date. And the opposite is true, too. We can think we've given a great performance, only to find that it didn't read quite so brilliantly to our spectators. What *we* experience and what *they* receive can be completely different realities. So we really need to *have a sense of perspective.* We have to be mindful as actors that, immediately after a performance, our senses are very heightened – and, therefore, they can be pretty unreliable. If anyone says anything too critical, we can't necessarily receive it constructively. If anyone says anything adulatory, it can sometimes give us a slanted stance on what actually happened. Feedback, praise and criticism are necessary parts of the dialogue, but they're best treated with an appropriate pinch of salt along with a peppering of perspective. And that also means *knowing whose feedback we trust.*

Post-performance practice 2: know whose feedback we trust

Knowing whose feedback we trust is very useful. For me *professionally*, it's the director (who has seen the work at various stages of the process and so has various yardsticks to go by), and my husband (who's a wonderful actor-director with a keen aesthetic taste). For me *personally*, it's my father (whose intelligence is sharp and whose ambition for me is sincere), and my agent (who has seen my evolution over more than twenty years). Beyond that, I keep an open-minded eye and ear on any other critique. Of course it's lovely if my loyal family and friends like it (and I've got some friends who hate everything). It's wonderful if the critics support it, but as we saw in Chapter 2, there's a certain caution there, too. Immediately after a performance, we need time for our creative pores to close before we can hear the feedback (good or bad) with any sense of objectivity. As Mike Alfreds understandingly reports an actor once telling him,

> 'Look, Mike, you've got to understand that when we're in the middle of the show or just at the end of it, our adrenaline is high. Whether or not we've given a good show, we've been out there working hard and seriously – and we're in no fit state to absorb anything you have to say. You must realise that when actors are performing, especially in the way you ask of

us, we're extremely vulnerable. And getting notes when we're in that state only makes us resentful and defensive – and angry with you. What we want now isn't notes, but a drink! Give us the notes tomorrow when we're in a receptive frame of mind to appreciate them.'[236]

Ain't that the truth?

Added to knowing whose feedback we trust, we should also consider that *our own truth is worth trusting.*

Post-performance practice 3: trust our own truth

Since our industry is so unpredictable and opinions are so variable, we ultimately have to have a *sense of our own truth*. We have to have a tiny kernel of honesty inside us that we can trust as a barometer of what went well and what needs working. If we can take time to develop our own best practices – physically, psychologically, and psychophysically – we can start to nurture that inner-truth barometer. Armed with our own sense of truth, we can begin to face, embrace, and ultimately diminish the monster of fear.

While the scary thing about stage fright is that it's really all in our heads, the wonderful thing about dealing with stage fright is that it *is* all in our heads! It's just another paradox of acting. We can take control over the choices we make, as well as the perspectives we take, and then we can start to relinquish stage fright's feverish grasp. At the end of the day, it really is up to us.

Overview

In this chapter, we've looked at a wide range of practical and philosophical strategies to enable us to develop our own practices. We've briefly addressed basic *physical* issues (including sleep, exercise, nutrition and avoidances). We've addressed some *psychophysical* issues (including breathing, meditation and yoga). We've negotiated three particular types of *preparation* (general approaches to our creative work; best practices for rehearsal; and best practices for performance). We've considered some *longer term strategies* for facing and embracing our fear. And we've ended with a few handy hints for adopting helpful mindsets towards *auditions* and *post-performance practices.*

Whether we try to do *all* of these, or *some* of these, or different ones at different times (depending on the role, issue or medium), we should each be close to developing a unique art of war. Armed with that knowledge, we're equipped to go out and face, embrace and overcome our stage fright.

Now that's a big achievement.

We're on the way!

Bravo!

Debrief

Among his five fundamental factors for the art of war, General Sun Tzu cites 'command': 'By command,' he writes, 'I mean the general's qualities of wisdom, sincerity, humanity, courage, and strictness.'[237]

At the end of this journey into the heart of stage fright, we've covered a wide terrain and assessed a multitude of strategies. We've also developed the qualities of a commanding general.

- We've developed *wisdom* about the nature of our fear and how it operates.
- *Sincerity* in our strategies for overcoming it.
- *Humanity* in seeing it as something to be embraced as much as something to be fought.
- *Courage* to realise that it's really ourselves who serve as our enemy.
- And *strictness* (or *focus*) in our thoughts and attention – to embrace our fear foes and, in doing so, overcome them.

We've developed these qualities by following a structured battle plan. We've looked at what stage fright is. We've understood its roots in the actor-audience relationship. We've probed how we learn and developed some strategies for memory. We've honoured the work that we do in the rehearsal room with our directors and our acting partners. And we've taken responsibility for how we can affect our creative well-being.

So where do we end as we face and embrace the Fear, and trust that we're well on our way to overcoming it? I propose we end with a new beginning...

A new acting paradigm

As actors, we know that we're our own instrument. We also know that that instrument changes every day. In fact, it changes every moment (as we saw in Chapter 3 with the dynamic activities of our autobiographical self).

And at the same time as the Tiny Picture of our individual instrument is changing, the Enormous Picture of science's understanding of human behaviour is also changing. We know that every day some new discovery is made about the mysteries of our brain. And whatever developments we make in *science* inevitably impact on *acting*.

One of the key developments in science at this point in the twenty-first century is what's known as 'the enactive approach'.[238] This term was introduced to me by pioneering actor-trainer and director, Phillip B. Zarrilli, in the summer of 2014. The enactive approach (or 'enactivism') has emerged over the last twenty years from cognitive science and philosophy of mind, and it has informed how our emotions, moods and feelings are studied. And we've touched upon it subtly throughout this book.

The basic premise with the enactive approach is that there's no difference between our emotions and our thoughts. We are what we are in each moment – be it in our thoughts, our senses, or our imagination. Any separation between our body and our brain is obsolete and unhelpful: 'Descartes' Error', as Antonio Damasio calls it.

So how does this affect us as actors facing stage fright?

It means that whatever we *experience* here-today-now is who we are, so use it. Whatever we *think* here-today-now is who we are, so use it. As enactive beings, we can use fear as a motivating energy – and thus we can transform it. After all, our brain only knows the nanosecond of 'Now'!

As we saw with 'meditation', we can change our thoughts.

As we saw with 'perception' we can change our thoughts.

As we saw with the mindsets of 'auditions', we can change our thoughts.

And because, according to enactivism, our thoughts and emotions are really the same thing, when we change our thoughts, we change our feelings. We can *think* ourselves into whatever we want to *feel*. We really can condition ourselves (as we saw in Chapters 1 and 3) to experience whatever we want whenever we want.

And we can do it now! At any one moment, we have the possibility to choose our thoughts, and to make decisions about our feelings and our actions.

Of course it doesn't mean that, if our character is in a state of murderous anger, we'll become angry murderers – because we know that the primary condition for us as actors is *dual consciousness*. (We merge with the character whilst also attending to all the technical conditions of the job.) But what it does mean is that we can think ourselves *into* stage fright – and, with wisdom, sincerity, humanity, courage, and focus – we can think ourselves *out* of stage fright.

So, is it too simplistic to say that Facing the Fear is simply 'Mind Over Matter'? Not really. Though we could put it this way: 'Do you want to be scared of what you love? Do you want to keep on hitting yourself over the head with a hammer? If so, then do it – and eventually you'll give it up.'

Or we could put it this way: 'Do you want celebrate this great art form and wonderful (if sometimes infuriating) profession, for which you've trained and to which you've devoted your professional life? If so, then do that, instead – and sustain a lifelong career!'

'*But*,' you may ask, 'if it really *is* so simple, why didn't you tell me that at the beginning of the book and save me two hundred and fifty pages?'

'*Because*,' I may reply, 'you wouldn't have believed me.' We needed to go on the journey – into the war room, out on the battlefield, into our brains, back in time, into the rehearsal room, out onto the stage, and in front of the camera. We needed to understand the enemy's manoeuvres and our own best battle strategies. We needed all that in order for us to feel we'd earned the right to say, 'I've been to the edge of the abyss, I've looked over, and I've returned.' The joy of 'being enactive' is that it enables us to be both *better actors in the role* (as we live and breathe through the circumstances of the character), and *better actors in life* (as we're no longer hounded by the imps of stage fright).

After three years of researching this book and ten years of considering my own stage fright, I actually find myself laughing. While I want to have the gracious command of a learned general, I really have the joyful chuckle of a Christmas elf. Having looked at stage fright from all angles – its history, its neuroscience, its manifestations both physiological and psychological – it seems absurd to be scared of something that we love so much. We might as well face our fears, embrace our fears, and for heaven's sake be done with them. Mightn't we? In a sobering moment, I once heard a young boy ask his mother, 'Who's Marilyn Monroe...?' Everything we do is ephemeral – so we might as well enjoy it while it lasts.

In which case, let's have the *wisdom* to be great storytellers.

The *sincerity* to honour our profession.

The *humanity* to reach out to our audiences.

The *courage* to work to the tips of our nerve endings.

And the *discipline* to coexist with our fear and to use it to our best creative ends.

We've been to the edge...

...we've looked over...

...now we're back again!

For good.

Compendium of Terms

AUTOBIOGRAPHICAL SELF – the complex juggling of all the neural networks that comprise our remembered past and our imagined future, and brings all those thoughts and images together into an existence that we experience as our life.

AMYGDALA – the brain's tiny security system, shaped like an almond, designed to ensure that we survive in dangerous situations by fleeing, freezing or fighting. It's our Vigilante!

CHOKING – when we perform worse than we know we can, and it usually affects our body and motor activities as much as our brain; the stakes usually have to be personally or professionally high to risk choking.

CIRCLES OF ATTENTION – Stanislavsky's tool for sharpening our focus on stage, from the biggest circle encompassing the whole auditorium down to the smallest circle of just 'us'.

CORE SELF – the part of our consciousness that knows that we're conscious, but without any perception of past or future: our sense of really living 'in the moment'.

CUED RECALL – the neurological match between what has been encoded in our brains (learnt) and what is later retrieved (remembered); if an actor doesn't give us the right line, there's a mismatch in our brain that can affect our cued recall.

DUAL CONSCIOUSNESS – the necessary balance between knowing that we're acting (and therefore getting on with all the technical work) while also allowing ourselves to commit to the moment-by-moment performance.

ELABORATE REHEARSAL – the process through which we give a piece of information 'meaning' so that we can more durably learn it. We need to give it personal value; we need to know the context of the information and its function in the situation, in order to elaborate it usefully.

ENCODING SPECIFICITY PRINCIPLE – Tulving's term to describe the process in which we remember something more easily if we put ourselves physically and emotionally into a similar state to the one that we were in at the time we originally learnt the information.

EXPANDING REHEARSAL (see SPACED RETRIEVAL)

FLOODING THERAPY – the act of disclosing something of which we're afraid in order to lessen our anxious thoughts.

FUNCTIONING SELF – the part of us that gets on with the task in hand (see OBSERVING SELF).

HIPPOCAMPUS – the seahorse-shaped region of the brain, which is highly active in our initial encoding of new information and our subsequent retrieving of that information (as memory). It's our Memory Master!

HOMEOSTASIS – our organism's physiological balance in the world.

IMAGINARY TRANSPOSITION – connected to empathy, the spectator puts themselves in the shoes of the person they're watching to understand why he or she might be experiencing that emotion.

IMAGINATIVE REHEARSAL – or 'mental rehearsal': a simple imagination process used particularly by sports psychologists so that athletes imagine the perfect match or race as a means of avoiding choking in performance.

LOCI METHOD OF RECALL – a method of learning a new speech, in which orators would picture an architectural structure and then place each new piece of information to be learned in particular rooms in a particular order.

LONG-TERM MEMORY – memory created by sufficient repetitions and practices for our brain to create a new brain map. It can last for hours, days, months, years, and even a lifetime.

MAINTENANCE REHEARSAL – the process of cramming information into our memory to retain it for a matter of hours.

MENTAL REHEARSAL (see IMAGINATIVE REHEARSAL)

MINDFUL NOTING – the process by which we translate our stressful feelings into words, so that we can bring some order to the mental and emotional chaos, and thereby reduce our stress.

MIRROR NEURONS – the firing of the same neurons in *our* brain as we watch *someone else* going through a particular activity or experiencing a particular emotion that enables us to feel empathy on a profound neurological level.

OBSERVING SELF – the psychological part of us that adjusts to the technical demands of performing (see FUNCTIONING SELF).

PARALYSIS BY ANALYSIS – when we consciously think too much about information that we had already lodged in our (unconscious) long-term memory. It is linked to CHOKING.

PEREZHIVANIE – Stanislavsky's term for 'experiencing' or 'living through' a role that can encompass all our feelings – those we're experiencing here-today-now as actors performing and those that are relevant to the character in the given circumstances.

PRACTICE-BASED RESEARCH – research based in action, rather than theory, and motivated by emotional, personal and subjective concerns.

PROTOSELF – the unconscious part of us that beavers away every moment of our lives, ensuring that our organism remains physiologically balanced.

SELF-ENTHRALLMENT – a moment of 'Aren't I good?' – a self-intoxication that can fracture our focus just as much as any negative, self-judging thought.

SEPARATION ANXIETY – the sensation suffered by small beings once they get over their self-enthrallment at being independent, and they suddenly realise their separation from their mother.

SHORT-TERM MEMORY – memory that lasts a few minutes to a few hours as we bring something consciously into our awareness, like a phone number or a last-minute script change.

SPACED RETRIEVAL – the process of allowing time between learning sessions for our brain to change the proteins and create new memory maps. Each space between retrievals should be longer, almost to the point of forgetting. Paradoxically, this makes our long-term memory of that information stronger.

STATE OF 'I AM' – Stanislavsky's term to describe the state of merging with the role in the moment of performance that encompasses all our feelings, including our own fear and consciousness.

TACTICAL BREATHING – a process of deep-breathing into the abdomen (usually on counts of four) to switch us from our sympathetic nervous system to our parasympathetic nervous system and calm us down; used by combat trainers.

TOXIC INTROJECTS – a psychological term referring to the self-interruptions in the flow of our lives, comprised of a *forbidden content* and a *catastrophic expectation* of what will happen if we don't listen to the toxic voice.

Confidence Checklist

- ✓ Focus on whatever you can control.
- ✓ Put in the preparation so that you can make good choices.

The physical practices

- ✓ Sleep seven to eight hours a night.
- ✓ Take regular sessions of aerobic exercise to cleanse the brain's toxins.
- ✓ Drink lots of water (around two litres a day).
- ✓ Eat the right foods (good carbs, nuts, fruits, leafy greens, grains, fish oils).
- ✓ Eat foods that you like.
- ✓ Eat around two hours before a performance.
- ✓ Avoid caffeine, alcohol, nicotine, recreational drugs, and sugar.

The psychological practices

- ✓ Make sure you have ways of physically and mentally relaxing.

- ✓ Focus on your breathing.
- ✓ Enjoy as many tasks as you can for their own sake, without agendas and expectations.

Basic principles for creative work

- ✓ Keep your choices simple.
- ✓ Don't have all your choices for your performance worked out in advance.
- ✓ Get out of your own way and let yourself truly listen to the playwright's words.
- ✓ Cultivate a constant state of inner improvisation.
- ✓ Know what you need to warm yourself up – for a class, rehearsal or performance.

Good line-learning practices

- ✓ Learn your lines on your feet as much as on your sofa.
- ✓ Give your lines your undivided attention.
- ✓ Learn your lines through repetition – as that's the way the brain knows this information is important enough for you to create some new neural maps.
- ✓ Have downtime – take breaks between line-learning sessions, almost to the point of forgetting what you've learned.
- ✓ Make sure you know what your lines mean – personally as well as literally.
- ✓ Repeat till you habituate (certainly for theatre).
- ✓ Be prepared to throw it all out of the window for film and television, and if they ask you to improvise, know that

you're well enough prepared to play about with the lines and the structure and the relationships – and have fun.

Good rehearsal practices

✓ Mine the text through detailed text analysis.

✓ Look for the physical clues within the language and rhythm.

✓ Look for the psychological clues of objectives and intentions.

✓ Look for the psychophysical 'bits of action'.

✓ Be sure (for theatre at least) you're dead-letter-perfect in your line-learning.

✓ Remember that 'cued recall' helps us all keep the flow going: be collaborative!

✓ Personalise the images so that they're much harder to forget.

✓ Turn a stressful rehearsal into a good opportunity to train under stress – just as a fireman or a soldier would.

✓ Speak to the director if the 'blocking' needs unlocking.

✓ Remain open to notes.

✓ Remember, rehearsal is play.

✓ Rehearsing is listening.

✓ Listening is incorporating and using whatever you're feeling here-today-now – nerves an' all!

✓ Understand that you and the character are already merged: the brain only knows 'now'.

Good performance practices

- ✓ Keep your attention on your partner (even if your partner is a prop or a sound cue).
- ✓ Get some perspective on your perception: your nightmare stage fright really won't ruin your career – the audience might not even notice!
- ✓ When cast in a small role, keep your expectations realistic: you're probably not going to experience a great sense of flow, so just enjoy the job for what it is.
- ✓ If you forget your lines mid-scene, just move (if possible). It doesn't have to be a major move, but you'll be switching channels in your brain from linguistic signals (of 'No! I've forgotten my lines!') to the spatial signals, so that you free up the linguistic channels for the lines of the text, rather than the Fear Voice.
- ✓ Rehearse your success in your imagination.

Long-term strategies for facing and embracing fear

- ✓ Acknowledge that your stage fright exists – get it out in the open somehow: the talking cure is invaluable.
- ✓ Understand that we can only be creative if we take risks. In other words, reframe your stage fright as a great chance for creative growth, rather than a will to run away.
- ✓ Care less! There's no such thing as a perfect performance, so release yourself from being full of cares about perfectionism.
- ✓ Understand that we need the dark times of unemployment. True creativity can only exist if we face the difficult times and appreciate their value.
- ✓ Talk back to the Fear Voice: tell it that you'll deal with it later, but you've got a job to do now.

- ✓ Reframe the 'problem that can beat you' as a 'challenge that can be overcome'.
- ✓ Reframe the stage fright in the light of humour. See it from a different angle. Laugh it into submission.

Mindsets for auditions

- ✓ They need you as much as you need them!
- ✓ Enjoy it for its own sake!
- ✓ There's no one like you in the whole world! So knock their socks off!

Good practices for post-performance

- ✓ Have a sense of perspective on the feedback – praise or critique: it's just someone's taste (and that includes the professional critics).
- ✓ Know whose feedback you trust.
- ✓ Trust your own sense of truth.

Endnotes

Preface

1. http://www.telegraph.co.uk/culture/theatre/theatre-news/10268514/Michael-Gambons-stage-fright-shows-actors-deserve-respect.html; http://www.dailymail.co.uk/tvshowbiz/article-2403635/Quentin-Letts-Stage-fright-Laurence-Olivier-Benedict-Cumberbatch-Michael-Gambon.html; http://www.thetimes.co.uk/tto/arts/stage/theatre/article3853070.ece.
2. Laurence Olivier, *On Acting* (New York: Simon and Schuster, 1986), p. 183.
3. Sara Solovitch, *Playing Scared: My Journey Through Stage Fright* (London: Bloomsbury, 2015).

Introduction

4. Stephen Wangh, *An Acrobat of the Heart* (New York: Vintage, 2000), p. 73.
5. Adolph Kielblock, *The Stage Fright, or How to Face an Audience* (Boston: Press of Geo. H. Ellis, 1891), cited by Nicholas Ridout, *Stage Fright, Animals and Other Theatrical Problems* (Cambridge: Cambridge University Press, 2006), p. 56.
6. Taylor Clark, *Nerve: Poise Under Pressure, Serenity Under Stress and the Brave New Science of Fear and Cool* (New York: Little, Brown and Company, 2011), p. 13.
7. *Ibid.*, p. 65.
8. Don Green, *Audition Success* (New York: Routledge, 2001), p. 23.

9. Sian Beilock, *Choke: What the Secrets of the Brain Reveal About Getting It Right When You Have To* (New York: Free Press, 2010), p. 160.
10. Clark (2011), p. 82.
11. Stefan Klein, *The Science of Happiness: How our Brains Make us Happy – and What We Can Do to Get Happier* (New York: Marlowe & Company, 2006), p. 153.
12. Neurologist Dr Dee Silver describes how 'Panic attacks are experienced in people who are fearful of having no control to protect or manage an event, that is being experienced. It is not realised by people experiencing panic attacks that the event actually presents no danger to anyone. Treatment for panic attacks, anxiety and fear is multiple, but cognitive therapy, medications and psychotherapy can be used to dampen the response to the attack or understand why the attack occurs.' (Personal correspondence between Dr Silver and the author, November 2015.)
13. Interview with Richard Seer, San Diego, California, August 2011.
14. Interview with Tim Orr, Boulder, Colorado, August 2012.
15. Estelle Barrett & Barbara Bolt (eds.), *Practice as Research: Approaches to Creative Arts Enquiry* (New York: I. B. Tauris, 2010), p. 4.
16. Cited in Mike Berry and Michael R. Edelstein (eds.), *Stage Fright: 40 Stars Tell You How They Beat America's #1 Fear* (Tuscon, Arizona: See Sharp Press, 2009), p. 46.

Chapter 1

17. Olivier (1986), p. 181.
18. Sun Tzu, *The Art of War*, trans. Samuel B. Griffith (London: Watkins Publishing, 2005), p. 125.
19. Antony Sher, *Primo Time* (London: Nick Hern Books, 2005), p. 59.
20. Donald Kaplan, 'On Stage Fright', *TDR* 14.1 (1969), cited by Ridout (2006), p. 59.
21. Anton Chekhov, *The Seagull*, trans. Michael Frayn (London: Methuen, 1986), p. 64.
22. Ridout (2006), p. 59.
23. Clark (2011), p. 168.
24. Klein (2006), p. 248.
25. *Ibid.*, p. 254.
26. Antony Sher, *Beside Myself* (London: Arrow Books, 2001), p. 127.
27. Cited by Solovitch (2015), p. 160.
28. Cited in Clark (2011), p. 202.

29. Stephen Nachmanovitch, *Free Play: Improvisation in Life and Art* (New York: Tarcher Penguin, 1990), p. 138.
30. Edward W.L. Smith cited in Robert B. Marchesani & E. Mark Stern (eds.), *Frightful Stages: From the Primitive to the Therapeutic* (New York: Haworth Press, Inc., 2001), p. 113.
31. Glen O. Gabbard on self-enthrallment, cited by Ridout (2006), p. 61.
32. Solovitch (2015), p. 30.
33. Beilock (2010), pp. 5–6.
34. Alvin R. Mahrer, 'You Will Have These Awe-Full Moments When You Have Your Own Experiential Session', cited in Marchesani & Stern (eds.) (2001) p. 139.
35. Beilock (2010), p. 252. [My emphasis.]
36. *Ibid.*, p. 254. [My emphasis.]
37. Cited in Clark (2011), p. 136.
38. *Ibid.*, pp. 12, 15, 16.
39. *Ibid.*, p. 136.
40. Eric R. Kandel, *In Search of Memory: The Emergence of the New Science of the Mind* (New York: W. W. Norton and Company, 2006), p. 388.
41. *Ibid.*, p. 342.
42. Clark (2011), p. 181.
43. *Ibid.*, p. 244.
44. *Ibid.*, p. 65.
45. David Roland, *The Confident Performer* (London: Nick Hern Books, 2001), p. 22.
46. Beilock (2010), p. 153.
47. Klein (2006), p. 188.
48. Antonio R. Damasio, *Self Comes to Mind: Constructing the Conscious Brain* (New York: Pantheon, 2010), p. 210.
49. Antonio R. Damasio, *The Feeling of What Happens: Body and Emotion in the Making of Consciousness* (New York: Harcourt Brace, 1999), p. 225.
50. *Ibid.*
51. Joseph Chaikin, *The Presence of the Actor* (New York: Theatre Communications Group, 1991), p. 21.
52. Constantin Stanislavski, *Building a Character*, trans. Elizabeth Reynolds Hapgood (London: Methuen, 2002), p. 21.
53. Mihaly Csikszentmihalyi, *Flow: The Psychology of Optimal Experience* (New York: HarperCollins *Publishers*, 2008), p. 37.
54. Stephen Aaron, *Stage Fright: Its Role in Acting* (Chicago: University of Chicago, 1986), p. 65.

55. Kirk J. Schneider, 'Standing in Awe: The Cosmic Dimensions of Effective Psychotherapy,' cited in Marchesani & Stern (eds.) (2001) p. 126.
56. Cited by Berry and Edelstein (eds.) *Stage Fright: 40 Stars Tell You How They Beat America's #1 Fear* (Tucson, Arizona: See Sharp Press, 2009), p. 103.
57. Olivier (1986), p. 186.
58. Ingemar Lindh, *Stepping Stones*, trans. Benno Plassmann, Marlene Schranz & Magdelena Pietruska (Wroclow: Icarus Publishers, 2010), p. 10.
59. David Mamet, *True and False: Heresy and Common Sense for the Actor* (London: Faber and Faber, 1998), p. 30.
60. Nachmanovitch (1990), p. 166.
61. Mamet (1998), p. 59.
62. Cited by Berry and Edelstein (eds.) (2009), p. 101.
63. Jean Benedetti, *Stanislavsky: His Life and Art* (London: Methuen, 1999), p. 40.
64. Constantin Stanislavski, *An Actor Prepares*, trans. Elizabeth Reynolds Hapgood, Bloomsbury Revelations Edition (London: Bloomsbury, 2013), p. 6.
65. Cited by Benedetti (1999), p. 228 from *Sobranie Sochinenii Volume VII* pp. 610, 611.
66. *Ibid.*
67. Rose Whyman, *Stanislavski: The Basics* (Abingdon: Routledge, 2013), p. 11.
68. Ridout (2006), p. 40.
69. Lee Strasberg, *The Dream of Passion: The Development of the Method* (London: Methuen, 1989), p. 57.
70. *Ibid.*, p. 101.

Chapter 2

71. Cited by Donald Spoto in *Marilyn Monroe: A biography* (New York: Cooper Square Press, 1993), p. 265.
72. Ridout (2006), p. 3.
73. Elias Canetti, *Crowds and Power*, trans. Carol Stewart (New York: Farrer, Straus and Giroux, 1984), p. 26.
74. Ian McKellen, 'I Always Wanted to be on Broadway', *The New York Times*, 27 September 1981, cited by Jane Goodall, *Stage Presence* (Abingdon: Routledge, 2008), p. 31.
75. Stanislavski (2013), p. 9.

76. Cited by Maria Ignatieva, *Stanislavsky and Female Actors: Women in Stanislavsky's Life and Art* (Lanham: University Press of America, 2008), p. 42.
77. Ridout (2006), pp. 85–9.
78. Goodall (2008), p. 153.
79. http://www.chinatopix.com/articles/61118/20150810/benedict-cumberbatch-mortified-by-audiences-avid-filming-as-he-stages-hamlet.htm#ixzz3iReu5TFP.
80. http://www.playbill.com/news/article/patti-lupone-putting-battle-gear-on-questions-stage-career-after-cell-phone-incident-352959.
81. Tiffany Stern, *Rehearsals from Shakespeare to Sheridan* (Oxford: Oxford University Press, 2000), p. 113.
82. Peter Hall, 'Godotmania', http://www.theguardian.com/stage/2003/jan/04/theatre.beckettat100.
83. Dan Rebellato, *1956 and All That* (London: Routledge, 1999), p. 107.
84. *Ibid.*, p. 112.
85. Stanislavski (2013), p. 69.
86. Ian McKellen, 'The Awful Hell of Stage Fright', *The Times*, February 1996.
87. http://latimesblogs.latimes.com/technology/2011/12/theaters-tweet-seats-twitter.html.
88. Sher (2001), p. 178.
89. *Ibid.*
90. Aaron (1986), p. 68.
91. Michael Billington, 'My showdown with Nick Hytner', *Guardian*, May 21 2007.
92. Helen Freshwater in *Theatre and Audience* (Basingstoke: Palgrave Macmillan, 2009), p. 3.
93. Chaikin (1991), p. 140.
94. Bruce McConachie, *Theatre and Mind* (Basingstoke: Palgrave MacMillan, 2013), p, 15.
95. *Ibid.*, pp. 15–16. [My emphasis.]
96. *Ibid.*, p. 16.
97. Cited in Berry and Edelstein (eds.) (2009), p. 93.
98. http://www.thefreelibrary.com/Rebirth+of+renaissance+man%3B+As+well+as+appearing+in+three+of...-a065212740.
99. *Ibid.*
100. Cited by Berry and Edelstein (eds.) (2009), p. 103.

Chapter 3

101. Derek Jacobi, *As Luck Would Have It* (London: HarperCollins *Publishers*, 2013), p. 224.
102. Michael Crawford in *Sydney Morning Herald*, May 5 1992, cited by Roland (2001), p. 3.
103. S.W. Little & A. Cantor, *The Playmakers* (New York: W.W. Norton & Company, 1970), p. 111, cited by Aaron (1986), p. 71.
104. Cited in Berry and Edelstein (2009), p. 244.
105. Interview with Donald Carrier, San Diego, August 2011.
106. Damasio (1999), p. 220. [My emphasis.]
107. Cited in Jonathan K. Foster, *Memory: A Very Short Introduction* (Oxford: Oxford University Press, 2009), p. 2.
108. Email correspondence with Tanya Moodie, March 2015.
109. Foster (2009), p. 28.
110. *Ibid.*, p. 29.
111. Personal correspondence with Dr Dee Silver, November 2015.
112. *Ibid.*
113. http://www.bbc.com/news/health-16086233.
114. Damasio (2010), p. 87.
115. Klein (2006), p. 62. [My emphasis.]
116. Interview with Jonno Roberts, San Diego, August 2011.
117. Interview with Jay Whittaker, San Diego, August 2011.
118. Foster (2009) pp. 118–9.
119. *Ibid.*, p. 119.
120. *Ibid.*.
121. Email correspondence with Tanya Moodie, March 2015.
122. Sher (2001), p. 143.
123. Foster (2009) p. 118. [My emphasis.]
124. *Ibid.*, p. 120.
125. *Ibid.* p. 121.
126. Larry. R. Squire, & Eric R. Kandel, *Memory: From Mind to Molecules* (New York: Scientific American Library, 2000), p. 26.
127. http://www.huffingtonpost.com/2014/05/15/robert-duvall-marlon-brando-cue-cards_n_5331270.html.
128. For an in-depth discussion of this, see Frances A. Yates's wonderful book, *The Art of Memory* (London: Pimlico, 1998) pp. 135–74.
129. De Witt's drawing is for the Swan Theatre, though it provides some possibilities of what Shakespeare's Globe may have looked like. Although de Witt's sketch doesn't show the five columns, etc., a detailed description of Fludd's work and his impact of theatre architecture can be found in Yates (1998), pp. 310–54.

130. Clark (2011), p. 36.
131. *Ibid.*, p. 41.
132. Psychologist Michael Davis cited by Clark, *Ibid.*, p. 45.
133. *Ibid.*, p. 46.
134. Cited in Solovitch (2015), p. 82.
135. Interview with Sam Graham, Leeds, May 2004.
136. *Ibid.*
137. *Ibid.*
138. *Ibid.*
139. Sher (2001), p. 128.
140. Interview with Matthew Dunster, Oxford, May 2004.
141. Kenneth Branagh, *Beginning* (London: Pan Books, 1990), p. 94.
142. Squire & Kandel (2000), p. 48.
143. *Ibid.*
144. Klein (2006), p. 62.
145. *Ibid.*, p. 37.
146. Cited in Solovitch (2015), p. 186.
147. Klein (2006), p. 68.
148. Jacobi (2013), p. 227.
149. *Ibid.*, pp. 231–2. [My emphasis.]
150. Interview with Donald Carrier, San Diego, August 2011.

Chapter 4

151. Robert Benedetti, *The Actor At Work*, 7th edition (New York: Alyn and Bacon, 1997), p. 220. [My emphasis.]
152. Max Stafford-Clark, *Letters to George* (London: Nick Hern Books, 1997), p. 40.
153. Skype interview with Mike Alfreds, London–Los Angeles, April 2015.
154. Mike Alfreds, *Different Every Night: Freeing the Actor* (London: Nick Hern Books, 2007), p. 313.
155. Sher (2001), p. 141.
156. Email correspondence with Rufus Norris, April 2015.
157. Skype interview with Mike Alfreds, London–Los Angeles, April 2015.
158. Alfreds (2007), pp. 313–334, in which he address actors' fears and directors' fears.
159. Sher (2001), pp. 118–9.
160. Skype interview with Mike Alfreds, London–Los Angeles, April 2015.

161. Aaron (1986), p. 3.
162. Iain McGilchrist, *The Master and His Emissary: The Divided Brain and the Meaning of the Western World* (New York: Yale University Press, reprint edition 2012).
163. Interview with Miles Anderson, August 2011.
164. Glen O. Gabbard, 'Stage Fright', *International Journal of Psychoanalysis*, 60 (1979), p. 390, cited by Ridout (2006), p. 60.
165. Interview with John Cariani, San Diego, August 2011.
166. https://www.youtube.com/watch?v=9e-ud9zhVuc.
167. http://www.vanityfair.com/hollywood/2015/08/benedict-cumberbatch-hamlet-leaks.
168. Skype interview with Mike Alfreds, London–Los Angeles, April 2015.
169. Cited by Jean Benedetti (ed. & trans.), *Moscow Art Theatre Letters* (London: Methuen, 1991), p. 155.
170. David Magarshack, *Stanislavsky: A Life* (London: Faber and Faber, 1986), p. 415.
171. Interview with Don Carrier, San Diego, August 2011.
172. *Ibid.*
173. *Ibid.*
174. *Ibid.*
175. Sher (2001), p. 148.
176. Interview with John Cariani, San Diego, August 2011.
177. Email correspondence with Max Stafford-Clark, April 2015.
178. Email correspondence with Tanya Moodie, April 2015.
179. Konstantin Stanislavsky, cited by Rose Whyman, *The Stanislavsky System of Acting* (Cambridge: Cambridge University Press, 2008), p. 254.
180. Interview with Jay Whittaker, San Diego, August 2011.
181. *Ibid.*
182. Jacobi (2013), p. 223.
183. Cited by Clark (2011), p. 237.
184. *Ibid.*, pp. 237, 238.
185. Solovitch (2015), p. 76.
186. Cited by Oliver Ford Davies, *Performing Shakespeare* (London: Nick Hern Books, 2007), p. 217.
187. Wangh (2000) p. 73. [My emphasis.]
188. *Ibid., p.* 124.
189. *Ibid.*
190. Cited by Ford Davies (2007), p. 164.
191. *Ibid.*

192. Ridout (2006). p. 59.
193. Wangh (2000) pp. 72–73.
194. Cited by Berry and Edelstein (eds.) (2009), p. 103.

Chapter 5

195. Cited by Berry and Edelstein (eds.) (2009), p. 101.
196. Equity and Spotlight Professional Development Day, May 2014, Los Angeles.
197. Sun Tzu (2005), p. 217.
198. David Roland's *The Confident Performer* (London: Nick Hern Books, 2001), is a lively and useful resource detailing the components of good nutrition, sleep and exercise.
199. Daniel G. Amen, *Making a Good Brain Great* (New York: Three Rivers Press, 2005), p. 16.
200. Sher (2001), p. 160.
201. Clark (2011), p. 254.
202. Roland (2001), p. 25.
203. Lindh (2010), p. 96.
204. Wangh (2000), pp. 26, 36.
205. Interview with Matthew Dunster, Oxford, May 2004.
206. Bella Merlin, *The Complete Stanislavsky Toolkit* (London: Nick Hern Books, 2nd Edition, 2014).
207. Beilock (2010), p. 57.
208. Foster (2009), pp. 59–60.
209. *Ibid*, p. 51.
210. *Ibid.*, p. 50.
211. Cited in Berry and Edelstein (eds.) (2009), pp. 89–90.
212. Clark (2011), p. 274.
213. Skype interview with David Annen, London–Los Angeles, August 2014.
214. *Ibid.*
215. Amen (2005), p. 147. [My emphasis.]
216. *Ibid.*
217. Skype interview with David Annen, London–Los Angeles, August 2014.
218. *Ibid.*
219. Mihaly Csikszentmihalyi, *Flow: the psychology of optimal experience*, New York: HarperPerennial, 1990), p. 3.
220. Interview with Jonno Roberts, San Diego, August 2011.
221. Interview with Jay Whittaker, San Diego, August 2011.

222. Beilock (2010), p. 130.
223. Clark (2011), p. 71.
224. *Ibid.*, p. 266.
225. Mihaly Csikszentmihalyi, *Creativity: Flow and the Psychology of Discovery and Invention* (New York: HarperPerennial, 1997), p. 11.
226. Nachmanovitch (1990), p. 154.
227. *Ibid.*, p. 158.
228. Green (2001), p. 23.
229. Roland (2001) p. 14.
230. Green (2001), p. 30.
231. Cited by Clark (2011), p. 125.
232. *Ibid.*
233. Nick Hern, private correspondence, April 2015.
234. Michael Shurtleff, *Audition: Everything an Actor Needs to Know to Get the Part* (New York: Walker and Company, 1978), p. 114.
235. *Ibid.*, p. 4.
236. Alfreds (2007), pp. 330–1.

Debrief

237. Sun Tzu (2005), p. 93.
238. See Giovanna Colombetti's compelling study of the enactive approach in *The Feeling Body: Affective Science Meets the Enactive Mind* (Massachusetts: MIT Press, 2014).